W9-DGM-634

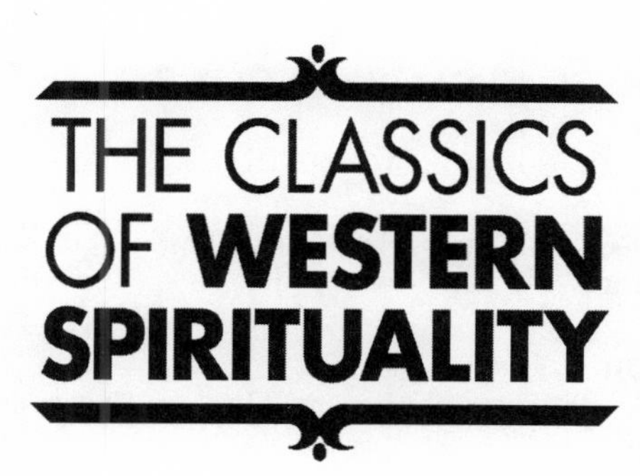
THE CLASSICS
OF WESTERN
SPIRITUALITY

THE CLASSICS OF WESTERN SPIRITUALITY
A Library of the Great Spiritual Masters

Seyyed Hossein Nasr—Professor of Islamic Studies, George Washington University, Washington, D.C.

Heiko A. Oberman—Professor for Medieval, Renaissance, and Reformation History, University of Arizona, Tucson, Ariz.

Raimon Panikkar—Professor Emeritus, Department of Religious Studies, University of California at Santa Barbara, Calif.

Jaroslav Pelikan—Sterling Professor of History and Religious Studies, Yale University, New Haven, Conn.

Sandra M. Schneiders—Professor of New Testament Studies and Spirituality, Jesuit School of Theology, Berkeley, Calif.

Michael A. Sells—Emily Judson Baugh and John Marshall Gest Professor of Comparative Religions, Haverford College, Haverford, Penn.

Huston Smith—Thomas J. Watson Professor of Religion Emeritus, Syracuse University, Syracuse, N.Y.

John R. Sommerfeldt—Professor of History, University of Dallas, Irving, Tex.

David Steindl-Rast—Spiritual Author, Benedictine Grange, West Redding, Conn.

David Tracy—Greeley Professor of Roman Catholic Studies, Divinity School, University of Chicago, Chicago, Ill.

The Rt. Rev. Rowan D. Williams—Bishop of Monmouth, Wales.

ʿUmar Ibn al-Fāriḍ

SUFI VERSE, SAINTLY LIFE

TRANSLATED AND INTRODUCED BY
TH. EMIL HOMERIN

PREFACE BY
MICHAEL A. SELLS

PAULIST PRESS
NEW YORK • MAHWAH, NJ

Cover Art: *Ts Selves* (147 x 66 x 6 cm; oil & acrylic on canvas) is part of Mark Staff Brandl's Metonymic Series in which he enlarges aspects of an image into apparent abstractions thereby transposing essential physical, visual, and spiritual continuities (hence, metonymy). *Ts Selves* is composed of three independent panels which resonate in their primary colors and enigmatic black shapes. The latter's resemblance to calligraphy is the key as each panel visually echoes one of the Arabic sounds **ta**, **ti**, or **tu**. In Arabic, the second person past tense is often formed by suffixing either the masculine **ta** or feminine **ti** to the verb, but changed to the first person it becomes **tu**, which may be either masculine or feminine. Here, Brandl refers directly to v. 218 of the *Poem of the Sufi Way* by Ibn al-Fāriḍ which underscores his central message that lovers in union transcend duality as "You" and "I" become "me." Brandl mirrors this syntax in his painting as the individual panels or "selves," with their own particular colors, unite in the black forms which compose and grow out of the central axis of the work, suggesting a quiet, guided chaos to creation and mystical union.

Since 1988, Mark Staff Brandl has lived with his wife Cornelia in Switzerland. An active international artist, theorist and critic, Brandl has had numerous exhibitions, and won a number of awards; he is a frequent contributor to *Art in America*.

Book design by Theresa M. Sparacio and Lynn Else.

Interior art by Valerie Petro.

Library of Congress Cataloging-in-Publication Data

Ibn al-Fāriḍ, ʿUmar ibn ʿAlī, 1181 or 2-1235.
[Dīwān. English]
ʿUmar Ibn al-Fāriḍ : Sufi verse, saintly life/ translated and introduced by Th. Emil Homerin.
p. cm.—(The classics of Western spirituality)
Includes English translation of the introduction to the Dīwān, known as Dībājah (The adorned proem) by Abū al-Ḥasan Nūr al-Dīn ʿAlī al-Miṣrī.
Includes bibliographical references and indexes.
ISBN 0-8091-0528-4 (cloth)—ISBN 0-8091-4008-X (pbk.)
1. Ibn al-Fāriḍ, ʿUmar ibn ʿAlī, 1181 or 2-1235 Criticism and interpretation. I. Title: Sufi verse, saintly life. II. Homerin, Th. Emil, 1955- III. Sibṭ Ibn al-Fāriḍ, fl. 1334. IV. Title. V. Series.

PJ7755.I18 A1713 2000
892.7′134

00-047884

Published by Paulist Press
997 Macarthur Boulevard
Mahwah, New Jersey 07430

www.paulistpress.com

Printed and bound in the United States of America

Contents

Translator of This Volume

TH. EMIL HOMERIN is Professor and Chair of the Department of Religion and Classics at the University of Rochester, where he teaches courses on Islam, classical Arabic literature, and mysticism. A native of Pekin, Illinois, Homerin is a graduate of the University of Illinois at Champaign-Urbana (B.A. '77, M.A. '78) and completed the Ph.D. with honors at the University of Chicago in 1987. He has lived and worked in Egypt for several years and has been the recipient of a number of grants and awards, including fellowships from the Mrs. Giles Whiting Foundation, the Fulbright Program, and most recently from the National Endowment for the Humanities and the American Research Center in Egypt. Among his honors and awards are the American Association of Teachers of Arabic Translation Prize and the Golden Key National Honor Society's recognition for his contributions to undergraduate education.

His research and publications focus on medieval Arabic poetry and mysticism, particularly in Egypt, and his previous work includes *From Arab Poet to Muslim Saint: Ibn al-Fāriḍ, His Verse and His Shrine* (1994); "A Bird Ascends the Night: Elegy and Immortality in Islam" (*Journal of the American Academy of Religion* 59:4 [1991]); and "Saving Muslim Souls: The Khānqāh and the Sufi Duty in Mamluk Lands" (*Mamlūk Studies Review* 3 [1999]).

Author of the Preface

MICHAEL A. SELLS is Emily Judson Baugh and John Marshall Gest Professor of Comparative Religions at Haverford College. He is the author of *Early Islamic Mysticism: Sufi, Qur'an, Miʿraj, Poetic, and Theological Writings* (Paulist Press Classics of Western Spirituality, 1996). In an earlier work, *Mystical Languages of Unsaying* (University of Chicago Press, 1994), he presents an analysis and theory of apophatic mystical writing in Plotinus, John the Scot Eriugena, Ibn ʿArabi, Meister Eckhart, and Marguerite Porete. Other writings by Michael Sells include: *Desert Tracings: Six Classic Arabian Odes* (Wesleyan University Press, 1989); *The Bridge Betrayed: Religion and Genocide in Bosnia* (University of California Press, 1994); and *The Cambridge History of Arabic Literature, al-Andalus* (Cambridge University Press, 2000), for which he is coeditor and contributor; and *Stations of Desire: Love Elegies from Ibn ʿArabi and New Poems* (Ibis Editions, 2000).

Dedication

To Nora, light in the feminine form,
To Luke, masculine light,
and Elias, one with the whirlwind.

Acknowledgments

The Publisher gratefully acknowledges use of the following: Excerpts from *The Poems of Saint John of the Cross.* Copyright 1972 by Willis Barnstone. Reprinted by permission of New Directions Publishing Corp. Excerpt from *The Narrow Road to the Deep North and Other Travel Sketches* by Matuso Basho, translated by Nobuyuki Yuasa (Penguin Classics, 1966). Copyright 1966 by Nobuyuki Yuasa. Used by permission of Penguin Books Ltd. Excerpt from *Laughing Lost in the Mountains: Poems of Wang Wei.* Copyright 1991 by Tony Barnstone, Willis Barnstone, and Xu Haixin (University Press of New England, 1991).

Preface

During a stay in Damascus, I attempted one evening to take one of the city's many minivan services to an outlying area. I asked someone waiting near the minivan station how to find the van to my destination. He responded that he was going in the same direction, and, after we were seated in the van, he asked me why I was in Syria. When I told him I was researching classical Islamic mysticism, he immediately asked what I thought of Ibn al-Fāriḍ. Then he asked what I thought of Ibn al-Fāriḍ's poem, the *Tā'īyah* (poem rhyming in T), referred to in this volume as "The Poem of the Sufi Way." Finally, he asked me what I thought about the interior or esoteric dimensions of the poem. When we reached his stop, he invited me to dinner, saying he would like to discuss the poetry of Ibn al-Fāriḍ with me at length. Unfortunately, my previous appointment did not allow us to continue with our conversation.

This minivan encounter encapsulated for me the fundamental role of poetry within Islam, the poetic nature of Islamic mystical life and thought, and the difficulty in translating (in the broad sense of the term) this heritage, so deeply and broadly cultivated, in a way that would render it accessible to the Western reader. Poetry in this world is a living tradition. Muslims in India and Pakistan engage in *mushāʿiras,* all-night poetry "jam sessions," where people of all walks of life compete with one another in reciting poetry by memory and in extemporizing, in meter and verse, their own poetry on the spot. The Arabic world abounds with poetry festivals. Iran's heritage of great love poetry is close on the lips and in the heart of a large percentage of Iranians. Throughout much of the classical Islamic world, poetry is at the center of cultural life.

It has been said that the Islamic mystical tradition utilized poetry as a vehicle to express mystical psychology and philosophy. However, the relationship between poetry and mysticism has been more intimate than such a model would allow. From the earliest mystical writings in Islam, poetic and mystical expressions have interacted intensely, influencing and transforming one another. In many literary texts the two expressions are so completely intertwined that it is impossible to discover where one begins and the other leaves off.

There is a moment during the recitation of a poem when the eyes of the reciter and audience moisten from a combination of aesthetic pleasure and remembrance of loss. The Arabic term for this moment—when body, mind, and breathing begin to feel a new, slower, rhythm—is *tarab*. The term has no single equivalent in English. *Tarab* refers to a deep sense of aesthetic appreciation, a kind of love intoxication, a sense of being overcome with waves of remembrance of what is at the core of one's being and lies too deep for other modes of thought to engage.

This world of *tarab* remains largely unperceived in the West. The lack of recognition is not due to any lack of analogue in Western culture. Popular Western love songs echo the lyrics of Islamic poetry in the lover's complaint, the polemic against the beloved, and the madness of love. It is no surprise then that the Majnūn Laylā story inspired one of the most popular songs in modern Western music, Eric Clapton's "Layla." In addition, the role in the West of love lyric as a milestone of remembrance and emotion across a lifetime parallels its role within the Islamic world (though in the last century, the West has tended to associate such intimate use of love lyric with songs rather than with poetry that stands alone without musical accompaniment). Nor is the lack of recognition due to any weakness or invisibility of the *tarab* world of culture within Islamic civilization. Recite the first verse of a well-loved poem anywhere from Marrakech to Bukhara, and you will likely find your conversation partner reciting the rest of the poem by heart.

Difficulty of translation is a major factor in the recognition gap. Translations of Islamic love poetry into English commonly lose the intertextuality central to the poetic meaning. Although the major themes of love poetry are universal, the partially overlapping poetic traditions of the Islamic world are based upon networks of tradition-specific associations and allusions. A single poem may echo other poems extending back through the history of the poetic tradition, to the Qur'an, and other aspects of Arabic and Islamic heritage. Textbooks can offer an overview of the major ritual obligations, the major historical periods, the various dynasties, the great figures, and the social organizations of Islam. The appreciation of the poetic element of Islamic culture, however, is a matter of both cultivation and sensibility, what Muslims call *dhawq* or taste. While Muslims would both wish and expect an interested non-Muslim to be conversant with the former areas, they are frequently astonished and deeply moved when the latter elements of the poetic tradition, profound yet profoundly neglected in Western societies, are recognized.

Within the tradition of mystical poetry in Arabic, the Egyptian ʿUmar Ibn al-Fāriḍ is in terms of centrality and influence, without equal. And of all of Ibn al-Fāriḍ's verse, the "Poem of the Sufi Way" places the most demands upon the reader's understanding of the intercultural worlds in which it is placed. Indeed, the poem epitomizes almost every aspect of the Arabic and Islamic heritage in general, and of Islamic mystical heritage in particular.

Ibn al-Fāriḍ's verse is nourished by the Arabic poetic tradition, the Qur'an and the Sunna (the Islamic tradition based upon the life and words of the prophet and his companions), and centuries of cultivation of mystical experience and expression. In the present volume Emil Homerin offers a major advance in our understanding of Islamic spirituality. Homerin succeeds in making this epochal figure and his poems, their *tarab* and their *dhawq*, more accessible to an international and multireligious readership.

A major virtue of this volume is its organization of the stages of our journey into the spirituality of Ibn al-Fāriḍ. Emil Homerin begins with an elegant and economical overview of the literary and cultural worlds in which Ibn al-Fāriḍ's poetry is grounded. The introduction opens, appropriately, with the ruins of the lost beloved's campsite (*aṭlāl*), the motif that begins the classical Arabic ode (*qaṣīdah*). These ruins epitomize as well the translation gap between Islamic spirituality and its appreciation (or lack thereof) in Western scholarship and popular culture. The subtlest allusion to this, the *aṭlāl,* in any form of cultural expression is recognized immediately in the Islamic world and placed within multiple frames of meaning and possibility.

Yet, for over two centuries studies of Islamic mysticism have tended to divorce it from the poetic tradition exemplified by the *aṭlāl*, even though Islamic mystics were steeped in the poetics and spirituality of these ruins. One reason for this divorce is the rigid boundary imposed by many scholars between the worlds of Sufism and Islam more generally, and between the worlds of religion and poetry. Many Western scholars claimed that Sufism was not grounded in Islam at all, but was instead an import from Christianity or Indian religions. Some of the same scholars claimed that love itself was an import into Islam from Christianity, since the tradition of love poetry in which Islamic conceptions of love are grounded was consigned by them to the realm of the secular and thus not taken seriously as an element within religion. To break out of such artificial boundaries requires more than refutation. It requires a complex set of translations. The poem itself, its rhythms, tone, meter, assonance, and other qualities must be rendered in an English style that can create an analogous effect in a difference discursive world. In addition, a wider act of translation requires an accessible and economical, yet thorough, contextualization of the poem within its tradition. Emil Homerin's discussions of classical Arabic poetry, the Qur'an and hadith, mystical interpretations of the Qur'an, and intimate interactions between religion and poetry (within society and within the life, hagiography, and psychology of Ibn al-Fāriḍ) offer a contextual overview vital for the reading of the poetry and commentaries that follow.

The elegant translation of Ibn al-Fāriḍ's famous *Wine Song* invites us into the world of Islamic lyrical spirituality. What are we to make of the poet-persona's refusal to specify the wine as spiritual or as earthly, the use of motifs (the ancient vintage, the magical qualities of the wine) associated with the notorious court poet Abū Nuwās, and the poem's reveling in apparent irreverence? The above features are found throughout much of the most loved poetry of the Islamic world, from the Arabic love odes of Ibn al-Fāriḍ and Ibn al-ʿArabī to the *ghazal*, a genre of love poetry that has been compared to the European sonnet. Homerin's introduction to the *Wine Song* and his translation grant the previously uninitiated reader access into this pervasive and treasured aspect of culture and sensibility in the Islamic world.

Following the translation of the *Wine Song*, Homerin presents translations of selected entries in the commentaries on the poem by al-Farghānī and al-Nābulūsī. This tradition of theosophical commentary on love poetry illustrates the cultural importance of a poem that can ground entire traditions of commentary, much as the Song of Songs generated similar commentary in the Jewish and Christian traditions of medieval Europe. Homerin's introduction warns us of the trap in reading the poem as a mechanical set of substitutions for the theosophical categories of the commentaries. The introduction also highlights the significance of the commentaries in their own right. For the reader accustomed to modern close readings of poetry, these commentaries might seem to stretch the boundaries of interpretation, with their quick and apodictic moves from a kiss or drop of wine to a station within the psychology of mystical experience and advanced theosophical cosmology. Yet for generations of Muslims, both the lyrical understanding of the poem and the theosophical and psychological allegory have existed fully present at the same time.

"The Poem of the Sufi Way" embraces the mannerist (*badīʿa*) poetics of the time, including the propensity for complex puns based on permutations of the three-consonant radical of most Arabic words. The resultant figures of speech, so grounded in the visual and sonic features of the Arabic, are notoriously difficult to translate. Indeed, the translator is forced, at the risk of falling into forced English syntax, to abandon the search for an immediate analogue for many of these effects. The process of finding compensations for them in the host language, bringing across the wit of the particular wordplay, and preserving the tone and delicacy places extraordinary demands upon the translator: upon his understanding of the Arabic original, sensitivity to the poetic idiom of the host language into which he is translating, and willingness to experiment and remain patient over a long span of attempts and revisions.

Equally challenging is the range of the poem. "The Poem of the Sufi Way" is a microcosm of Islamic tradition at the time of Ibn al-Fāriḍ. A preliminary list of central themes of the poem would include the following: the famous lovers of classical Arabic poetry; key themes and passages from the Qur'an and from the hadith, the stories of the Qur'anic prophets; the stories of the four "rightly guided" Caliphs; mystical interpretations of Qur'anic passage and the motifs that grew out of these interpretations, such as the pre-eternal covenant; worlds of esoteric science (alchemy, astrology, divination, numerology); the psychology of Sufi states of altered consciousness; the stations of Muḥammad's *miʿrāj,* or journey through the heavenly spheres to the divine throne; the stations of the mystic in his or her journey to the divine beloved; and interpretations of key mystical concepts such as *fanā'*—the passing-away of the human self in mystical union with the divine.

The general introduction, the introduction to the poem, and the running commentary provide us with the clues we need to follow these allusions. Of special interest is the poetic "I," a subject persona that is at times clearly human, at times divine, and at times seems to indicate the moment of union between the two. Homerin offers intriguing comparisons of this persona with poems from the Western tradition. We might add to these analogues the "I" of Walt Whitman's *Leaves of Grass*. The contrasts between Whitman's world and that of Ibn al-Fāriḍ are obvious. But those very contrasts might allow us one more way of viewing a complex subject persona that can be, depending upon the particular verse and the interpretation, both individual and collective, both mortal and eternal, both human and divine. In the case of "The Poem of the Sufi Way," this doubled referent (or fused referent when the voice speaks from the perspective of mystical union) results in a remarkably sustained reflection upon the hadith, quoted and explained by Homerin, in which God becomes the very faculties (hearing, seeing, touch, movement, speech) of the servant loved by God.

In following the movement of the subject voice of the poem, I found myself making connections among the *aṭlāl* (those ruins of the lost beloved's campsite that lie at the origin of poetic consciousness); the pre-eternal covenant (in which the human and divine were together and to which the human strives to return); and the pre-eternal wine (that existed before the creation of the vine). The *aṭlāl* and ancient wine are marks of the lost union with the beloved, a lost paradise. In the pre-eternal convenant Sufism brings together the poetic sense of lost garden and Qur'anic notions of lost and promised moments of union. As the subject voice of the poem, the "I" moves back and forth from the eternal to the temporal, from the perspective of mystical union to that of separation, this interweaving is thickened. These are some personal connections I have made while reading the poem. Others will no doubt find other connections; and the number of possible connections to be made in a poem of this range and depth is vast.

In this volume, the spirituality of Ibn al-Fāriḍ has been refracted for us into panels of various cultural and literary color: allusion and subtext; lyricism; the love poem's allegorical and theosophical parallel universe; and a subject persona at once majestic and intimate. The final refraction is the hagiography of Ibn al-Fāriḍ composed by his grandson. Here we are brought into the process of the formation or construction of a saint. By this time, with the acculturation that we have encountered previously in the volume, we are better prepared to understand the stories in which Ibn al-Fāriḍ collapses, shrieks, is driven into ecstasy, or tears off his clothes and runs near-naked through the street—all upon hearing a few verses of love poetry. And we are better prepared to understand why and how such events would be singled out by a hagiographer within Islam as key moments in the development and recognition of a saint.

Michael A. Sells

Note to the Reader

ʿUmar Ibn al-Fāriḍ (d. 632/1235) is the most venerated mystical poet in Arabic, comparable to John Donne in English or John of the Cross in Spanish. Two of his poems, in particular, have long been considered classics of Islamic mystical literature: the *Wine Ode (al-Khamrīyah)*, and the extraordinary *Poem of the Sufi Way (Naẓm al-sulūk/al-Tāʾīyah al-kubrā)*. In these and other works, Ibn al-Fāriḍ deftly employed the Arabic poetic tradition for religious ends to voice the spiritual ideas and feelings of many of his contemporaries, and his poems have been the focus of mystical commentaries for centuries. A major contribution to this tradition was the definitive *Dīwān*, or edition, of Ibn al-Fāriḍ's verse made by his grandson ʿAlī, who prefaced this collection with a reverential account of his grandfather's pious life, known as the *Adorned Proem (Dībājah)*. This popular work promoted Ibn al-Fāriḍ's saintly status throughout the Islamic world, where his verse continues to be recited as a living testimony to his enduring reputation as both a master poet and spiritual guide.

On Translation

My translations in this volume are the final stage in a process that necessarily depends upon close reading and analysis of the Arabic originals, so that one may grasp their meaning and spirit. This essential foundation has been laid, in large part, by Professor Jaroslav Stetkevych, whose erudition and love of classical Arabic poetry have left their impression not only on me, but on an entire generation of scholars. Dr. Stetkevych is also to be commended for the virtue of true patience, which I again ask of him and other readers, for all translations in this volume—together with any mistakes—are my own unless otherwise noted.

The translation of ʿAlī's *Proem to the Dīwān* poses few problems; translating his grandfather's poetry, however, is more challenging. Since many of Ibn al-Fāriḍ's originals are still regarded as poetic masterpieces, they deserve at least a reasonable counterpart in English, and so, when translating his verse, I have been concerned not only with form and content but also with the poems' tones, moods, and deeper meanings. Toward this end, my own method of translation generally follows that laid out by Robert Bly in *The Eight Stages of Translation* (Boston: Rowan Tree Press [1983], 13–49). The final stages of a translation are particularly crucial, and here I was especially helped by Deans Richard Aslin and William Scott Green, the Department of English, and Edward Wierenga, then chair of the Department of Religion and Classics at the University of Rochester, who collaborated to make a Bridge Grant possible. This grant allowed me to undertake a semester of intensive study of poetry in English by working closely with two accomplished poets in Rochester's English Department, Barbara Jordan and Jarold Ramsey. They judiciously read drafts of my translations, suggested revisions, and graciously shared with me their knowledge and love of poetry. Finally, Michael Sells of Haverford College read the last drafts of the poems and offered invaluable suggestions in light of his deep knowledge and appreciation of Arabic poetry and Islamic mysticism.

Clearly, good translations must stand on their own as poems that can be enjoyed and appreciated with a minimum of notes and commentary. Nevertheless, a translation is a "bringing over" of material from one culture and language to another and, as such, a conscious exercise in interpretation potentially relevant to interested individuals in a variety of fields. Therefore, I have tried to clarify thorny issues of translation and meaning in the introduction and commentary specific to each translation. For those wishing to pursue more detailed study of Ibn al- iḍ's Arabic verse and its Sufi import, a number of pertinent works are listed in the bibliography, to which I would add my own forthcoming study of the poet, tentatively entitled *Passion Before Me, My Fate Behind: Ibn al-Fāriḍ and the Poetry of Recollection.*

Matters of Form

In these translations I have attempted to present the original Arabic material in forms congenial to English and its readers. In the *Proem*, for instance, I have created paragraphs and added punctuation, though both are largely absent in the manuscripts. As for Arabic poetry, the originals are composed of verses bearing a consistent meter and end-rhyme, with each line divided into two nearly equal half lines. Further, much of this poetry is characterized by the presence of paradox and parallel constructions, reinforced by the repetition of words and sounds. After a number of experiments in form, I decided to translate each Arabic verse into a four-line stanza, which, I felt, encouraged the parallel and paradoxical play of the original. Additionally, in a number of places within the translation of the *Poem of the Sufi Way,* I use shifting margins within groups of stanzas to underscore dialog (e.g., vv. 8–116), as well as prominent Arabic rhetorical features, including parallelism (e.g., vv. 139–47), and structural patterning (vv. 537–74).

Although this volume aims to introduce Ibn al-Fāriḍ's thought and verse to a broad, contemporary audience, certain key Arabic terms are cited in the commentaries, along with their translations, in order to alert the reader to multiple meanings, word plays, and subtle relationships among important word clusters. The transliteration of these words follows the system used for Arabic by the Library of Congress. Well-known words and names, however, are generally cited in their common English forms (e.g., Sufi, not Ṣūfī; Cairo, not al-Qāhirah; Moses, not Mūsā).

When pronouncing these key words and names, the reader should be aware that Arabic vowels and consonants approximate those of English. There are three short Arabic vowels: (1) *a* as in "bat," (2) *i* as in "bit," (3) *u* as in "put." Long vowels are usually lengthened short vowels. There are two Arabic diphthongs: (1) *ay* as in the *i* of "bite," and (2) *aw* as in "cow." The majority of Arabic consonants sound like their English equivalents with the following additions: the hamzah (') is a glottal stop; the ʿayn (ʿ) is produced by "swallowing" the vowel immediately preceding or following it (e.g., maʿārif, ʿUmar); *kh* approximates the *ch* of "loch" or "Bach"; *ḥ* resembles a breathy, whispered "ha!" In addition, there are four velarized or "emphatic" consonants: *ṣ, ḍ, ṭ, ẓ;* they give a "darker" quality to the surrounding vowels (e.g., Arabic *s* is pronounced like the English "sad," while *ṣ* approximates "sod." The emphatics are of importance to this work since the Sufi poet's name is Ibn al-Fāriḍ; the emphatic *ḍ* gives the *ā* the sound of a prolonged *a* as in "father."

Texts

Despite many published editions, Ibn al-Fāriḍ's *Dīwān* has yet to be properly edited from manuscript, and there is even a lack of consensus regarding the number of its poems. My translations of the *Wine Ode*, the *Poem of the Sufi Way*, and the *Adorned Proem* are based primarily on the Arabic edition of Ibn al-Fāriḍ's *Dīwān* as compiled by the poet's grandson, and most recently edited by ʿAbd al-Khāliq Maḥmūd (Cairo: Dār al-Maʿārif, 1984). However, the Maḥmūd edition, too, has errors and omissions, and so I have made corrections and additions based on several manuscripts of the work, especially ms 3968 (Adab) and ms 1965 (Adab) from Cairo's Dār al-Kutub al-Miṣrīyah, together with a microfilm of the oldest known manuscript of ʿAlī's edition—#1559 (Shiʿr) of ms 238, Tehran: Kitābkhānah Markazī (Cairo: Arab League Manuscript Institute, 775/1393)—which I discovered during several years of research in Cairo, generously supported by the Fulbright program, the American Research Center in Egypt, and Egypt's Dār al-Kutub and the Arab League Manuscript Institute. A fourth manuscript was also consulted, the Chester Beatty Library ms Ar3643 (i)/5473 (former Arabic ms 472), which is an edition of Ibn al-Fāriḍ's *Dīwān* based on a line of transmission independent of the poet's grandson ʿAlī. The Chester Beatty Library graciously provided me with a microfilm of this manuscript, which was partially edited and published in transliteration by A. J. Arberry (Chester Beatty Monographs, no. 4 [1952]).

NOTE TO THE READER

Dates

Many classical Arabic sources are arranged according to Islamic "Hijrī" dates, and so all dates cited in this work prior to the twentieth century are given in the Islamic years followed by their Common Era equivalents (e.g., 632/1235).

Acknowledgments

I remain indebted to earlier studies and translations of Ibn al-Fāriḍ, especially those of R. A. Nicholson and A. J. Arberry, and to friends and colleagues who have made this a better work through their assistance, comments, and corrections. In particular, I wish to thank again Mark Brandl, William Cleveland, Bruce Craig, Robert Dankoff, Frederick de Jong, Carl Ernst, Iymān Fu'ād Sayyid, Aḥmad Ḥarīdī, Barbara Jordan, Paul Lowsensky, Heshmet Moayyad, Séan O'Feahy, Ruth Ost, the late Fazlur Rahman, Jerry Ramsey, Paula Saffire, Michael Sells, Jaroslav and Suzanne Stetkevych, John Swanson, and Nora Walter. I am also grateful to Paulist Press, especially to copyeditor Joan LaFlamme, and to editor Kathleen Walsh, whose wit and humor added a touch of fun to the tedious task of proofreading and editing.

Finally, I want to add that I first met the cover artist, Mark Brandl, in my hometown of Pekin, Illinois when we were both ten years old. A fast friendship immediately ensued when we learned that we were born approximately ten hours and ten miles apart on the same day—May 19, 1955. Since then we have crossed paths repeatedly, and, over the last twenty-five years, have collaborated on numerous reviews, articles, and projects involving art and mysticism, including the painting *Ts Selves* about which may be added this final note. When the mysticism series, Classics of Western Spirituality, began in 1978, I, as a first-year graduate student, was heard to remark, "I'll be in that series someday." To which Brandl reportedly said, "And I'll paint your cover." No doubt we spoke from naivete, even hubris, but then, here we are.

Introduction

In memory of the beloved
we drank a wine;
we were drunk with it
before creation of the vine.

This opening verse to the renowned *Wine Ode* by ʿUmar Ibn al-Fāriḍ begins with the invocation of the beloved and memory of her, and ends in the intoxication produced by a timeless vintage. Ibn al-Fāriḍ has assembled this scene from several essential elements that appear throughout his poetry: wine, love, the beloved, and, above all, the act of recollection. In this, he shares much with earlier Arab poets who composed moving poems lamenting the loss of love and life. Traditionally, standing amid the ruins of the beloved's desert campsite, the poet questions his fate as he recalls his beloved's final departure:

Whose encampments are these
which you came upon at al-Anʿum,
whose dappled traces appear
like the markings of the speckled snake?

The east wind had played with them
so they were hard to recognize,
save for the remains of a trench,
its sides caved in.

They were the abode of a girl
with a broad white smile, soft and tender,
with slender hips and firm forearms
where the bracelets go round.

But she listened to those who slandered us
and cut the bonds to you,
and now she has gone off with your neighbors
on the road to Syria.

So here you are brokenhearted,
overwhelmed by love desire
and flowing passion,
reeling like a madman.

Why not forget your grief
with a strong she-camel,
brisk as the wild ass,
like a bite-scarred camel stallion,

One strutting with her saddle,
trustworthy on the night journey,
proudly flipping her tail,
and breaking stones with her notched hooves?

Ask Tamīm and ʿĀmir
of their wars with us;
is a man who knows nothing
equal to one seasoned by experience?[1]

The fading traces of an encampment, a water trench, charred hearthstones, or other remains may empower a poet to evoke the blissful union of days gone by and to ponder his destiny. As in these verses by Bishr ibn Abī Khāzim (fl. 6th C.E.), there is an Orphic quality to such poetry as the poet summons an image of his beloved, only to lose her again in the harsh reality of separation and death. Although Ibn al-Fāriḍ rarely speaks of war, his poetic landscape is still very much the same, filled with the desert flora and fauna of the pre-Islamic bedouin poets, and with their longing:

O driver of the caravan,
halt for a moment at the spring encampment
that I might see or hear
the gazelles in the winding valley.

For if I cannot see them
or hear them recalled,
then I have no use
for eyes or ears.[2]

Ibn al-Fāriḍ's desert is also the locus for other powerful forces, and specific landmarks show that his dunes, valleys, and their gazelles are near Mecca and Medina, the holiest Muslim land. In such a context, Ibn al-Fāriḍ's *dhikr*, his "recollection," becomes more than the shaman-poet's conjuring of his beloved's shade, for *dhikr* is the Sufi practice of meditation undertaken to induce ecstasy and, perhaps, too, the beatific vision. Ibn al-Fāriḍ's poetry, then, blends two traditions, that of classical Arabic poetry together with Islamic mysticism, to intimate deeper spiritual dimensions within life and to call his listeners to set out on a pilgrimage leading back to God:

O my night companion,
refresh my spirit,
singing of Mecca
if you wish to cheer me,

For her courtyard has my herds,
her soil is my grassland,
and her torrent channel is my place
for water and provisions.

In her was my intimacy,
and the ascent of my sanctity:
my station was Abraham's,[3]
and the enlightenment clear.

But the fortunes carried me
    away from her;
        cut off from water
            my drinking could not last.

If only time
    would permit a return,
        perhaps then my festive days
            would return to me.[4]

A Sweet Spring of Arabic

Ibn al-Fāriḍ's love of the Mecca and Medina stemmed in part from the years he spent there as a young man and his later return on the pilgrimage. Nevertheless, he passed the majority of his life in Cairo, where he taught the traditions of the prophet Muḥammad *(ḥadīth)* and poetry. Several of his students wrote short accounts of him, including the Andalusian *ḥadīth* scholar, mystic, and litterateur Muḥammad ibn Yūsuf Ibn Musdī (598–663/1202–65):

> ʿUmar ibn Abī al-Ḥasan [ʿAlī] ibn al-Murshid ibn ʿAlī, a descendent of the Saʿd tribe, Abū al-Qāsim and Abū Ḥafs. His father was originally from Hama, [while ʿUmar] was born and resided in Egypt and known as Ibn al-Fāriḍ, for his father was a women's advocate *[fāriḍ]* before the governor of Egypt. His father was among the people of religious knowledge and scholarship, and he gave his son a broad education in belles lettres *[adab]*. [Ibn al-Fāriḍ] was of gentle nature, a sweet pool and spring, of pure Arabic in expression, refined of allusion, fluent and sublime in pronunciation and quotation. He then decided to undertake the study of Sufism, and so he became like a variegated meadow, perfumed by beauty, clad with good nature, gathering from the generosity of the self all varieties [of good things]. He lived in Mecca and then returned to his country [of Egypt] and took up residence in the Azhar congregational mosque. He heard *[ḥadīth]* from Abū [Muḥammad]

al-Qāsim ibn ʿAlī al-ʿAsākirī[5] and others, and he taught *ḥadīth*. I heard something of that and some of his poetry.[6]

Ibn Musdī adds that Ibn al-Fāriḍ was born in 576/1181 and died in 632/1235; several other students noted that Ibn al-Fāriḍ had been a member of the Shāfiʿī legal school, and that his grave was in Cairo's al-Qarāfah cemetery. These notices by Ibn al-Fāriḍ's contemporaries provide only limited information about him, but they nevertheless draw attention to his three areas of scholarly interest: *ḥadīth,* mysticism, and poetry. In fact, Ibn al-Fāriḍ's recognized expertise in Arabic poetry led to his adjudicating a famous literary dispute in Cairo, while one of his odes was said to have so impressed the Ayyubid sultan al-Malik al-Kāmil (r. 615–35/1218–38) that the sultan sent the poet a large sum of money and later sought his permission to erect a shrine for him. The story goes that Ibn al-Fāriḍ refused the sultan's lavish offers, choosing to trust in God and not some earthly sovereign to meet his needs.[7]

One may question the validity of such stories, yet there are strong indications that Ibn al-Fāriḍ may have shunned the public life of the royal court. Several noted poets of his day, including Ibn Sanāʿ al-Mulk (550–608/1155–1211), Ibn ʿUnayn (549–630/1154–1232), Bahā al-Dīn Zuhayr (581–656/1186–1258), and Ibn Matrūḥ (592–649/1196–1251), actively pursued courtly favor by composing panegyrics and other poems on a ruler's behalf. These poets often worked in the Dīwān al-Inshā' (Ministry of Information) and frequently rose to positions of power, such as vizier.[8] However, there is no evidence that Ibn al-Fāriḍ ever composed panegyric or political verse, or held a ministerial position. On the contrary, the religious nature of his occupation as an *ḥadīth* scholar is underscored by his residence at the Azhar mosque, where he also appears to have taught poetry. By this means, Ibn al-Fāriḍ supported his family, which included at least three children, while avoiding the moral and aesthetic compromise expected of a court poet, along with the political intrigues of the period, as the Ayyubid princes fought among themselves and the Crusaders for the right to rule Egypt, Syria, and the Holy Lands around Jerusalem and in Arabia.[9]

Ibn al-Fāriḍ did, however, resemble the court poets of his time in one respect, namely, their shared poetic style, commonly known as *badīʿ*. By the seventh/thirteenth century, Arabic poetry had entered a period of pronounced mannerism. A primary subject of this verse was the poetic tradition itself, as poets paid homage to past masters while seeking to surpass them by means of rhetorical strategies meant to amaze and delight their audiences, and praise their patrons:

Al-Malik al-ʿĀdil,
the "just king"
whose regal names honor
the pulpits of all domains,

His copious justice
has summoned forth in every land
a garden like paradise, well-watered
by his call for flowing generosity!

Due to his justice,
the wolf passes the night
famished with knotted stomach,
though the tawny gazelle is in his sight.

No true believer
can be troubled to doubt
about Abū Bakr,
that best of men![10]

These verses are from a long panegyric composed in praise of the Ayyubid ruler and counter-crusader Abū Bakr al-Malik al-ʿĀdil (d. 615/1216) by the poet Ibn ʿUnayn, who has drawn from nothing less than the Qur'ān and Islamic tradition to praise his lord. Just as God's Beautiful Names (including al-ʿAdl, "the Just") are recited in the mosque, so, too, are the ruler's name and titles read during the Friday sermon as the congregation prays for his well-being. But Ibn ʿUnayn implies that al-ʿĀdil's name has the power of its divine counterpart and so may serve as an instrument of creation. For the peace and prosperity that the sultan's beneficence brings to his domains have transformed the land into a verdant garden, like the garden of paradise watered by the heavenly river Kawthar. Further, the sultan's justice has reached not only his human subjects, but all of nature as the wolf holds back from devouring the gazelle, a clear parallel to the lion lying down with the lamb. Then, Ibn ʿUnayn plays on the sultan's name, Abū Bakr, which was also the name of the first caliph and one of the prophet Muḥammad's most trusted companions, to exalt the sultan's piety and holy mission as the defender of the faith, and the poet declares his master to be *khayr al-warā*, "the best of men," a title traditionally referring to the prophet Muḥammad.[11]

Ibn ʿUnayn's laud of al-ʿĀdil was praised for its charm and elegance by his learned contemporaries, but this complex poetic style in the hands of lesser poets and in obsequious praise of minor officials soon threatened to smother poetic creativity with a rhetorical excess of baroque proportions. Nevertheless, the *badīʿ* style, at its best, challenged familiar modes of perception through metaphorical inversions, antithesis, and word play in order to present a world where the seemingly ordinary might suddenly reveal the miraculous.[12] With this in mind, Ibn al-Fāriḍ perfected his own particular *badīʿ* style to articulate his views of a reality in which all of creation, when seen aright, is bathed in the glow of love's supernal light:

Every charming man,
  every pretty girl,
    their loveliness is lent to them
      from her beauty.

For her, Qays was mad for Lubnā,
  and just so all the other lovers
    like Laylā and Majnūn,
      ʿAzzah and Kuthayyir.

Each of them desired the quality
  she had wrapped
    in a form of loveliness shining forth
      in a loveliness of form.

Because she appeared
in outward forms they supposed
were someone else
though she revealed herself there.

In veils she came forth,
hidden by external guise,
each showing shaded
with shape shifting.[13]

Kissing the Cup's Lip

In respect to his aesthetic and spiritual ends, Ibn al-Fāriḍ resembles such Buddhist and Taoist poets as the Japanese Haiku master Matsuo Bashō (1644–94) and the Chinese poet and painter Wang Wei (699 or 701–59 or 61). Verse by both Asian poets takes the form of a quiet meditation on the human condition, and on nature, which serves as a polished mirror to reflect often unseen mystical realities. By approaching nature with a mind free of ideas and opinions, they lose themselves and so find a profound stillness:

Breaking the silence
Of an ancient pond,
A frog leaps into water—
A deep resonance.
—Bashō[14]

On branch tips the hibiscus bloom.
The mountains show off red calices.
Nobody. A silent cottage in the valley.
One by one flowers open, then fall.
—Wang Wei[15]

Ibn al-Fāriḍ also senses a deeper mystery in the natural world, but unlike Wang Wei and Bashō, he rarely pauses for long over any single object or image. Rather, he pushes on to encounter his beloved anew in yet some other trace of love's inner presence:

Though he be absent from me
   every grasping sense sees him
in every subtle sense,
   lovely and pure:

In the melody
   of the lyre and gentle flute
when they embrace
   in trilling notes of song,

In the meadows
   of the forest gazelle
in twilight's cool
   and daybreak's glow,

Where the mist
   falls from clouds
on a blossoming carpet
   woven from flowers,

Where the zephyr
   sweeps its skirts,
guiding to me at dawn
   the sweetest scent,

And in my kissing
   the cup's lip,
sipping wine drops
   in pure pleasure.

I never knew exile
   while he was with me,
and wherever we were
   my mind was at quiet rest.[16]

Here, the scene slowly unfolds to reveal the lover from dawn to dusk, listening to moving music as he drinks wine in memory of his beloved. Ibn al-Fāriḍ has carefully arranged a series of nouns, their supporting participles, and several verbs within repeating and symmetrical syntactical forms to highlight the beloved's emanation throughout the world of the lover's senses, a result, no doubt, of their former union recalled in the final verse. This dense weave of a highly rhetorical poetic form together with themes of love, longing, and union is characteristic of Ibn al-Fāriḍ's poetry, as are its dramatic and introspective qualities. In this respect, Ibn al-Fāriḍ's verse resembles closely that of the English metaphysical poets John Donne (d. 1631), George Herbert (d. 1633), and Henry Vaughan (d. 1695), with their search for illumination both in nature, and especially within the human soul:

Here musing long, I heard
A rushing wind
Which still increas'd, but whence it stirr'd
No where I could find;

I turn'd me round, and to each shade
Dispatch'd an Eye,
To see, if any leafe had made
Least motion, or Reply,
But while listening I sought
My mind to ease
By knowing, where 'twas, or where not,
It whisper'd; *Where I please.*

Lord, then said I, *on me one breath,*
And let me dye before my death!
—Henry Vaughan[17]

To hasten a spiritual awakening or, as in these verses, the coming of the Holy Spirit, Vaughan, Donne, and other Christian poets of the seventeenth century practiced meditation exercises, including those of Ignatius of Loyola (d. 1556), and this clearly contributed to the devotional and mystical character of their verse as well as to its formal composition.[18]

Similarly, as an accomplished Sufi, Ibn al-Fāriḍ was well-versed in the practice of *dhikr* ("recollection, meditation"), which he regarded as an essential tool for moral purification and spiritual ecstasy.[19] Ibn al-Fāriḍ's poetry, then, may be considered one of meditation, as the act of recollection beginning the poems initiates an interior drama in which the poet "projects a self upon an inner stage, and there comes to know that self in the light of a divine presence."[20]

At this point an obvious parallel should be drawn between Ibn al-Fāriḍ and another great poet of mystical love, the Spanish monk John of the Cross (1542–91), whose *Cántico espiritual* has several stanzas built on nouns and adjectives and which convey a tone and mood similar to Ibn al-Fāriḍ's meditation quoted above:

> My love, the mountains and
> the solitary wooded valleys
> the unexpected islands,
> the loud sonorous rivers,
> the whistling of the loving winds.
>
> The night of total calm
> before the rising winds of dawn,
> the music of a silence,
> the sounding of a solitude,
> the supper that renews our love.[21]

Ibn al-Fāriḍ and John of the Cross stress the negative way toward union, as the lover must eradicate his selfish ways in total obedience to the beloved's will, and both poets map the *via negativa* to be followed by lovers aspiring to union and illumination. In his poems, John of the Cross turned to Italian verse, popular songs in Spanish and Portuguese, and, above all, to the Bible's Song of Songs for much of his love imagery, while Ibn al-Fāriḍ drew from the Qur'ān and, more often, from Classical Arabic poetry and ancient Arab love legends. The beautiful love poems composed by both men certainly encourage a mystical reading, though overt theological and mystical references are generally absent. This calls attention to the important fact that the mystical ideas of Ibn al-Fāriḍ and John of the Cross are intimately connected to love and its poetic expression, to the extent that they should not be, indeed, cannot be separated. To speak in the age-old tradition of wine, the poem is not a vessel into which is poured a mystical substance to be consumed and the cup discarded. Rather, mysticism is the wine and poetry the sweet water that blend together to produce an invigorating and refreshing drink different and, perhaps, superior to either alone.[22]

Nevertheless, both poets have left us a cipher to the mystical ideas pervading their verse. John of the Cross wrote four substantial commentaries interpreting the mystical meanings and implications of his three major love poems, *Cántico espirtual*, *Noche oscura*, and *Oh Llama de amor viva*, while composing about a dozen other poems whose religious themes are more readily apparent.[23] The number of authentic poems by Ibn al-Fāriḍ is likewise modest, consisting of seven love poems *(ghazal)*, seven odes *(qaṣīdah)*, a wine ode *(khamrīyah)*, and several dozen quatrains and riddles.[24] Among his odes, however, is the *al-Tā'īyah al-kubrā (Ode in T Major)*, also known as the *Naẓm al-sulūk (Poem of the Sufi Way)*. This poem is unprecedented in the history of Arabic mystical verse, for while Sufis had drawn inspiration from and contributed to the larger Arabic poetic tradition for centuries, no one before Ibn al-Fāriḍ had ever made such a grand poetic presentation of mystical thought in Arabic.

Spanning seven hundred and sixty verses, the *Poem of the Sufi Way* is one of the longer poems ever composed in Arabic and the most famous one rhyming in "T." Yet in contrast to other lengthy Arabic poems, such as those on grammar or law, this ode is not confined to a didactic presentation of its subject, as Ibn al-Fāriḍ frequently employs highly lyrical language to speak of mystical love and life. Indeed, the first 163 verses of the *Poem of the Sufi Way* are little different from several of Ibn al-Fāriḍ's longer love poems, but, then, the poet ends his *ghazal*, declaring that the time is right to examine the mystical elements composing many of his poetic themes and images. Taking the form of a guide for the perplexed, the next six hundred verses range over a number of crucial concerns confronting the seeker on the Sufi path, and, in the role of the enlightened spiritual guide, Ibn al-Fāriḍ instructs his student on such mystical matters as selfless love, spiritual intoxication and enlightened sobriety, and union. But no matter the issue, Ibn al-Fāriḍ continues to display his considerable poetic skill throughout the poem while, at the same time, drawing attention to his broad knowledge and profound understanding of Sufism.

He Loves Them, and They Love Him

Often referred to in Arabic as *taṣawwuf* ("following the Sufi path"), Sufism, or Islamic mysticism, designates the study of experiences within Islam characterized by ineffability, a noetic quality, and transience, and frequently by a positive sense of passivity, timelessness, and unity. Sufism also includes the methods to attain and refine these experiences, the theories and doctrines regarding their origin and significance, and the place of these experiences within the lives of individuals and their societies. Given its spiritual concerns, Sufism clearly has much in common with other mystical traditions, but some similarities also stem, in part, from the fact that in the seventh century Islam came to light and flourished in an environment saturated with religious beliefs and practices flowing from a number of sources, including Judaism, Christianity, and Zoroastrianism, and fed by a variety of Hellenistic religious currents. Islam was undoubtedly influenced to some degree by the many ascetic and mystical practices in the region, including the wearing of a simple frock made of wool *(ṣūf)*, from which Sufism derives its name. Still, Islamic mysticism has always drawn its sustenance primarily from the Qur'ān and the traditions of the prophet Muḥammad.[25] Though the Qur'ān is justly renowned for its powerful vision of the Last Day and divine judgment, many passages reveal a God of mercy and compassion whose living presence is always around us:

> To God belongs the east and west; wherever you turn, there is the face of God. (2:115)
>
> If my servants inquire of you concerning Me, lo, I am near. (2:186)
>
> We are nearer [to the human being] than his jugular vein. (50:16)

The Qur'ān calls humanity to bear witness to God's oneness and to worship only Him, and as a sign of love and mercy for His creation, God has sent prophets to remind human beings of their obligations. Those who answer the call will find their reward with their Lord:

> Say [to them, Muḥammad]: "If you love God, then follow me, that He may love you and forgive your sins, for God is forgiving and merciful." (3:31)

> God loves those who depend upon Him completely. (3:159)

> O self at peace, return to your Lord, contented and pleasing. Enter among My servants and enter My garden. (89:27–30)

> The paradise promised to the God-fearing is like a garden flowing with rivers of ever pure water and delicious milk, with rivers of wine delightful to those who drink, and rivers of pure honey. Every kind of fruit is there for them, and forgiveness from their Lord. (47:15)

But humanity need not wait until the Judgment Day to encounter God's blessings, for He has revealed the Qur'ān to guide them, while He generously showers His favors upon sincere believers, especially during the mysterious Night of Power:

> Truly We sent down [the Qur'ān] on the Night of Power. What will convey to you what the Night of Power is? The Night of Power is better than a thousand months! The angels and the Spirit [of Revelation] descend then with every decree by permission of their Lord. Peace there is until the rise of dawn! (97:1–5)

These and other verses were a source of inspiration for Ibn al-Fāriḍ and other Muslim mystics in their quest for a close relationship with God. Similarly influential have been the many Qur'ānic accounts of human and divine encounters, often found in stories of the prophets, such as Moses on Sinai and his standing before the Burning Bush, Abraham's conversations with God, and the miracles of Jesus. Moses' meeting with a mysterious stranger possessing esoteric wisdom became a mystical paradigm in Islam, as did Joseph's beauty and spiritual knowledge, and Jacob's faith. But of paramount significance has been the life of the prophet Muḥammad (ca. 570–11/632), and Qur'ānic references to such important events as Muḥammad's early victory against a larger heathen force at Badr and his moments of spiritual revelation:

> Blessed be he who took his servant [Muḥammad] by night from the sacred mosque to the furthest mosque, whose precincts We have blessed, that We might show him Our signs. (17:1)
>
> Truly this [Qur'ān] is a revelation inspired, taught to [Muḥammad] by one strong, powerful, possessing intellect who set himself on the farthest horizon and then drew close and descended to within two bows' length or nearer, and he revealed to his servant [Muḥammad] what he revealed. The heart did not lie about what it saw, so will you wrangle about what he saw? [Muḥammad] saw him descend again, near the furthest lote tree where the Garden of Sanctuary is, where there enveloped the lote tree what enveloped it. [Muḥammad's] vision did not turn away or transgress, and truly, he saw one the greatest signs of his Lord! (53:4–18)[26]

These two passages have been joined in Muslim tradition to form the basis for Muḥammad's *al-Isrā' wa-al-Miʿrāj*, his miraculous Night Journey from Mecca to Jerusalem and his subsequent ascension to heaven accompanied by the archangel Gabriel, where the prophet met with various prophets and, ultimately, with God. Though the Qur'ān gives no details beyond the passages cited above—which do not, in fact, speak of an ascension at all—later Muslim recensions are full of details supported by prophetic *ḥadīth (al-ḥadīth al-nabawī)*, accounts of Muḥammad's sayings and actions, and a second foundational source of Islamic mysticism. In addition to elaborating on Muḥammad's heavenly ascension and other archetypal aspects of his pious life and ascetic ways, the *ḥadīth* collections also convey instructions on ritual and legal matters, as well as aphorisms and advice for those who would follow a path of love and devotion toward God:

> [Muḥammad] the Apostle of God—God's blessings and peace be upon him—said: "Sincerity is that you worship God as if you see Him, and if you do not see Him, know that He sees you."
>
> The Prophet—God's blessings and peace be upon him—said: "Not one of you truly believes until you love for your brother what you love for yourself."
>
> A man came to the Prophet—God's blessings and peace be upon him—and said: "O Messenger of God, guide me to an act that if I do it, God will love me, and the people will love me." So he replied: "Renounce this world, and God will love you; renounce what people possess, and people will love you."
>
> The Messenger of God—God's blessings and peace be upon him—said: "Be in this world as if you were a stranger or wayfarer."[27]

Beside the prophetic *ḥadīth* is a smaller body of traditions known as Divine Sayings *(al-ḥadīth al-qudsī*, *al-ḥadīth al-illāhī*, or *al-ḥadīth al-rabbānī)*. They purport to be the words of God revealed to Muḥammad but, for various reasons, not found in the Qur'ān, and a number of these traditions directly address mystical matters:[28]

> The Messenger of God—God's blessings and peace be upon him—said:
>
> God said: "My servant draws near to Me by nothing more dear to Me than by the religious obligations that I have imposed upon him, and My servant continues to draw near to Me by willing acts of devotion such that I love him. Then, when I love him, I become the ear with which he hears, the eye with which he sees, the hand with which he grasps, and the foot

with which he walks. Surely were he to request something of Me, I would give it, and if he were to seek My protection, I would shelter him."[29]

Ibn al-Fāriḍ alludes to this Divine Saying, known as "The Tradition of Willing Devotions" *(Ḥadīth al-Nawāfil)* several times in his *Poem of the Sufi Way*. Yet, already in the third/ninth century, this Divine Saying was popular among Sufi masters, who frequently quoted it in their penetrating discussions on mystical union. Earlier, however, the mystical strains present in the Qur'ān and *ḥadīth* were probably less developed, subsumed within a more general ascetic piety *(dīn)*, which sought immediate solutions to pressing needs. For in the first-second/seventh-eighth centuries, nascent Islam faced rapidly changing conditions that generated a series of questions regarding nearly every aspect of life and society. Religious thinkers of the period, such as the ascetic and preacher al-Ḥasan al-Baṣrī (21–110/642–728) and the legal expert Abū Ḥanīfah (ca. 80–150/699–767), worked to establish and regulate proper ritual, the obligations of the faith, and law, in a more traditional sense, which was often an ad hoc affair aimed to aid in the administration of an ever-expanding empire. Similarly, faced with Christian polemics and continued dissension within the Muslim community, these and other scholars undertook to defend the faith and more precisely determine what constituted correct belief.[30]

Inevitably, the scholarly community became more specialized, and by the second-third/eighth-ninth centuries, distinct religious disciplines formed to develop and advance various aspects of Islamic belief and practice. The third/ninth century, in particular, witnessed the emergence of the major schools of law *(sharīʿah)*, along with the collection and codification of *ḥadīth*. Distinctive movements in Qur'ānic commentary *(tafsīr)*, theology *(kalām)*, and philosophy *(falsafah)* also arose at this time, as did attempts to explore more fully and articulate mystical ideas and practice. Mystically inclined religious scholars, including al-Ḥārith al-Muḥāsibī (d. 243/857), Dhū al-Nūn of Egypt (d. 245/860), Abū Yazīd al-Bisṭāmī (d. 261/875), and Aḥmad al-Kharrāz (d. 286/899) mapped out for their disciples some of the psychological states *(ḥāl/aḥwāl)*, and ethical and cognitive stages *(maqām/maqāmāt)* to be encountered along the way toward the annihilation of selfishness *(fanā')* and, ultimately, abiding in God's will and living presence *(baqā')*.

The Day of the Covenant

A key figure in developing the science of Sufism was al-Junayd of Baghdad (d. 297/910), whose explorations in mystical theology and psychology were passed on to his friends and disciples in a series of influential letters and epistles.[31] Like many Sufis before and after him, al-Junayd thought deeply on Qur'ān 7:172 in order to better understand the complex relationship between creation and its divine creator:

> And when your Lord drew from the loins of the children of Adam their progeny and made them bear witness against themselves: "Am I not your Lord?" They said: "Indeed, Yes! We so witness!"

In Sufi circles, this dramatic event became known as the *Yawm al-Mīthāq*, or Day of the Covenant. Al-Junayd believed that on this "day" in pre-eternity, God called forth the spirits *(rūḥ*/pl. *arwāḥ)* of humanity within His will and prior to their existence in creation, in order to take the covenant from them. Al-Junayd went on to state that God had, in fact, taken the covenant from Himself, for He must have answered Himself on behalf of the spirits whose contingent being was derived from His necessary one. God's willing of the spirits and the covenant, then, while suggesting plurality, became the means for His self-manifestation of His oneness. This interpretation of the Primordial Covenant further implies that God's oneness dwells within *(bāṭin)* His outward creation *(ẓāhir)*, suggesting the possibility of an esoteric as well as exoteric knowledge, and a union of sorts between creature and Creator, a view succinctly expressed by Ibn al-Fāriḍ:

For the secret of "Indeed, Yes!"
is the mirror of God's unveiling,
and the meaning of union is confirmed
with the denial of "withness."[32]

According to al-Junayd, following the Covenant, God made the spirits forget their former bliss as He sent them out into creation. Once there, the spirits enjoy their own human individuality but, as a result, they grow self-centered within material existence, which veils them from their original state of perfection. Helping to bind each spirit to the material world is the *nafs*, the "self," which in al-Junayd's psychology is not an ontological entity like a soul, so much as it is an ethical principle equivalent to the "self" in selfishness, or concupiscence. Again, the Qur'ān serves as the basis for this notion of the human being as composed of a divine spirit *(rūḥ)* and a more material self *(nafs)*. Speaking of the creation of Adam, the Qur'ān states:

> [God] proportioned him and breathed His spirit into him, and He gave you ears and eyes and hearts. (32:9)

Yet, despite humanity's illustrious origins, the Qur'ān warns that the human self *(nafs)* is "prone to evil" (12:53), for it tempts the individual toward unrestrained physical gratification. These base tendencies must be checked by developing a sense of conscience and by following God's guidance, so that the self becomes "at peace" and pleasing to God (89:27–30). The Qur'ān declares:

> So fear God as much as you can, and listen, obey, and spend [on charity] for your own good, for whoever is saved from his own selfishness *[shuḥḥa nafsihi]* will be among the prosperous. (64:16)

Each individual, then, must choose whether to be obedient to God and true to the covenant to worship Him alone, or to fall victim to selfish desires. This constitutes God's test *(balā')* of humanity, which, for al-Junayd, is the source of tribulation *(balā')* for the spirit longing to return to its heavenly home. Yet, this tribulation initiates the mystic's spiritual struggle to subdue selfish tendencies, which include not only the desires of the body, but those of the intellect as well. For this reason, al-Junayd paid particular attention to the state of mystical intoxication *(sukr)*. In rare moments, a mystic may lose all sense of self in an expansion *(basṭ)* of consciousness, yet this obvious spiritual achievement, if unchecked, could lead to a dangerous selfish pride. Therefore, al-Junayd focused on a subsequent state of sobriety *(ṣaḥw)*, in which exhilarating moments of illumination are stabilized within a selfless life of enlightenment, and Ibn al-Fāriḍ clearly embraced this view in his *Poem of the Sufi Way*:

I imagined sobriety
as my perigee, and intoxication
my ascent to her, with effacement
my lote tree's end in space.

But when I cleared the clouds away,
I found myself up and awake,
while my inner spring
refreshed my eyes,

And from my drunken poverty
I recovered, grew rich
in my second separation,
union like oneness to me.[33]

But this enlightened life is possible only if God fully annihilates the mystic's selfish will *(fanā')* and graces him with the highest mystical experience of *baqā'*. Al-Junayd likened this final state of "abiding" in God to the spirits' first moment in pre-eternity, for in this ultimate mystical stage God overwhelms His worshiper and assumes his will and actions, becoming the sole actor as declared in the Tradition of Willing Devotions. This is the true witnessing to the *tawḥīd Allāh*, which means not only "monotheism," but God's absolute oneness, such that mystical union is not the joining of two separate and distinct essences or natures, but rather, it is the realization of the divine unity of all existence, as Ibn al-Fāriḍ declares:

The tongues of all beings—
if you listen close—
witness with eloquence
to my unity,

While about my union
  a tradition has come,
    its transmission clear
      without doubt,

Declaring true love
  for those who draw near Him
    by willing devotions
      or those decreed.

The point of its teaching
  is clear
    as noonday light:
      "I am his ear...."[34]

Muḥammad's Light

Clearly, Ibn al-Fāriḍ was influenced by the mystical doctrines elaborated by al-Junayd and other early Sufis, whose teachings were passed down through their students, though at times sharp differences of opinion did arise among them. For instance, al-Ḥusayn ibn Manṣūr al-Ḥallāj (d. 304/922), a former student of al-Junayd, was accused of promoting a doctrine of union resembling incarnation *(ḥulūl)*, as two substances, one divine, the other human, came to dwell together in one body. Al-Ḥallāj was eventually executed, though his case involved political as well as religious issues. Yet this tragic episode suggests the political tensions and perhaps, too, the intellectual conservatism of the fourth-fifth/tenth-eleventh centuries. This period was also conservative in the positive sense that attempts were made to preserve the religious heritage of earlier centuries. Sufi scholars, including al-Sarrāj (d. 378/988), al-Kalābādhī (d. 385/995), al-Sulamī (d. 412/1021), al-Qushayrī (d. 465/1037), and al-Ḥujwīrī (d. 469/1077), composed Qur'ānic commentaries and guidebooks containing mystical lexicons, biographies, spiritual genealogies, and detailed explanations of Sufi thought and practice. Asserting the Qur'ānic and prophetic basis for Islamic mysticism, their works attempt to systematize Sufism and to situate it within a larger, increasingly specialized and divided Islamic tradition.[35]

Influenced by several of these scholars, Abū Ḥāmid Muḥammad al-Ghazālī (d. 505/1111) sought to build a consensus among the Muslim community regarding not only the range for specific fields of religious study, such as Sufism, but for faith in general.[36] A theologian with mystical proclivities, al-Ghazālī wrote extensively; his most influential work remains the *Iḥyā' ʿulūm al-dīn (The Revivification of the Religious Sciences)*, whose title is indicative of his mission. In this and other writings, al-Ghazālī examined various branches of religious studies, including law, theology, and mysticism, and assessed their worth to Muslim life. Throughout, al-Ghazālī stressed *dīn* ("religion") in a holistic sense reminiscent of the first Islamic centuries and, toward this end, he utilized Sufism's emphasis on personal experience to revitalize the letter of the law and to enliven the God of theology.

This was not, however, a case of the law *vs.* the spirit, or orthodoxy *vs.* heresy. Rather, the efforts of al-Ghazālī are representative of scholars in the sixth-ninth/twelfth-fifteenth centuries who worked to assemble the various parts of Islam into a coherent and meaningful faith in which each dimension was given its proper place and value, depending to some degree, of course, on a scholar's own particular expertise and concerns. Law *(sharīʿah)* was a foundational component for any acceptable system, and al-Ghazālī and respected Sufi masters made adherence to it a necessary basis for further spiritual development. Only after mastering the rules and obligations regulating such important matters as the canonical prayers, fasting, and proper behavior, could an adept proceed to the Sufi path *(ṭarīqah)*, with its additional stipulations regarding mystical devotions, personal conduct, and communal life. Even then, it was only the exceptional individual who, graced by God, might experience union and an enlightened vision of creation in its relation to God *(ḥaqīqah)*.

From this perspective, belief, ritual, law, and mystical experience are all essential for the individual seeking the inner truth *(bāṭin)* behind the world of exterior form *(ẓāhir)*, and here again, al-Ghazālī and the Sufis would point to the Qur'ān to support their views:

> God is the light of the heavens and the earth. The semblance of His light is like a niche in which is a lamp, the lamp in a

> glass. The glass is like a shining star lit from a blessed tree, an olive, of neither east nor west, whose oil would seem to shine even if not touched by fire. Light upon light, God guides to His light whom He wills, and God strikes parables for humanity, for God knows everything! (24:35)

In his *Mishkāt al-anwār (The Niche for Lights)*, al-Ghazālī interprets this passage in neo-Platonic terms, as God's light overflows into various levels of the universe, including the world of materiality.[37] Further, these emanations are shaped by God's divine names and attributes, which appear in different forms and combinations, and in the *Poem of the Sufi Way*, in an incredible display of syntactical parallelism and patterning, Ibn al-Fāriḍ details this process of divine emanation and its outer and inner effects throughout a multilevel cosmos (vv. 537—75). Ibn al-Fāriḍ may have drawn several of his ideas and images from al-Ghazālī, though Sufi theories of the divine light and its emanation may be found as early as the third/ninth century, especially in the work of Sahl al-Tustarī (d. 283/896), who also interpreted the Qur'ān's "Light Verse" to elucidate his own views.[38]

A key component of al-Tustarī's doctrine is the Light of Muḥammad *(Nūr al-Muḥammad)*, a type of Logos principle, also referred to by later Sufis as the Muḥammadan Reality *(al-Ḥaqīqah al-Muḥammadīyah)*. This Prophetic Light was believed to be God's first emanation and the instrument of all subsequent creation, which began on the Day of the Covenant. According to one *ḥadīth,* Muḥammad said: "I was a prophet when Adam was still between water and clay," and in a Divine Saying, God says to Muḥammad: "If not for you, I would not have created the heavens." These and other Sayings and traditions have often been cited by Ibn al-Fāriḍ and other Sufis to support their notions of the Light's role in creation and its progressive manifestation among the prophets culminating in their seal, the historical Muḥammad. Moreover, even after the death of the human Muḥammad, the Prophetic Light continues to appear on earth among the gnostics and friends of God:[39]

> And the secrets of all of them before
> were brought and bestowed on us
> by him who was their seal
> in prophecy's due time.

Only by following after him
and by his leave
did any prophet ever call
his people to the truth.

So now our legal scholar
is like their prophets of long ago,
while any one of us calling to the truth
undertakes the acts of an apostle.

Our gnostic in this Muslim time
is like those prophets
with firm resolve
holding to God's decree,

And what was once a miracle among them,
after him became a gracious gift of grace
given to a caliph
or one sincere and true.

Humanity no longer needs
the Messenger;
they have his family and companions,
and his followers leading in the faith.[40]

Remember Me

Illumined by the Light of Muḥammad, those mystics so graced by God attain mystical union and enlightenment and thus become the perfect guides to lead others to the truth. To aid their students in this quest, Sufi masters developed a number of rules and practices, including fasting, seclusion, and devotional prayers. But among the Sufis perhaps the most respected and widespread means to purify oneself in preparation for a mystical experience has been the practice of *dhikr* ("recollection").[41] Assuming a variety of forms and often accompanied by specific procedures involving breath control, posture, movement, and dance, the *dhikr* ritual revolves around the repetition of God's divine names, and/or of religious formulas, whether said aloud or in silence, among a group or alone in seclusion. This Sufi practice, too, is grounded in the Qur'ān, which repeatedly calls humanity to *dhikr*, to remembrance of God and His blessings to them:

> O humanity, recall the blessings upon you from your Lord. Is there another creator other than God, who sends sustenance to you from the sky and the earth? There is no god but Him, so how can you turn away? (35:3)
>
> O you who believe, remember God often, and praise Him morning and evening! (33:41–42)
>
> Recite the name of your Lord, morning and evening, and bow down to Him for part of the night, and praise Him long into the night. (76:25–26)

While all Muslims are to remember God during their daily prayers and on other religious occasions, Sufis have sought to recollect God constantly as a means of self-purification and total obedience to Him. To further their efforts, novices and their superiors have gathered together to perform the *dhikr* and to recite the Qur'ān, and sometimes verse, in what came to be known as *samāʿ* ("audition"), a term derived, perhaps, from the divine command to "listen intently" when God and His revelation are recalled:

> When the Qur'ān is recited, be silent and listen to it that, perhaps, you all may be graced. Remember your Lord within yourself, humbly and with trepidation, reciting quietly at dawn and just before sunset; do not be among the heedless ones. Truly those who are in the presence of their Lord are not too proud to worship Him, praise Him, and bow down to Him! (7:204–6)
>
> The true believers are only those who, when God's name is recalled, their hearts fill with fear, and when His verses are recited to them, their faith increases, for they trust only in their Lord! (8:2)

A cherished goal of *dhikr* and *samāʿ* is an ecstatic trance in which the individual's will and desires are assumed by God in accord with the Tradition of Willing Devotions and His promise in Qur'ān 2:152: "When you remember Me, I remember you." Further, the Qur'ān directly links the notion of recollection with the Day of the Covenant *(mīthāq)*:

> Recall the blessings upon you from your Lord and His covenant that He confirmed with you when you said: "We hear and obey!" (5:7)

For al-Junayd and other Sufi masters, then, the state of rapture experienced through recollection marked the mystic's inner return, if only for a moment, to the Day of the Covenant. Memories of this sacred pre-eternal state lie dormant within the spirit, waiting to be awakened by a focused and sustained act of recollection, as Ibn al-Fāriḍ elegantly recounts in his *Poem of the Sufi Way*:

A child—though he may grow
  into a man dull and slow—
    will reveal my state to you
      by instinct and intuition.

When the infant moans
  from the tight swaddling wrap
    and restlessly yearns
      for relief from distress,

He is soothed by lullabies and lays aside
  the burden that covered him;
    he listens silently
      to one who soothes him.

The sweet speech makes him
  forget his bitter state
    and remember a secret whisper
      of covenants in pre-eternity.

His state makes clear
  the conditions of audition
    and confirms the dance
      to be free of error.

For when he burns with desire
  from lullabies,
    anxious to fly
      to his first abodes,

He is calmed
  by his rocking cradle
    as the hands of his nurse
      gently sway it.

I have found in gripping rapture
  when she is recalled
    in the chanter's tones
      and the singer's tunes,

What a suffering man feels
  when he gives up his soul,
    when the messengers of death
      come to take him.

One finding pain
  in being driven asunder
    is like one pained in rapture
      longing for friends.

The soul pitied the body
  where it first appeared,
    and my spirit rose
      to its high beginnings,

And my spirit soared past the gate
opening to beyond my union
where there is no veil
in communion.[42]

Close Encounters

The practice of *dhikr* and *samāʿ* was a major activity for Sufi novices and adepts who had, for centuries, loosely gathered around recognized masters and their teachings. Then, in the sixth/twelfth century, many of these Sufi circles coalesced into distinct religious brotherhoods *(ṭarīqah*/pl. *ṭuruq)*, with their own particular spiritual lineage, doctrine, and ritual; often, members lived and worked together for a time under an established religious rule.[43] Though several of the major Sufi orders rose to prominence during Ibn al-Fāriḍ's lifetime, there is no indication that he was ever a member of an organized brotherhood, or that he founded one of his own. But a grandson claimed that, late in life, Ibn al-Fāriḍ did meet the renowned Sufi ʿUmar al-Suhrawardī (d. 632/1235), who gave the frock of his order to two sons of the poet. In the same story, Ibn al-Fāriḍ's grandson noted how al-Suhrawardī was adored by the masses, but that it was his grandfather who possessed the rare gift of spiritual vision. Fantastic elements within this story undermine its credibility, but it does draw attention to another important religious development within medieval Islam, namely, the veneration of holy men and women, and an increasingly popular cult of the saints, which came to include al-Suhrawardī, Ibn al-Fāriḍ, and another of their contemporaries, Muḥyī al-Dīn Ibn al-ʿArabī (d. 638/1240).[44]

A subtle thinker and prolific writer, Ibn al-ʿArabī had a tremendous impact on the Sufi tradition, and his mystical vision of reality has dominated Islamic metaphysical thought for centuries. A major focus of this vision is *wujūd* ("being," "existence") and its underlying oneness. Later referred to as *waḥdat al-wujūd* ("the unity of being"), this doctrine asserts that the existence of anything is identical to its relation to necessary being, God. Contingent existence, then, is relational to this necessary being, which it reflects, if only in a limited and transient way. Therefore, the task of the sincere mystic is to discover his own relativity, and that of all things, in order to witness the permanent ground of being within its continual self-disclosure *(tajallī)* by means of the divine names and attributes.[45]

Ibn al-ʿArabī developed these and related ideas in a number of books and epistles, most notably in his *Fuṣūṣ al-ḥikam (The Bezels of Wisdom)*, and the voluminous *al-Futūḥāt al-Makkīyah (The Meccan Revelations)*. Concerning this later work a story was told that Ibn al-ʿArabī once wrote to Ibn al-Fāriḍ asking permission to comment on the *Poem of the Sufi Way*, to which Ibn al-Fāriḍ was said to have replied, "Your book entitled *The Meccan Revelations* is a commentary on it." While this story is almost certainly apocryphal, it highlights the close association of the two mystics within the later Sufi tradition. This was largely the result of commentaries written on the *Poem of the Sufi Way* and the *Wine Ode* by several of Ibn al-ʿArabī's followers, who read and analyzed the poems in terms of their master's teachings on existence *(wujūd)* and the perfectly realized human being *(al-insān al-kāmil)*. This common link aside, there is little evidence that Ibn al-Fāriḍ and Ibn al-ʿArabī even knew of each other, not to mention corresponded.[46]

The writings of both mystics, however, convey a strikingly similar view of a unified reality, whose self-disclosure occurs on the Day of the Covenant. As the spiritual seeker purifies himself, he is able to recollect and witness this self-disclosure, and once enlightened, with his will and senses assumed by God, he may become an active conduit for gnosis. Despite these important similarities, several recent studies have pointed out key differences in the mystical terms used by Ibn al-Fāriḍ, and Ibn al-ʿArabī and his disciples. This strongly suggests that such themes and ideas common to the works of Ibn al-Fāriḍ and Ibn al-ʿArabī did not result from direct influence between the two men but from their shared Sufi heritage, which included the works of al-Tustarī, al-Junayd, al-Ghazālī, and many other well-known and respected Sufi masters.[47]

But variations in terminology are also a natural consequence of differences in form and language, between Ibn al-ʿArabī's dense prose, as encountered in *The Meccan Revelations*, and the sophisticated poetic style of Ibn al-Fāriḍ's *Poem of the Sufi Way* and *Wine Ode*. Further complicating the situation, medieval and modern commentators have persisted in reading the *Poem of the Sufi Way* as a spiritual autobiography.[48]

While many have correctly noted the mystical transformation of the "I" of the poem from a self-centered lover to the universal self of the Light of Muḥammad, they have failed to appreciate the presence of the lyric "I," that dramatic persona so essential to a poet's craft.[49] This is not to deny that Ibn al-Fāriḍ probably experienced mystical states of consciousness, some of them quite powerful and profound, or that he strongly identified with the Sufi tradition. But many sections of the poem, such as that on divine emanation and the various levels of existence, would appear to be more the product of doctrine, reason, and reflection than of personal mystical experience. Pious legends and romantic readings aside, the mannered and highly nuanced language of the *Poem of the Sufi Way*, its multiple voices, and its openly didactic character argue against it being a spontaneous, almost manic oracle, or a biographically accurate account of Ibn al-Fāriḍ's mystical ascension to union with the Prophetic Light of Muḥammad.

Yet, whatever its autobiographical substance, the lyric persona's emotive force energizes Ibn al-Fāriḍ's verse, which has continued to influence and shape Arabic poetry and Islamic mysticism for over five hundred years. Whether in the role of the suffering lover, the Sufi guide, or the Prophetic Light, Ibn al-Fāriḍ bears witness to the transformative power of love, while urging his listeners, both the Sufi devotees of the past and, ultimately, those of us in the present, to undertake a journey of personal exploration and mystical discovery:

It is love, so guard your heart,
  passion is not easy;
    wasted by it, would you choose it,
      if you had reason?

Live free of love,
  for love's ease is hard:
    it begins in sickness,
      and ends in death.

But to me, death in love
  by drowning desire,
    is life revived
      by my beloved.

I have warned you,
knowing passion and my enemy;
so choose for yourself
what is sweet.

But if you want to live well,
then die love's martyr,
and if not, well,
love has its worthy ones.

Not to die in love
is not to live by love;
before you harvest honey,
you must surely face the bees.[50]

Sufi Verse

Wine Ode

Heaven's Wine

From its pre-Islamic inception, Arabic verse on wine has been closely linked to blood and the powers of life and death. Related themes of love and loss have also blended with this verse as the beloved's lips promise an intoxicating kiss, while her sudden departure calls for wine's consolation. Over the centuries, sacramental and spiritual dimensions of wine were increasingly explored by both Christian and Muslim poets, and, perhaps reflecting the transformative power of the Eucharist, wine's miraculous abilities to cure the sick and revive the spiritually dead were praised by poets. Wine was emblematic of immortality, and though the Qur'ān forbids the consumption of earthly wine, in many verses it declares a heavenly vintage to be the drink of paradise:

> Those brought near in gardens of bliss, a group from earlier times and a few from times thereafter, they recline face to face on brocade couches, as immortal youths pass round to them bowls, pitchers, and cups flowing with a sparkling wine! (56:11–18)

> Witness those brought near. They will certainly be in bliss, face to face on couches, and you will recognize on their faces the heavenly glow, as they are served a choice wine sealed with musk. So let those who aspire for the best, aspire for this! (83:21–26)

Muslim mystics added further to the poetic allegories of wine, since sobriety and intoxication had long served as metaphors for states of consciousness and moments of ecstasy. Thus wine almost naturally came to symbolize the eternal love flowing between God and His worshipers, and Sufi manuals often cite wine verse to allude to this intimate relationship. Like most early Sufi verse, that on wine rarely exceeded a verse or two, but by the sixth/eleventh century, longer wine poems were composed by Sufis, including Ibn al-Shahrazūrī (d. 511/1117), Yaḥyā al-Suhrawardī (d. 587/1191), and Abū Madyan (d. 594/1197). Ibn al-Fāriḍ knew this tradition well, and he detailed the amazing spiritual qualities of wine in what has come to be regarded as the finest poem on mystical wine in Islam.[1]

The *Wine Ode* begins in praise of a wine that intoxicated the poet and his companions as they drank in remembrance of their beloved. But this was no earthly vintage, for it made them drunk prior to material creation. The shining wine then takes form as the sun itself, with its cup the full moon holding its reflection; bubbles form from mixing wine with water, just as stars appear when light turns into night. A whiff of its bouquet and a sudden flash of its splendor have led the poet to conceive of this heavenly wine and seek it out (vv. 1–3). But in this world below, not a drop is here to drink, only a rare fragrance lingers, yet what marvels would appear if a single jar of this elusive vintage could ever be found. In an elaborate rhetorical display, Ibn al-Fāriḍ enumerates the bouquet, flavor, and other aspects of this wine; its goblet, strainer, and additional accessories; and the particular powers of each for cleansing the senses and healing the body, psyche, and spirit (vv. 8–20). Such miracles, however, will not take place; the wine is gone. Still, the mere mention of the wine's name is enough to intoxicate its seekers, who call the poet to describe the wine, since he is its experienced connoisseur. The poet answers their request, but obliquely (vv. 21–23):

They say to me: "Do describe it,
for you know its character well!"
Indeed, I have word
of its attributes:

Purity not water,
subtlety not air,
light but not fire,
spirit without body.

Lovely features guiding
those describing it to praise;
how fine their prose and poetry
on wine.

Then the poet further underscores the heavenly nature of his drink by denying that he has sinned by drinking any wine at all. He was drunk prior to his creation and will remain so long after his bones have turned to dust (vv. 24–25).

Having described the wine, its vessels, accessories, and effects, Ibn al-Fāriḍ next turns to those gathering to drink. He praises the residents of the monastery, who often serve as the wine source in Classical Arabic literature; these folk, too, are intoxicated by the wine, though they have never tasted it. He charges his companions to search for the wine in the tavern, with its music and joyful reverie. They should drink the wine straight or, if they must, then, let them mix it with water, but they should never turn away from the beloved's bright smile. In Arabic poetry the wetness of the beloved's lips and mouth has often been compared to a powerful wine, a taste of which will conquer time. Though this intoxication is fleeting, to refuse the wine offered by the beloved's moist, red lips is to abandon love, union, and ecstasy, and so live life in vain (vv. 24–31).[2]

At the end of his poem, as in the beginning, Ibn al-Fāriḍ joins wine to the beloved, and throughout he refers to his subject by the feminine pronoun *hā* ("her"; "it"), which can refer to either wine or a beloved. Further linking the two is the ever-present process of *dhikr* and recollection (vv. 1, 5–6, 11, 24). In fact, several medieval commentators have interpreted Ibn al-Fāriḍ's *Wine Ode* to be a testament to the power of the *dhikr* ritual, as Sufis gather together in joy and song to invoke the name of God and experience the all-pervasive inner and outer effects of mystical recollection. Various commentators have likewise pointed out Ibn al-Fāriḍ's several allusions to the Day of the Covenant (vv. 1, 27), and the astral imagery (v. 2) that resonates with passages found in his *Poem of the*

Sufi Way revolving around Muḥammad's Prophetic Light (e.g., vv. 431–41). This, combined with Ibn al-Fāriḍ's other references to the Qur'ān and Sufi doctrines of love and union, encourages readings of his *Wine Ode* as an extended meditation on the presence of divine love within the universe and the lover's momentary return to his beloved through recollection and mystical union.[3]

Text and Commentary

My translation of the *Wine Ode* is based on the Arabic text found in Ibn al-Fāriḍ's *Dīwān*, edited by ʿAbd al-Khāliq Maḥmūd (Cairo: Dār al-Maʿārif, 1984), 189–92, with two notable exceptions. I follow the majority and some of the oldest manuscripts of the *Dīwān* regarding the order of vv. 5–6, and that of vv. 15 and 20, which, in both cases, are transposed in the Maḥmūd edition. Further, I have not included in this translation eight verses normally numbered vv. 23–30 in many printed editions. These verses were not included in the version of the poem collected by Ibn al-Fāriḍ's grandson, ʿAlī, who knew of them but thought them to be of dubious authenticity.[4] These verses are also absent from manuscripts of the oldest commentaries on the *Wine Ode*. A brief discussion and sample of this commentary tradition follows the translation.

ʿUmar Ibn al-Fāriḍ
Wine Ode
(al-Khamrīyah)

sharibnā 'alā dhikri-l-ḥabībi mudāmata
sakirnā bihā min qabli an yukhlaqa-l-karmu

In memory of the beloved
we drank a wine;
we were drunk with it
before creation of the vine.

The full moon its glass, the wine
a sun circled by a crescent;
when it is mixed,
how many stars appear!

If not for its bouquet,
I would not have found its tavern;
if not for its flashing gleam,
how could imagination picture it?

Time preserved nothing of it
save one last breath,
concealed like a secret
in the breasts of wise men.

But if it is recalled among the tribe, *5*
the worthy ones
are drunk by morn
without shame or sin.

From the depths of the jars
it arose, though truly,
nothing remained
save a name.

Yet if one day
it crosses a man's mind,
then joy will dwell in him,
and anxiety depart.

Could the tavern mates see
the seal of its jar,
without the wine that seal alone
would make them drunk,

And could they sprinkle it
on a dead man's earth,
the spirit would return to him,
his body revived.

Could they fling *10*
into the shadow of its trellised vine
a sick man on the point of death,
disease would flee him;

Could they bring a cripple
near its tavern, he would walk,
and from mention of its flavor,
the dumb would talk.

Could breaths of its bouquet
spread out in the east,
one stuffed-up in the west
would smell again;

And were a touching palm
tinged by its cup,
one would not stray at night,
a star in hand.

Could it be unveiled in secret
  to the blind, he would see,
    and from the strainer's sound,
  the deaf would hear.

Were the riders *15*
  to seek its soil
    with one scorpion-stung among them,
  the poison would not harm him.

Could the wizard write
  the letters of its name
    on the brow of one struck by the jinn,
  the tracings would cure and cleanse him,

And were its name inscribed
  upon the army's standard,
    all beneath that banner
  would fall drunk from the sign.

It refines the morals
  of the tavern mates
    and guides the irresolute
  to resolution's path;

He whose hand never knew munificence
  is generous,
    while one lacking in forbearance
  bears the rage of anger,

And could the stupid one among the folk *20*
  win a kiss from its strainer,
    he would sense the hidden sense
  of its fine qualities.

They say to me: "Do describe it,
  for you know its character well!"
    Indeed, I have word
  of its attributes:

Purity not water,
  subtlety not air,
    light but not fire,
  spirit without body,

Lovely features guiding
  those describing it to praise;
    how fine their prose and poetry
  on wine.

One who never knew it
  is moved by its memory,
    just as one longing for Nuʿm
  is stirred when she is recalled.

But they said: "You've drunk sin!" *25*
  No, indeed, I drank only
    that whose abstention
  is sin to me.

So cheers to the monastery's folk!
  How often they were drunk with it
    though they never drank it,
  but only longed to,

While it made me drunk
  before my birth,
    abiding always with me
  though my bones be worn away.

So take it straight,
  though if you must, then mix it,
    but your turning away
  from the beloved's mouth is wrong.

Watch for it in the tavern,
  try to uncover it there
    amid melodious tunes
  where it becomes the prize.

It never dwells with anxiety *30*
  at any time or place,
    just as sorrow
  never lives with song.

Be drunk from it,
  if only for the life an hour,
    and you will see time a willing slave
  under your command.

For there is no life in this world
  for one who lives here sober;
    who does not die drunk on it,
  prudence has passed him by.

So let him weep for himself,
  one who wasted his life
    never having won a share
  or measure of this wine.

The Quest for Meaning: Sufi Commentary and the Wine Ode

Ibn al-Fāriḍ's *Wine Ode* can easily be read and understood as a Classical Arabic poem in praise of wine and as a love poem, too, without resort to mystical ideas and interpretations. Yet in light of Ibn al-Fāriḍ's *Poem of the Sufi Way*, the *Wine Ode* takes on a more ethereal glow, which over the centuries has been enhanced by the poet's prominent place within the Sufi canon. In this respect, a major contributor to the *Wine Ode*'s claim to mystical fame has been the commentary tradition. Ibn al-Fāriḍ's verse became the subject of commentaries soon after his death; and of the approximately twenty-five surviving commentaries, ten focus exclusively on the *Wine Ode*.

Some of these commentaries are grammatical in nature, and include references to poetic devices employed by Ibn al-Fāriḍ, such as alliteration and antithesis. Other commentaries, however, are concerned more with religious content than poetic form, and so, rather than regarding these works as literary criticism, we might more usefully construe them as forms of mystical exegesis. Indeed, the Sufi commentators prove insightful when they cite relevant passages from various religious sources, or when, occasionally, they base their interpretations of specific themes and images in Ibn al-Fāriḍ's *Wine Ode* on the poet's more explicit comments in the *Poem of the Sufi Way*. Nevertheless, many authors stretch beyond the limits of commentary in order to dissect and examine Ibn al-Fāriḍ's poems as mystical treatises in support of their own particular theosophical systems. These Sufi commentaries became the lenses through which most later generations have read Ibn al-Fāriḍ's verse. Several commentaries even became respected mystical works in their own right, especially the commentary on the *Poem of the Sufi Way* by al-Farghānī (d. 699/1300), ʿAbd al-Ghānī al-Nābulusī's (d. 1143/1731) massive commentary on Ibn al-Fāriḍ's entire *Dīwān*, and the commentary on the *Wine Ode* by Dā'ūd al-Qayṣarī (d. ca. 747/1346).[5]

Al-Qayṣarī's *Sharḥ al-Qaṣīdah al-Khamrīyah* (*Commentary on the*

Wine Ode) may have been the first commentary composed on the poem, and it has certainly been the most influential, as evidenced in the large number of surviving manuscripts of the work and in the later commentaries that depend directly on it.[6] Al-Qayṣarī was born in Anatolia and later resided in Cairo before returning to his native city of Kayseri. A follower of Ibn al-ʿArabī's mystical teachings, he studied with a second generation student of Ibn al-ʿArabī, ʿAbd al-Razzāq al-Kāshānī (d. 735/1334) and wrote under the strong influence of Ibn al-ʿArabī's adopted son and spiritual heir Ṣadr al-Dīn al-Qūnawī (d. 673/1274).

Al-Qayṣarī detailed his own related views on being and reality in several works, including an extensive introduction to his commentary on the *Wine Ode*. There, al-Qayṣarī states that the absolute Reality *(al-ḥaqq)* comprehends its own essence *(al-dhāt)* and essential perfections, thereby giving rise to essential love. This initiates the first level of divine emanation or effusion, known as the level of exclusive unity *(al-martabah al-aḥadīyah)*. At this point, there is no predication of any sort, as love is the source of the incomprehensible essence of exclusive unity. However, on the second level of inclusive unity *(al-wāḥidīyah)*, distinction occurs between the essence of love, and the divine names and attributes. Their diverse spiritual realities then appear on the third level, that of distinctive divine knowledge, with its immutable entities *(al-ʿayān al-thābitah)*, while the loci of their manifestations appear on the fourth level of the visible world of multiplicity.

Love's essence and the multiple levels of predication can only be comprehended experientially by the purified, perfected gnostics, who realize that the divine effusion is the primal cause of love, which pervades all levels of being, all existents, and all types of love. Even such low forms as physical human love and that of animals point back to their first cause, God, Who loves those who love Him. God guides His lovers back to Him via the straight path of Islam as charted by the best of all creation, the prophet Muḥammad, who alone possesses perfect love. By following the Prophet, the loving worshiper of God draws nearer to Him until God assumes His servant's senses and will, thereby plunging him into ecstasy and rapture, annihilating the lover's being and essence into His own, where the lover abides forever.[7]

Al-Qayṣarī's theosophical exposition is, for the most part, neither drawn from nor explicitly supported by Ibn al-Fāriḍ's *Wine Ode*. Nevertheless, it serves as the template for al-Qayṣarī's subsequent analysis of the ode, for which he employs a traditional method of commentary: he cites a verse or two from the poem, clarifies obscure or difficult words, and then renders an interpretive prose version of the verses in question. Al-Qayṣarī's mystical doctrines indelibly color his reading of the ode, though many of his observations and interpretations are plausible. Further, his mystical glosses of Arabic terms are certainly intriguing, as are his citations of possible allusions within the poem to the Qur'ān, *ḥadīth,* and Sufi ideas and practice, with which Ibn al-Fāriḍ was undoubtedly familiar.

Al-Qayṣarī's commentary, and those like it, cannot be fully understood and appreciated without a careful study of their own particular mystical concerns and positions. While aware of this fact, I have nevertheless selected and translated the following passages from al-Qayṣarī's commentary on the *Wine Ode* to illustrate interpretive strategies that have been pervasive among Muslim mystics, and to underscore their persistent reading of Ibn al-Fāriḍ's verse as an elaborate allegory of Sufi doctrine.[8]

Selections from al-Qayṣarī's Commentary on the *Wine Ode*:

[1] In memory of the beloved
we drank a wine;
we were drunk with it
before creation of the vine.

Commentary: What is meant by "the beloved" here is the true beloved who unites all causes for love, and He is the Real, all glory be to Him, Who creates all existent things, bringing them forth from the concealment and darkness of pre-eternity into the light of existence by means of His compassionate mercy. By means of His compassionate mercy, He assigns to each existent a particular perfection suitable for it, and among existents, He has bestowed the robe of nobility on the human species, having given in full to the believers among them the blessing of Islam, faith, right guidance, providence, and all perfections resulting from them, as He, most high, has said [in the Qur'ān 5:3]: "Today, I have perfected your religion for you and given to you in full My blessing, and I have approved Islam as a religion for you." Among believers, He has exalted His saints with the honor of proximity and perfection, and He has ascribed to them the attributes of beauty and majesty so that they might grasp experientially what they can of His lights, and understand what comes to them of His secrets. So they love Him with a love that causes their actions to disappear into His actions, consumes their attributes in His attributes, and effaces their essences in His essence!

What is meant by "wine" is the drink of Zanjabīl, and the spring of Salsabīl, which delights its drinker and intoxicates him, driving out his reason, and baffling his mind, as is indicated in the Lord's Word, that immortal text in which He, most high, has said [76:17–18]: "They will be given there [in paradise] a cup to drink whose blend is Zanjabīl from a spring named Salsabīl." By means of it, the drinker loses his sense of self as all of the properties of his human nature disappear along with his natural traits regarding the designations of actions, characteristics, and essence. For the ruling property of duality disappears from him as he becomes one then with the divine essence that was from the beginning when there was nothing with it. Just as he [the prophet Muḥammad]—God bless him and give him peace—has said: "God was, and there was nothing with Him!" with the passing away of him who was not, and the abiding of Him who never disappears. Just as the poet—may God sanctify his spirit and illuminate his grave—said in his *Ode in T Major* [v. 159]:

Passion annihilated
 the attributes here between us
  that had never abided there,
   so they passed away.

This drink's source is also mentioned in His, most high, saying [76:5–6]: "Lo, the righteous will drink from a cup whose blend is from Kāfūr, a spring from which God's servants drink as they cause it to flow abundantly." First, [the drink] is blended with Kāfūr, then with Zanjabīl, as indicated by the sequence in the Glorious Word. There, He mentions the Kāfūr mixture, to which He endowed the cool refreshingness of certainty, as belonging only to drinkers among the righteous as it abundantly flows to the spirits of lovers who shun multiplicity. He speaks of this a third time with respect to "those brought near" as having the choice, sealed wine, in His, most high, saying [83:25–27]: "They are served a choice wine sealed with musk. So let those who strive, strive for this! Its blend is from Tasnīm, a spring from which drink those brought near." Only "those brought near" Him will receive it. He said: "of a choice wine sealed with musk" whose fragrance perfumes the breaths of existence, and whose taste quenches the burning thirst of those parched for the beatific vision. He mentions Tasnīm [lit. "ascension"] as an indication of [the drink's] high place and exalted rank.

What is intended by "drinking" is the reception of the everlasting divine effusion that descends in levels over the entities and their capacities, [and which] is necessary for the manifestation of the perfections hidden in the unseen of the servant's entity. [These perfections] are the divine states concealed in the treasury of the unseen, firmly rooted in the servant's reality. As for [the poet's] saying, "in memory of the beloved," recollection of [the beloved] stirs up longing, stimulates rapture, perfects love, enhances passion, imparts a burning desire, and evokes wonder. These and similar effects are produced by love arising from the perfections in the entities of perfect people and from the spirits of those in union.

"Memory" [*dhikr*, also "recollection"] has levels, namely, those of the tongue, the heart, the spirit, and the innermost mystery. All of these recollections are the result of the Merciful's recollection of the entity of His servant, without which there would be no existence, manifestation, spirit, or joy. [Recollection] is an expression of the eternal essential knowledge attached to the entity of the servant in the state of his immutability in the presence of divine knowledge. In the presence of spiritual entification, the entity is the receptacle for divine self-manifestations contiguous with perfection. Whereas in the [higher] presence of divine knowledge, the servant's entity is annihilated in the entity of Him Who possesses beauty and majesty; [the servant's entity] calls for annihilation from the presence of exclusive unity, with the tongue of its capacity, drinking its choice, pure wine from the hands of the cup-bearers of the divine names and attributes in the gathering of unseen realities and visible spirits, prior to [the servant's] existence in this compound, elemental form. As He, most high, has said [7:172]: "And when your Lord drew from the loins of the children of Adam their progeny and made them bear witness against themselves, 'Am I not your Lord?' They said: 'Indeed, Yes! We so witness!' Lest they say on the Day of Resurrection: 'Indeed, we were unaware of this!'"

[The poet] said, "We were drunk with it before creation of the vine." That is to say, "We were enraptured in God's beauty due to God's eternal majesty, prior to the manifestation of this human form." Since this is the case for the entities of the spiritual elite and perfect people, and their spirits, too, [the poet] cited the plural form, saying "we drank," and "we were drunk."

[2] The full moon its glass, the wine
a sun circled by a crescent;
when it is mixed,
how many stars appear!

Commentary: "Its" refers to the wine, with the subject being "the full moon," and "cup" as the predicate, that is, "The full moon is the cup for it." The "crescent" is what goes around [the sun], while "how many" refers to the stars, that is, "Many are the stars that appear."

What is meant by "the full moon" is the spirit of the divine beloved with respect to manifest existence; this is the Muḥammadan Essence, which exists in true being. It is illuminated by the light of the sun of the essence of exclusive oneness via reflection due to the opposition between the two essences, which is the property of the two comprehensive levels of existence, namely, that of unity and that of differentiation. However, this [opposition] is not with respect to essential exclusive oneness since it has neither differentiation nor separation within it. Therefore, [the poet] made the full moon a cup, a drinking bowl full of drink, and thus something limited, which can only be in the world.

Just as he uses the word "full moon" metaphorically for the cup, he uses the "sun" as a metaphor for the spiritual drink due to the existence of the supra-sensory heat adhering to ecstasy, along with intoxication and the illumination that enlightens hearts and spirits, indeed, the whole world. In fact, the light of the visible sun is its form and manifestation in the sensory world. [The poet] uses the noun "crescent" as a metaphor for the cup-bearer, drawing on the association they both have to turning in a circle. While the crescent moon circles in terms of its form, the cup-bearer actually turns in a circle to pass the cup around among the companions. What is meant by [the "crescent"] is the Commander of the Faithful, [the fourth caliph, Muḥammad's cousin and son-in-law] ʿAlī ibn Abī Ṭālib [d. 40/660], may God honor him! [The poet] calls him a crescent moon metaphorically, for in relation the Prophet and his presence, God bless him and give him peace, [ʿAlī] was like a crescent compared to the full moon. Also, the crescent is a portion of the full moon, for due to its distance, the moon at first is only partially illuminated by the sun, and so is called a new moon. Similarly, due to their closeness, the Commander of the Faithful is like a portion of the Prophet, may God bless him and give him peace, as [the Prophet] said: "You [ʿAlī] are to me as Aaron was to Moses, for ʿAlī and I are of one light!" For during the time of God's apostle, may God bless him and give him peace, there was a full moon illuminating [the Prophet's] spirit with the Muḥammadan Light, and after him, ʿAlī was a perfect full moon illuminating the hearts of those traveling the spiritual path, and a cup-bearer bringing the wine of gnosis to the spirits of perfect people, until the Judgment Day. [The Prophet] made him the cup-bearer for the heavenly cistern and the river al-Kawthar [in paradise], and for this reason the spirits of the perfect saints and spiritual elite coming after [ʿAlī] have attached themselves to him like no other among [the Prophet's] closest companions, may God be pleased with all of them. The secrets of unity are revealed only by him!

As for the bubbles produced from blending the drink with water, [the poet] extends his earlier metaphor by comparing them to stars. Similarly, [the poet] Abū Nuwās [d. ca. 198/813] compared them to pearls when he said:

It is as if
the big and tiny bubbles
are pearls
strewn on earth of gold.

What is meant here is that which arises when the drink of true gnosis is blended with the water of the science of rational meanings and indisputable spiritual knowledge, and which may be perceived by spiritual vision, just as the stars may be perceived by the eyes. [This blend] enables those possessing rational perceptions and pure spiritual capacities to receive and drink [the wine] by their perception of it. For if [the wine] is unmixed, it destroys its drinker, making him appear in the form of an apostate and unbeliever, just as grape wine, if it is strong, will destroy the drinker who takes it straight. Undoubtedly, He, most high, speaks of a mixture as the drink of the righteous among the servants, ascetics, and those like them who do good and charitable deeds and keep their vows in the path of God, while fearing the Resurrection Day, [when He says]: "They will be given to drink there, a cup whose blend is Kāfūr," and, [again], as the drink of those perfect, consummate ones brought near "whose blend is from Tasnīm, a spring from which drink those brought near." Tasnīm is derived from *al-sanām* ("summit"), meaning the high station that is attained only by "those brought near." [God] gives [another] blend as the drink for those in the midst of the spiritual path and the gnostics declaring oneness who attain the station of the pious and more, as He, most high, has said [10:26]: "For those who do what is right, there is goodness, and more," a blend of Zanjabīl, since Zanjabīl is of medium heat, for it is from the third level. When the blending occurs, the stars of gnoses give rise to the sciences of certainty requisite for guiding seekers and leading those traveling the spiritual path, as He, most high, has said [16:16]: "And by the stars they are guided." In a similar fashion, al-Farrā' [a noted grammarian and scholar, d. 207/822] explains that al-Zanjabīl is the spring from which "those brought near" drink straight, while it is blended for the rest of Paradise.

[3] If not for its bouquet,
I would not have found its tavern;
if not for its flashing gleam,
how could imagination picture it?

Commentary: "Bouquet" is a pleasant fragrance, while "tavern" is a wine shop, the place where wine is purchased. The "flashing gleam" is brightness and light. "Its" throughout the verse refers to the wine.

What is intended by "the pleasant fragrance" is the traces of absolute beauty, that being the loveliness visible in the forms of engendered lovers. The tavern is the source of absolute beauty that adorns spiritual and physical existents with a single drop, as compared to the ocean of essential absolute beauty. That is to say, without [the wine's] pleasant fragrance, which is the vestigial love visible in the forms of handsome men and women, I would not have been rightly guided to the source of absolute beauty, which is the true beloved. As has been said in verse:

If not for you, I would not know love,
if not for love, I would not know you!

"If not for its lights and brightness in the forms of visible existents, I would not have had a way of arriving at the light of lights, which is absolute divine being." For at the time of the soul's annihilation in the figurative beloved—who is real from a point of view, as has been mentioned—and during its tribulation caused by [the beloved's] scourges and trials, [the soul] turns itself toward the true absolute beloved who is everlasting for all things and the refuge for every living thing. Then, He pours over it traces of His absolute beauty, thereby attracting [the soul], and taking it away from its figurative beloved out of His vigilant care for it. So He frees [the soul] from the straits of scourges and trials and turns its face toward His noble courtyard, the source of lights and the mine of perfection. Then the arrival at the divine presence comes to pass for [the lover], and [his] understanding is enlightened due to the soul's enlightenment. So [the understanding] comprehends universal affairs by its becoming, then, an intellect comprehending the universal principles. Therefore, it has been said: "One who does not love passionately, cannot possibly travel the Sufi way."

Following this line of commentary, al-Qayṣarī goes on to interpret subsequent images and figures in the *Wine Ode* in terms of his mystical doctrine of the effusion of divine love and its self-manifestations on the various levels of existence. He also draws particular attention to perfectly realized human beings and love's effects on them, including the spiritual states and mystical knowledge resulting from the practice of recollection. So blessed are these enlightened prophets, saints, and gnostics that if those blinded by material creation were to seek them out in search of love, they would find the cure for their spiritual maladies:

[16] Could the wizard write
the letters of its name
on the brow of one struck by the jinn,
the tracings would cure and cleanse him.

Commentary: By "the wizard" he means the gnostic, the spiritual guide, and by "one struck" he means the one who is veiled, who has been afflicted by the evil genies of self-delusion and the devils of concupiscence and passion. By "brow" he means the imaginal faculty in which is imprinted the images of perceptible things as well as evident and ideal rational concepts. For [this faculty] is located above the brow in the fore part of the frontal lobe of the brain, and among the philosophers it is termed the "collective sense" [i.e., the imagination]. What is intended by "name" is the appellation, while the "letters" consist of rational components, and material and sensory components that are the elements. That is to say, were the realized gnostic to trace and inscribe the meanings of [the letters'] rational components, the meanings of the elements, and their realities on the heart and imaginal faculty of one veiled and bowed down by the affliction of self-delusion and the temptation of devils and concupiscence, that inscription would cure him of whatever had befallen him, blinded him, and so caused him to become veiled and go astray. The point is: Could the gnostic freely administer the explication of the certain sciences and divine gnoses, which he possesses, to one veiled, and inscribe them upon his heart, [the veiled one] would be cleansed of all the evils in him. And God is the true guide!

[20] And could the stupid one among the folk
win a kiss from its strainer,
he would sense the hidden sense
of its fine qualities.

Commentary: "The stupid one among the folk" is their disgraceful ignoramus, while the "strainer" is what is pulled over the mouth, as is a veil wrap. However, the strainer is specifically to cover wine, while the veil is specifically for a person's mouth. A "kiss" is to touch with the lips, while "fine qualities" are praiseworthy character traits. That is to say: Could the ignorant numbskull touch the wine strainer with his lips, that kiss would bestow upon him the meaning of its character traits and attributes. The point is: Were one who does not know anything about divine gnoses and merciful realities to come to the realized gnostic, the perfect, perfecting one carrying the divine trust and drinking pure drink, and obey [the gnostic] and accept what [the gnostic] orders him to do on the path of sincerity and faith, and drink that overflows from [the gnostic], then that obedience and acceptance would allow [that person] to grasp meanings pertaining to the heart and certain sciences resulting from the effects of divine love and right gnoses. What is meant by "the stupid one" is the heedless person veiled from the realities, while [what is meant] by the "strainer" is the realized gnostic who is the ocean of the wine of gnoses and the drink of realities, for he is the one to bind or loose the strainer. Then [the poet], may God be satisfied with him, said:

[21] They say to me: "Do describe it,
for you know its character well!"
Indeed, I have word
of its attributes:

[22] Purity not water,
subtlety not air,
light but not fire,
spirit without body.

Commentary: Those veiled from the truth, though seeking it, say: "What is this wine whose attributes include these things mentioned? Describe it to us, because you have encountered it, while it remains concealed from us." Just so was it said to the Apostle of God [Muḥammad]—blessings and peace be upon him: "Relate to us your Lord's lineage"—that is: "Describe to us your Lord"—and, then, the chapter called "Sincerity" [112] was sent down. So [the poet] described the wine as the essence of purity and subtlety lest they fancy that it was from the soil. Then he said "not water…not air" lest they fancy that it was either of these; he then described it as luminous while declaring its being to be free of fire. Finally, he denied that it was in any way material and confirmed its existence as a spiritual affair by saying: "spirit without body." Therefore, one knows that the drinking [of this wine] is specifically for the heart and spirit, not the body. Thus, he clarified here what he meant by the aforementioned wine.

[26] So cheers to the monastery's folk!
How often they were drunk with it
though they never drank it,
but only longed to.

Commentary: He intends the "monastery's folk" to be the realized gnostics who drank the drink of love, while dwelling in the monastery of passionate love. That is: "Cheers to the realized gnostics who drank the drink of love [offered by] the divine attributes, and who were cheered and intoxicated by it!" Since essential love was the source of the essence, few are those among the gnostics who can realize it for certain, so that only the spiritual elite and peerless ones realize it. [The poet] said: "though they never drank it, but only longed to." That is: They aimed to drink it, but they were not able to. As to his attaching them to the monastery, this is a suitable metaphor since he has likened them to monks....

[27] While it made me drunk
before my birth,
abiding always with me
though my bones be worn away.

Commentary: That is: "From the wine of love and the drink of gnosis, I was completely drunk before elemental formation"—that is, in pre-eternity—"and that intoxication abides with me forever, though my bones wear away." [In this verse] is an indication of [the poet's] realization of the station of the perfect, perfected human beings.

[32] For there is no life in this world
for one who lives here sober;
who does not die drunk on it,
prudence has passed him by.

Commentary: That is to say: If the seeker is drunk from it even a single time, then there will come to him this everlasting happiness and eternal authority that make life good. For there is no life for one who lives sober in this world, veiled from reality and its meanings, seduced by this world and its abodes. One who does not voluntarily put to death his engendered state by being drunk from [the wine] is passed over by prudence and reason. For that death gives everlasting life, while the life of this world bequeaths eternal death. Thus, one who chooses the ephemeral over the permanent and death over life has no reason. Also know that what is intended by sobriety here is the first sobriety of those who are veiled, and it is the sobriety that exists prior to intoxication and the arrival at the station of union. This is not the second sobriety, which belongs to the perfect and perfecting [gnostic] after intoxication and the arrival at the station of union, and which surely is the highest station and most exalted degree. Then the poet, may God be satisfied with him, said:

[33] So let him weep for himself,
 one who wasted his life
 never having won a share
 or measure of this wine.

Commentary: Surely, he loses this world and the next, due to what has slipped from his hand, of life and the capacity that makes possible the acquisition of happiness in both worlds and the attainment of abundance in both places. But he who wasted his life in attaining the ephemeral, his commerce was not profitable, nor was he rightly guided, as "he lost this world and the next, and that, indeed, is a clear loss" [22:11]. So his soul will say: "What a pity that I abandoned God!" [39:56]. We ask God to protect us from that, to place us among the God-fearing, and to bless us and the rest of the lovers with the stations of the gnostics and the perfections of those with hope, for He is the most merciful giver of mercy. Praise be to God, the lord of the worlds, and God's perpetual blessings upon our master, Muḥammad, and all of his family and companions, until the Day of Judgment.

Poem of the Sufi Way

The Pilgrim's Path to God

As in the *Wine Ode*, Ibn al-Fāriḍ opens his *Poem of the Sufi Way* in the tavern, but the focus of this ode is not the heavenly wine of love, but the lover's life of deprivation, transformation, and eventual union. The poet/lover tells us that he once saw his beloved's lovely face and desired to be intoxicated again by her beauty (vv. 1–7). So, in a long address to his beloved, he detailed his great sufferings, which, he believed, had made him worthy of her affection (vv. 8–83). But the beloved would have none of his melodramatic complaints, and she denounced his claims to love as the delusions of a lover in love with himself, not with her; had he been true, he would have given up all vestiges of will and desire in total obedience to her alone (vv. 84–102). Duly chastened, the poet/lover replied by renewing his pledge to prove worthy of her love, as his tone changes from a boisterous one of proud suffering to that of humble submission (vv. 103–17). Then, the poet recounts how he kept his promise and annihilated his will and desires such that only the beloved remained in his heart and entire being (vv. 117–47). Significantly, the climax of union occurs during the pilgrimage to Mecca and the holy sanctuary enclosing the Kaʿbah. In Arabic love lore, the pilgrimage provided an opportunity for lovers to meet, often illicitly, while religious traditions proclaimed the rites and rituals of the pilgrimage to be the surest means possible on this earth for a human and divine encounter. Ibn al-Fāriḍ draws from both sources as he recounts the lover's union and return to the Day of the Covenant (vv. 148–63).

Throughout this opening love poem, Ibn al-Fāriḍ uses the past tense, signaling, once again, that his verse is one of studied recollection and meditation. His mystical concerns and ideas then become more overt as the poet assumes the role of the spiritual master instructing his disciple regarding the *via negativa* (vv. 164–96). Citing his own previous struggle with asceticism and spiritual poverty, the guide relates how he gradually reined in his unruly and selfish nature *(nafs)* and so found union. He gives several analogies to help the aspirant grasp the meaning of this union and the superiority of enlightened sobriety over the intoxication of ecstacy (vv. 197–238). But, above all, he tells the seeker to become sensitive to the divine beauty within all of existence and its shifting self-manifestation among lovers (vv. 239–64). While oneness is at the heart of existence, plurality, though transient, demands that one lead a religious life, and in the guide's case, this led him to the highest station of identification with the Prophetic Light of Muḥammad (vv. 265–333).

Ibn al-Fāriḍ then circles back to speak anew on the annihilation of selfishness and the mystic's ascent to the divine Beloved, who assumes the senses of His lover now abiding in His presence (vv. 334–427). This is possible, the guide declares, because memory of the Covenant may be recovered through recollection, which is the goal of the Sufis and their *samāʿ* (vv. 428–41). Then, going beyond the duality of union, the guide speaks of oneness, and the Prophetic Light's emanation throughout the universe, especially within the mystic (442–502). In fact, the initial obstacle to selfless union, the mystic's own individual self *(nafs)* becomes the locus of divine self-disclosure once it is shorn of its selfish ways and brought into a tranquil repose in the beloved (vv. 503–32). This is yet another example of God's emanation via His divine names and attributes as they appear and coalesce to form the spiritual and material levels of the cosmos (vv. 533–74). Again, the poet/guide speaks as the Light of Muḥammad, which directs this process of divine manifestation and forges an indivisible chain of revelation, linking God to His prophets, saints, scholars and, especially, to His realized gnostics (vv. 575–650).

The guide warns the novice not to regard this emanation as a form of reincarnation or the divine's incarnation into human form. Such views limit the divine, numbering it as a thing among other things when, in fact, God is all that exists in reality. Just as one's self has many roles and guises, though it is in essence one, so, too, does the diversity of the manifest world depend on one inner reality. In an extraordinary parable, Ibn al-Fāriḍ likens this situation to a shadow play; shadow shapes appear to move and act, but when the screen is raised, one actor stands revealed (vv. 651–706). Thus, the Light initiates and flows through all of creation, which, in turn, seeks to better see the Light and thereby find union. This is the truth underlying the mystic's quest as well as all religions, though many have gone astray by limiting the Light to a single form (vv. 706–42). Still, their efforts are sincere, and the compassionate God has sent the Qur'ān, the prophets, and this very Light to recall the Covenant to true lovers and so reveal to them the way back to the beloved (743–61).

This thematic map may help the reader explore Ibn al-Fāriḍ's *Poem of the Sufi Way* with its dense poetic style and diction, which an earlier translator of the ode, A. J. Arberry, compared to an arabesque:

> The aesthetic effect created by this sharp contrast between the repetition of strongly dominating themes and their almost endless elaboration in minute detail of patterned variation is precisely similar to the impression conveyed by a monumental building decorated with delicate arabesque tracery. The resemblance is not accidental; for Ibn al-Fāriḍ's style, not excelled in its kind by any other Arab poet, represents the consummation of the same artistic impulse which culminated (with building materials instead of words and images) in the Alhambra's perfect balance between strength and subtlety.[1]

Issa Boullata has built upon Arberry's observations in one of the few serious studies of the relationship between meaning and style in Ibn al-Fāriḍ's poetry. Boullata focuses on vv. 549–74 of the ode, which are among the most intellectually and rhetorically abstruse verses of the poem. Carefully mapping their morphological and syntactical symmetry in light of their mystical content, Boullata demonstrates how various stylistic elements of the ode, particularly its verbal patterning, contribute to the poem's overall effect and meaning:

> As the structure begins to build up a montage of semantic effects, one begins to sense that the patterning of ideas and words leads to a construction of a harmonious whole. Artistic symmetry and balance begin to express spiritual harmony and order. A Sufi vision of the world emerges. Based on Islamic tenets, it expresses a mystic view of God and the universe in which art and thought blend to create impressions of unity and infinity as they comprehend physical plurality and phenomenal multiplicity within an eternity of harmony and order that evoke no other art as strongly as they do the arabesque.[2]

These comparisons of Ibn al-Fāriḍ's verse to an arabesque highlight the "abstractions based on rhythm and repetition" apparent in both.[3] Yet, there is a prominent evolutionary course to the *Poem of the Sufi Way* that may be obscured by the arabesque motif with its riot of motion. I would compare Ibn al-Fāriḍ's ode to a spiral, whose curving line sweeps out in progressively broader and higher circles as the poet returns to earlier themes and images to speak of love and life in increasingly rarified ways. Further, like the labyrinths followed in age-old rites of spiritual initiation, this poem leads its reader through a difficult and dynamic maze of mystical death and spiritual transformation. Involved is a process of both involution and evolution as the lover rises from his obscure earthly state to a refulgent one of cosmic splendor as the prophetic Light of Muḥammad:

I embraced my lights
  and so was their guide;
    how wondrous a soul
      illuminating lights!

My full moon never waned;
  my sun, it never set,
    and all the blazing stars
      followed my lead.

By my leave, in my realm
planets moved,
and angels bowed
to my dominion.[4]

Though readers will at times lose their way as this ode twists and turns, still they can follow the thread of love to the poem's end. There they may look back and trace the circuitous route to enlightenment against the background of Ibn al-Fāriḍ's unitary vision of existence. But here again the *Poem of the Sufi Way* resembles the spiral or cylindrical helix, which when unfolded into a plane becomes a straight line, a fact that Ibn al-Fāriḍ might well have appreciated:

The celestial spheres turn on me,
so marvel at the pole of their turning,
a central point
that circles them all.

So do not go beyond my straight line
for in the corners
are hidden things;
seize your best chance now![5]

Text and Commentary

As was the case with the *Wine Ode*, my translation of *Poem of the Sufi Way* is based on the Arabic text found in the Maḥmūd edition of the *Dīwān* (83–172) and read in consultation with a number of the earliest manuscripts of Ibn al-Fāriḍ's verse, all noted in the bibliography. The *Poem of the Sufi Way* is certainly Ibn al-Fāriḍ's most celebrated work, and amid its rising popularity, the poem became the stuff of legends. According to one tale related by the poet's grandson ʿAlī, Ibn al-Fāriḍ would fall into deathlike trances for days, then recover and spontaneously recite verses directly inspired by God; these verses were then collected to form this long ode. Similarly, in a second story ʿAlī told how the prophet Muḥammad appeared in a dream to Ibn al-Fāriḍ and ordered the poet to name this poem the *Naẓm al-sulūk*. Through double-entendre this title can mean "Stringing the Strings of Poetry's Pearls," "Poem of the Sufi Way," or "Order of the Spiritual Life," and these multiple meanings underscore the poem's subject of the pilgrim's progress while asserting Ibn al-Fāriḍ's posthumous reputation as a great poet, gnostic, and spiritual guide.[6]

Such tales were an early and integral part of the commentary tradition that asserted the inspired, perhaps even sacred character of the *Poem of the Sufi Way*, and these stories were also cited by admirers of the ode to defend Ibn al-Fāriḍ against occasional charges of heresy stemming from his vision of divine unity and, above all, from his use of the feminine gender to refer to God. But what undoubtedly drew scholarly attention was the ode's length and overt Sufi themes, and four major commentaries were composed in the century following the poet's death. Like many of the commentaries on the *Wine Ode*, three of the four originated from followers of Ibn al-ʿArabī, in this case, from Saʿīd al-Dīn al-Farghānī, ʿAfīf al-Dīn al-Tilimsānī (d. 690/1291), and al-Qayṣarī, while the fourth commentary by ʿIzz al-Dīn al-Kāshānī (d. 735/1344) interprets the poem in similar, if somewhat different, monistic terms. These four works served as the foundation for later medieval commentaries and studies, including those of al-Nābulusī, who attempted to define further Ibn al-Fāriḍ's religious experiences and beliefs.[7]

As was the case with the *Wine Ode*, I have drawn from this commentary tradition for a nuanced Sufi reading of the *Poem of the Sufi Way*. Yet, while the *Wine Ode* easily stands on its own without extensive commentary, the length and complexity of the *Poem of the Sufi Way* demands, I believe, a running commentary. Therefore, readers will find facing my translation of the poem a verse-by-verse commentary, which may easily be covered to avoid distraction when reading the poem. The aim of my commentary is to illuminate both the aesthetic and mystical dimensions of the ode, while trying to avoid highly speculative Sufi exegesis resulting from overly zealous, if sincere, efforts to uncover profound secrets within every word of the text.

ʿUmar Ibn al-Fāriḍ
Poem of the Sufi Way
(Ode in T Major)
(Naẓm al-sulūk/al-Tāʾīyah al-kubrā)

1: The poet likens his eye, which beheld the beloved, to a cup-bearer who gives him the strong wine in a chalice reflecting the beloved's beautiful countenance.

2: The poet is not intoxicated by wine but by a single glance at his beloved's face. Another possible reading is that the poet fooled his companions by means of "my glance." In Arabic love theory and poetry, however, it is the morally questionable "glance" *(naẓar/naẓrah)* at the beloved that ensnares the lover.

4: With structurally parallel phrases, Ibn al-Fāriḍ alludes to intoxication's mixing of time and place as the tavern of the poet's drunkenness *(ḥāni sukrī)* became the time for his thanksgiving *(ḥāna shukrī)*.

5: Well-known Sufi terms suggest the spiritual dimensions of this love and union *(waṣl)*, as intoxication (*sukr*; v. 4) leads to an expanding exhilaration (*basṭ*; also "reaching out"), while sobriety *(ṣaḥw)* may result in a gripping fear *(qabḍ)*. Also see vv. 164, 269, 646–48.

6: The poet's seemingly reprehensible intoxication and shameless gaze on the beloved are acceptable during the unveiling of the bride in the bridal chamber *(jalwah)*. Ibn al-Fāriḍ underscores this very private, intimate encounter by using the term *khalwah* ("seclusion"), which in Sufism refers to a period of solitary retreat; also compare vv. 209–12, 559–60. In courtly love poetry, the spy guards the beloved, and the term may refer to the continual presence of society's restrictions on love and relationships, though several commentators have interpreted the spy here *(raqību baqā ḥaẓẓin)* as the poet's former narcissistic self-regard; see vv. 20, 50–52, 137, 367.

saqatnī ḥumayyā-l-ḥubbi rāḥatu muqlatī
wa-ka'sī muḥayyā man 'ani-l-ḥusni jallati

The palm of my eye handed me
love's heady wine to drink,
and my glass was a face
of one revealing loveliness.

Drunk by my glance I caused
my companions to suppose
that drinking their wine
had brought my heart joy.

But by the dark pupils of the eyes
I did without my drinking bowl;
from the eyes' fine qualities, not cool wine,
came my intoxication.

So in the tavern of my drunkenness
was the time of my thanks to brave young men,
for despite my infamy,
I completely hid my love with them.

Then, when sobriety ceased, *5*
I sought union with her;
shame's grip did not seize me
as I stretched out for her.

There was no one present with me there—
no persistent spy of fortune—
in the seclusion of the bridal chamber
where I revealed my all to her.

7: Again, terms from the Sufi lexicon describe the poet's condition (*ḥāl*; also a "mystical state") as in flux between finding his beloved in a rapture *(wajd)*, which effaces *(māḥīya)* him, and losing her by her absence *(faqd)*, which confines and disables *(muthbit)* him.

9: Ibn al-Fāriḍ refers to Qur'ān 7:142–43, which recounts Moses' experience at Sinai when he said: "My Lord, appear to me that I may gaze upon you." To this God replied: "You will never see Me!" God then revealed His splendor to the mountain, which crumbled, sending Moses into a swoon; see vv. 11, 308–14, 327–28, 478–79.

13: Qur'ān 21:51–71 tells of how the prophet Abraham was thrown into a fire by his relatives after he destroyed their idols. God cooled the flames to protect his messenger; see vv. 606–7, and, for Noah, see Qur'ān 71:1–28; 11:25–48; 23:23–41; 26:105–22, and vv. 602–4.

POEM OF THE SUFI WAY

With my state as witness to rushing love—
my finding her effacing me,
losing her transfixing me—
I said:

"Before love annihilates
what remains of me to see you,
allow me
one backward glance,

"Or if you forbid my seeing you,
bless my ear with:
'You'll never see me!'—
words sweet to one before me.

"For could I wake *10*
from my intoxication
my heart would not break,
but for passion.

"Had Sinai and the mountains
contained what is in me,
they would have come crashing down
before the unveiling:

"A passion betrayed
by telling tears;
a grief inflamed by burning pains
consuming me with their disease.

"Noah's flood is like
my wailing tears,
Abraham's blazing fire like
my pangs of love.

15: Regarding Jacob's sorrow for his lost son Joseph, see Qur'ān 12:84–87, 93–96, and also vv. 610–11. For the Qur'ānic account of Job, see 21:83–84; 38:41–44.

20: By concealing his love for the beloved, the lover is emaciated by love-sickness, a condition that, paradoxically, reveals his true state to others. In an alternate reading: "In complaining of emaciation *[fī shakwā al-nuḥūli]*, I confided to my spy...." The spy/overseer/censor *(murāqib)* might allude to larger society or to some aspect of the lover himself, such as the intellect or conscience; see v. 6. In either case, the spy appears as an alter-ego of the poet.

"If not for my deep sighs,
  these tears would drown me;
    if not for shedding tears,
      my sighs would scorch me.

"Jacob did not divulge *15*
  the least of my grief,
    while all of Job's affliction
      is but some of mine.

"What pushed impassioned lovers
  to ruin in the end
    is but a part of what befell me
      as my trial began.

"Had the caravan's guide
  heard my groaning
    caused by sickening pains
      wracking my body,

"My torment would have brought to mind
  the ruined life of those left behind
    when the riders set out
      on the bridled brown camels.

"For affliction had distressed
  and destroyed me
    as emaciation laid bare
      the hidden secret of my being.

"Drunk and wasted, I confided *20*
  to emaciation—my spy—
    all my secrets
      and details of my way.

24: Those of the quarter or "the tribe" may refer to the lover's relations or those of his beloved, who guard her from unwanted advances. Within a Sufi context, the folk or tribe often alludes to the brotherhood of fellow mystics.

25: Qur'ān 82:10–12: "Indeed there are guardians over you, generous and recording, knowing what you do."

"I appeared a mere trace to him
who could not see my essential self,
tried and worn out
by love's chronic pain.

"Though my tongue did not tell,
my soul's whispers
revealed to his ear
the secret it had concealed,

"And his ear turned
into a mind for my thought
to turn in;
he had no need to see.

"So he told the tribe of me
making plain the hidden
nature of my affair—
he was of those who knew—

"As though recording angels *25*
had descended upon his heart
revealing life's register
written for my part.

"Yet he would not have known
what I concealed
nor the guarded secret
buried deep within

"Had not the veil—my body—
been ripped away revealing
what had been screened from him:
the mystery of my heart.

32–33: Ibn al-Fāriḍ makes several references to the Sufi concept of *fanā'* ("passing away," "annihilation") to stress the lover's claims to have totally eradicated any lingering thoughts of himself or his own welfare before the beloved, who may reject or accept him as she wills.

"I was hidden from him there
in my secret joy,
but spent by wasting,
my moaning laid it bare.

"Sickness dissolved me,
and so divulged me to him;
passion brings to pass
every wondrous thing.

"Distress despatched me, *30*
its touch effacing
tales of a soul
treacherous as tears.

"Had hateful death sought me out,
it would not have known my place,
as hiding love of you,
hid me.

"Between longing and craving,
I passed away
bearing rejection,
revealing majesty.

"Yet, could my heart
be passed back to me
by my passing from your courtyard,
still, it would not want an exile's camp.

"The title of my condition?
I have divulged but a part to you,
for what lies below this disclosure
is beyond my power to impart.

41: This is one of a number of direct references within the poem to the popular Muslim view of the human being as composed of a pre-eternal spirit *(rūḥ)* and a corporeal body with a psychological and volitional self *(nafs)*. Traditionally, the spirit is regarded as existing before the body's creation, as well as after its dissolution. See the Introduction and below, especially vv. 108, 145, 195–202, 208–10, 400–401, 425–41, 537–38.

"I say nothing, *35*
powerless in many affairs
never to be told in words,
though could I speak, they would be few.

"My cure was on the verge of death,
a death rapture had decreed,
as cooling my violent thirst
excited the fever burning me.

"My condition was more worn
than my robes of patience;
being was bound to my delight
in being nothing.

"Had those who came to visit me
been shown the light,
and come to know from heaven's slate
what flowing love had left of me,

"Their eyes would have witnessed
nothing save a spirit
passing through
a dead man's clothes.

"After my traces were effaced *40*
and I wandered away,
I wondered about my existence,
but thought could not snare my being.

"Then my case with you
stood by itself—
my proof: my spirit
came before my body.

ʿUMAR IBN AL-FĀRIḌ

"I did not relate
  my condition in loving you
    tired and tied by anxiety;
      only, my grief needs release.

"Displaying endurance to the foe
  is proper indeed,
    but before lovers
      only weakness will do.

"My fine patience forbids my complaining,
  but had I complained to my enemies
    of what I feel,
      even they would have helped me.

"Impassioned with you, *45*
  my patience leads to praise
    if you I bear
      without holding back.

"Whatever grief afflicts me
  is a gift,
    since my resolve was safe
      from breaking the bond.

"So for every pain in love
  that appears from you,
    I give thanks
      in place of complaint.

"Yes, passion's pain
  when it attacks me
    is reckoned
      as one of love's blessings.

49: The lover apparently rejects the term "misery" *(shaqā')* to describe his ordeal since it is, in fact, cause for happiness.

50: "My ancient allegiance" *(qadīmu walā'ī)* may allude to God's pre-eternal Covenant with the spirits of humanity, and in Arabic love poetry, this may signify that lovers were meant for each other since pre-eternity. Based on Qur'ān 7:172, Muslim tradition holds that this Covenant, taken prior to creation, attests to God's lordship, and to humanity's dependence on and servitude toward Him. See the Introduction, and vv. 68–69, 156–58, 430–41, 456–57, 495–509, 549–52.

50–52: The "wicked young slaves" correspond to the slanderer *(wāshin)* and blamer *(lāḥin; lā'im)* found in many Classical Arabic love poems, including those of Ibn al-Fāriḍ. Along with the spy, they are among the lover's protagonists who seek to thwart his goal of union with the beloved; the slanderer denigrates the lover as unworthy of love, while the blamer criticizes him for wasting his time and tries to deceive the lover into believing that the beloved is beneath him. Like the spy, the slanderer and blamer may be read in terms of the lover's psyche, as the first pushes the lover to further spiritual self-sacrifice, while the latter would pull him down into more selfish sensual pursuits. In addition, some commentators have interpreted the slanderer as a guardian angel, and the deceiving blamer as Satan. See vv. 6, 20, 135, 166, 366–67, 389–90, 397–402, 408.

"My misery—no, my tribulation—
is a bounty from you;
my wearing misfortune for your sake
is ample blessing.

"My ancient allegiance to you *50*
led me to see those wicked young slaves
you entrusted to me
as great and guarded treasures:

"One is a deceiver
leading blindly to recklessness;
the other, jealous, raves on,
weaving lies against me.

"I break with the first and his blame
out of righteousness,
while tactfully, I appear to bond
with the second, low-born and mean.

"No terror I met,
no savage force that struck me
ever turned my face
from your path,

"Yet there is no praise,
no glory, for my love;
I had no forbearance in bearing
what fell to me for you.

"Your beauty, calling all to worship you, *55*
decreed bearing what I have told
and what is far beyond
the telling of my tale.

61: To highlight love's rocky road, in contrast to the easy path toward a wayward life, Ibn al-Fāriḍ makes a direct reference to a well-known *ḥadīth*: "The Garden is enclosed by hateful things, while enclosing hell are things of lust." Compare v. 499.

"And this is it:
you appeared to my eyes
with the most perfect qualities
surpassing even loveliness.

"Then you decked me with affliction
and turned it loose on me,
but from you,
it was a most lovely adornment.

"He who tangles with beauty,
I think will see
his soul thrown down
from precious life to ruin.

"But a soul that thinks
it will not see trouble in love
is turned away
when it turns to passion.

"For no stable spirit *60*
ever won its wish;
no soul loving the quiet life
ever wished for love.

"Where is tranquility?
Far from the lover's life;
enclosing Eden's garden
are hateful, horrible things.

"Yet I have a freeman's soul;
could you give it what is beyond desire
to forget you,
it would not be moved.

64–65: To stress that love is the lover's guide and ultimate goal, Ibn al-Fāriḍ plays on several Muslim legal and sectarian terms: *madhhab* ("a school of religious law"; "a road, or orientation"), *millah* ("a religious community"), and *riddah* ("apostasy").

68–69: Ibn al-Fāriḍ invokes the *mīthāq*, the Primordial Covenant between God and the spirits of humanity taken before creation of their bodies. He alludes to its timelessness with antithesis and parallel structures as the prior covenant *(sābiqi ʿahdin)* is followed by his subsequent bond *(lāḥiqi ʿaqdin)*. While the covenant is that of pre-eternity, the subsequent bond may represent the lover's initial experience of union and his abiding love for his beloved. Interpreted religiously, the bond might represent the devotee's mystical experiences or, perhaps, the ties between various communities and their prophets. In light of Ibn al-Fāriḍ's other poems, however, this subsequent bond may also refer to the Day of Resurrection, when humanity will again come face to face with its creator following its intervening time of trial *(fatrah)* on earth. See the Introduction, and vv. 50, 156–58, 430–33, 456–57, 495–509, 549–52.

"It will not let go of love,
though it be exiled far away,
shunned, forsaken, despised,
cut off from hope.

"I have no way to leave
my path in love,
and if one day I turn away,
I have lost my true religion;

"If ever an urge for other than you *65*
slips through my mind,
I will die
in apostasy.

"You are judge of my affair,
do as you will,
but my desire
has been for you alone.

"By love's strong bond between us
never weakened
with thought of being broken—
the best of oaths;

"By your taking the covenant of love
where I did not appear
in the soul's manifest disguise
in the passing shadow of my clay;

"By the priority of a pact
unbroken since I pledged it,
and a subsequent bond beyond
being loosed by intervening time;

70–76: A panegyric, or section of praise *(madḥ),* often concludes many Classical Arabic odes, as the poet entreats his patron on behalf of himself, his tribe, or cause. Here, Ibn al-Fāriḍ's praise of the beloved forms the central part of the lover's oath of fidelity and final plea for acceptance.

71–73: Ibn al-Fāriḍ again raises the beloved to divine status, this time, by ascribing to her the attributes *(waṣf)* of perfection *(kamāl)*, majesty *(jalāl)*, and beauty *(jamāl)*, attributes normally predicated together of God. God is necessarily perfect, and His majesty and beauty have been seen by Muslims as contrasting states within this perfection; *jalāl* ("majesty") is associated with God's wrath *(mysterium tremendum)* while *jamāl* ("beauty") expresses His satisfaction and kindness *(mysterium fascinans).* Further, among these attributes, Ibn al-Fāriḍ designates perfection as the ultimate support for the finest *(aḥsan)* and soundest *(aqwām)* created form *(ṣūrah)*, namely, the human being, the crown of creation, as mentioned in Qur'ān 40:64, and 95:4: "Indeed We created the human being with the finest stature." Also see vv. 646–48.

75: The term translated throughout as "subtle sense" is *maʿnā*. This word may signify the meaning or hidden sense of something (e.g., the meaning or sense of a word), as well as a poetic motif. By extension, Ibn al-Fāriḍ frequently uses the term to point toward the "idea" or "reality" manifest by or within a form as, in this case, where physical beauty appears to give way or point toward a deeper spiritual sense. Also see vv. 643–45.

"By the rays rising *70*
in your glowing face—
from their splendor all full moons
will soon disappear—

"And the attribute of your perfection,
from which creation's fairest form
and most straight in stature
sought support;

"By the quality of your majesty—
near it, my suffering is savory,
my slaughter sweet,
before it—

"And by the secret of your beauty
with which every luminous face
arose in all the worlds
and waxed full;

"By a loveliness captivating reason,
leading me to a passion
making my weakness lovely
before your strength,

"And by a subtle sense in you *75*
beneath that loveliness—
by it I saw it, as it was too fine
for the grasp of even an insightful eye—

"Truly you are my heart's desire,
my farthest wish,
my final aim,
my choice and chosen.

77: This verse is not found in some early editions of the poem and is considered by many to be a later addition. According to one account, Ibn al-Fāriḍ appeared in a dream to a man reading the poem, and instructed him to add it after v. 76. See *Dīwān*, Maḥmūd ed., 92–93 (n. 77).

78: This verse continues the use of legal technical terminology found earlier (64–66), as the lover's obligation or duty *(farḍ)* and custom *(sunnah)* demand his total abasement before his beloved.

82: In contrast to ascetics who give up the pleasures of this life in hopes of God's mercy and reward in the afterlife, the true lover is enthralled with all aspects of his beloved, whether they bring him pleasure or pain. Also see vv. 304, 324, 443.

"I stripped off my modesty
making no excuses,
and wrapped myself in depravity,
enjoying disrobing and my robe.

"Stripping off restraint
is my duty to you,
and depravity is my custom
though my folk despise to come near me.

"But they are no folk of mine so long
as they find fault with me exposed,
showing their hatred, seeing fit
to rough me up for your sake.

"In passion's faith, *80*
love's nobles are my family;
they approved my nakedness
and found joy in my exposure.

"So whoever is angry, let them be,
but not you;
there is no harm when noble friends
are satisfied with me.

"If some of your fine qualities
roused the ascetics, well,
all of you imposed
temptation's unrest on me.

"Yet I was never lost until I chose
loving you as my way;
if not for you,
what a waste, my confusion!"

84: Ibn al-Fāriḍ underscores the beloved's demand for absolute obedience with references to the pilgrimage and to the straight path (*sawā'*, i.e., *sawā' al-sabīl*), which suggests the straight path of obedience to God mentioned in the oft-repeated opening chapter of the Qur'ān (1:5).

88: A "faint star," literally, *al-Suhā*, a faint star in Ursa Major used by the Arabs to test one's vision.

But she said:
"You aimed for another's love
and fell short, blind
to the straight pilgrim's path to me.

"You were seduced *85*
by a fickle soul's disguise
till you said what you said
and dressed in an ugly lie.

"For you coveted
the most precious thing
with an aggressive soul,
transgressing beyond its bounds.

"How can you win my love,
that most beautiful friendship,
with lying pretense,
that ugliest fraud?

"Your desires deceived you;
how can one born blind, confused,
diverted from his design,
find a faint star to guide him?

"So you settled on a station
beyond your power to reach
on feet that never could
step beyond their lot.

"You craved a thing *90*
toward which so many folk
have craned their necks,
only to lose their heads.

91: Qur'ān 2:189 forbids Muslims returning from the pilgrimage from "entering tents from their back," as was the custom among the pre-Islamic Arabs. In context of the beloved's rebuke, this Qur'ānic reference may be accusing the presumptuous lover of trying to meet with her by deception and stealth, and of being unworthy of her, just as pagans were not worthy to enter the tents of Muslims.

92: This verse echoes Qur'ān 58:12–13, which calls believers to make an offering before their private meetings with the prophet Muḥammad. But in contrast to the sincere alms *(ṣadaqah)* requested by the Qur'ān are the lover's *zukhruf*, his bombast or "golden lies."

93: Though the lover may be morally pure, his narcissism makes him unfit for true, unselfish love. In contrast to the lover's "bright face" is the "black face" of humility; a tradition ascribed to the prophet Muḥammad declares: "Poverty is a black face in both worlds" *(al-faqru sawādu-l-wajhi fī al-dārayn).*

94: To illustrate the proper passivity and humility of the lover before his beloved, Ibn al-Fāriḍ turns to Arabic calligraphy where a small line, called a *kasrah*, falls below the dot marking the letter *B* leading to its pronunciation as *bi* or, in this case, *bī* (i.e., "in/by/with me").

"You went to tents
not to be entered from the back,
their doors shut to the knocking
of one like you,

"And before confiding
love's secrets,
you offered golden lies,
craving an impossible glory.

"You came bright-faced, proud,
without a blemish
in this world or the next,
to woo my purity.

"But had you been with me
like the line beneath the dot of B,
you would have risen up to where
no scheme could ever take you,

"Where you could see that you will not see *95*
what you have counted on,
and that your big plans
were poor provisions.

"The open road to me is plain to see
for one right-guided,
but commonly lust
blinds and leads astray.

"So now I will expose your passion
and who it is who has worn you out;
I will sweep away your pretense
to my love.

98: The beloved charges the lover with being in love with love, not with her. He has permitted some part of himself to remain in order to experience love's pleasure (as he, the lover, had desired in v. 8).

99: Again, Ibn al-Fāriḍ refers to the Sufi technical term *fanāʾ* ("annihilation," "passing away") as he stresses the lover's need for union in order to discover the beloved's form *(ṣūrah)* within.

"You are love's ally, all right,
but for its sake, not mine;
as my proof, you have saved
an attribute of yours.

"For you never loved me
so long as you were not lost in me,
and you will never be lost
without my form in you revealed.

"So give up claim to love, *100*
call your heart to something else,
and drive away your erring ways
with that.

"Shun the courtyard of union,
that was not to be—
here you are living;
die if you are true!

"Such is love: if you do not die
you will derive nothing from it;
so decide on death
or leave my love alone."

So I replied to her:
"My spirit is yours, yours to take;
why should I care
if it is mine to hold?

"I am not afraid
to die from love;
my faithful nature
fears all else.

108: The "soul" or "self" *(nafs)* in Ibn al-Fāriḍ's poems usually designates the volitional self characterized by a wayward and selfish nature, and not the spiritual dimension of humans, which he often refers to as the *rūḥ* ("spirit"). Thus, the lover must be ready and willing to sacrifice his self-centered and selfish nature if he truly aspires to the beloved and not merely to love of himself. See the Introduction and vv. 41, 108, 145, 195–210, 400–401, 415–42, 458–64, 656–715.

"What should be said of me save: *105*
'So and so died of love!'
Who will grant me this,
my earnest wish?

"Yes, I will be satisfied with my death,
its end in deep affection
though short of union,
if my right to loving you is true.

"But if I truly fail to win
this bond with you, so rare,
then my repute for having tried
is glory enough for me.

"Still, if I end unknown, in pain,
you have done no wrong
to a soul finding joy
in martyrdom.

"Even if you waste my blood
so I do not die a martyr,
it is enough I know
who called down my fate.

"For, I see my spirit's sacrifice *110*
falls short of union with you;
how different a precious robe
from shabby, worn-out clothes.

"Yet, before the crush of death,
I stand straight and firm,
while those who fear it,
their supports come tumbling down.

113: This "good sign" or omen is the destruction of the *nafs* ("the volitional self" or "soul") with its proud and deceptive nature.

114–115: The beloved's power vis-à-vis her lover is stressed by contrasting her "judgment" *(qaḍā)* with her "satisfaction" *(riḍā)*, her "threat" *(waʿīd)* of destruction with the "promise" *(waʿd)* of eternal life; these or related terms occur throughout the Qur'ān, particularly in pronouncements of God's omnipotence and His grace on the Day of Judgment (e.g., 43:77; 3:15; 31:9; 50:20).

117: Ibn al-Fāriḍ continues his metaphor of martyrdom, but with additional allusions to Islamic law (*sharīʿah*, also meaning "path" or "way to water") and to entering *(sālik)* the Sufi path of past spiritual masters. Also see the numerous references in the Qur'ān concerning fighting and following in the "way of God" (e.g., 5:54; 9:20).

"By slaying my soul
you will not be unjust.
No, you will grant its wish
if you lay my heart to waste.

"If this good sign from you is true,
then you have raised me high,
exalted my stature,
increased my worth.

"So here I am appealing
for your judgment and satisfaction;
I will not delay
my appointed time.

"Your threat is my promise, *115*
its execution a gift to a friend
steady under any affliction
save separation.

"I have come to hope
for what is feared;
so make a dead man happy
whose spirit is ready to live!"

May I be her ransom,
for I gave my soul for her,
entering the way of the forefathers
who scorned any path but mine.

In each tribe how many victims
has she condemned to pain;
not once did they win
a glance at her,

122: Having been rebuked for harboring a love of himself, the lover begins his tale of how he purged this last remnant of self-regard out of love for his beloved.

And how many mortals like me
has she put to death by love;
were she to glance at them with grace,
life would come again.

If she lets my blood *120*
be shed for her love,
then she will set my rank
on glory's peaks and high places.

I swear if I lose my life loving her,
I profit;
if she infects my heart,
she will cure it.

She humbled me among the tribe
until I found myself;
their least achievement
was far above my high ambition.

Submitting to them
reduced me to a faint obscurity,
so they did not see lowly me
as a site fit for service.

From the heights of glory,
I—puffed up with pride—
slid down
to depths of abasement.

No one knocked at my door *125*
or placed hope in my standing;
no neighbor sought my shelter
for I had lost my defenses,

127: Ibn al-Fāriḍ refers here to the popular belief that the *jinn* ("genies") cause madness through possession. Thus critics of the lover chide his impertinence for aspiring for the beloved. Her phantom did not visit his dreams as was believed to happen with true lovers; rather, a genie has possessed him. For another reference to possession, see vv. 223–25, and also see vv. 664–71.

129: Earlier (vv. 19–29, 43) the imperfect lover gave away the secret of his love as he made his boastful claims, and took pleasure in his pain. But now as the lover purges his spiritual and psychological state *(ḥāl)* in true humility and love, he is careful to keep love's secret free of reductive thoughts and selfish desires.

130: Love is ineffable, which is to say that it must be experienced to be truly known. Although the intellect *(raqība ḥijan)* may try to uncover love's secret by stealth, its efforts are doomed to failure. Similarly within Sufism, the heart *(qalb)* or secret/inner heart *(sirr)*—not the brain—is the site of inspiration, following the example of the prophet Muḥammad, upon whose heart Gabriel, the spirit of revelation, brought the Qur'ān (e.g., Qur'ān 26:192–94; 2:97). See vv. 751–53.

132: In medieval love theory, keeping love's secret, even if by lies and deception, was considered a sign of the lover's sincerity.

As if I had never been
  eminent among them,
    but always in their eyes a wretch
      in both my fortune and distress.

Had someone asked: "Who do you love?"
  and I clearly spoke her name,
    they would have said: "He means another,"
      or "The phantom jinn has touched him!"

But had disgrace for her sake been too hard,
  I would not have found passion so sweet;
    if not for love,
      I would have no glory in humility.

For her, my state was adorned
  with an absent mind,
    broken health,
      and infamy.

In a place without the spying mind, *130*
  the soul whispered secretly
    within my heart alone
      the hidden desire to love her.

Then I guarded against the tale
  tracing through the rest of me,
    fearing that my shedding tears
      would clearly speak my secret.

To keep it safe, part of me
  misled another part,
    and in hiding it,
      my deception spoke true.

133–34: Ibn al-Fāriḍ again implies that love's gnosis is outside the range of the human intellect, imagination, and reflection.

137: The "guard" or spy *(murāqib)* may represent the lover's self-regard or intellectual faculties, which obstruct his experiencing selfless love; see vv. 6, 20, 367.

138: Ibn al-Fāriḍ refers to the recurring poetic motif of the beloved's phantom visiting the poet in a dream. Also see vv. 127, 146.

139: With language echoing vv. 5–8, Ibn al-Fāriḍ contrasts the lover's contrite state of passive humility with his earlier manic and impetuous actions toward the beloved.

When my intuition refused
to reveal it to my ribs,
I shielded it
from my reflection.

Relentlessly, I hid it,
forgot it, and forgotten
was my keeping this secret
revealed to me.

If I pick the fruit of torment *135*
after planting my desires,
then God bless the tormented soul
dying in desire.

For the sweetest of love's cravings
is that she decreed the soul's torment,
she who brought forth these desires
then made them disappear.

For her, from me, against me
she set a guard to watch
over my heart's stirrings
in case they draw near love.

So if at night they slip secretly
into my mind unbound from fantasy,
I am silent, head down
awed in reverence.

My eyes are shut
if I desire a glance;
my hand is stopped
if it stretches out to touch.

141–47: This passage links the lover's devotion to his beloved with *dhikr*, prayer through "remembrance" or "recollection" of God, and the subsequent trance induced by its practice. Often the devotee begins by repeating aloud one of God's divine names (Allāh; the Merciful, etc.), and then advancing to the stage of silent repetition within the heart. See the Introduction and vv. 271–72, 407, 411, 420–41, 515–20, 528–29, 560, 731, 759.

145: While the lover's spirit *(rūḥ)* is rapt in ecstasy with the beloved, his volitional conscious self *(nafs)* still desires to see or possess the beloved. Also see vv. 41, 108, 400–401, 425–26, 537–38.

146: As the lover advances on his quest, even those blaming him for his shortcomings aid him, for this blame enables him to picture his beloved, who comes to him as a phantom in his dreams. Also see vv. 127, 139.

In my body's every member *140*
is desire's bold advance
and a drawing back in fear,
dreading presumption.

My mouth and ear show signs
of rivalry for her,
though choosing between the two
seemed to me a blessing:

When my tongue recites her name
and my listening ear
arrives to hear,
my tongue falls silent,

While my ear goes deaf
when my tongue,
no slave to silence,
guides her mention to my heart.

I guard her with a jealous rage
consuming me in love with her,
but I know my place and worth,
and renounce my jealousy.

Then the spirit is carried away *145*
to rest in joy with her,
though I cannot absolve my soul
from conjuring desire still.

While she is far from sight,
my ear sees her
in the phantom form of blame
visiting my waking state,

147–54: Reference in v. 147 to the beloved causing a part of the lover to "pass away" leads to an account of a unitive experience with the beloved, which occurs during the annual pilgrimage, near the Kaʿbah at a time for prayer. Also compare vv. 486–88 where the true lover's last selfish residue is finally obliterated.

148: In union, wherever the lover faces becomes his direction *(wijhah)* for prayer, just as the Qur'ān declares in 2:115: "Wherever you turn, there is the face *[wajh]* of God." An *imām*, or prayer leader, stands before the congregation to lead the proper prayer ritual.

150: According to a tradition God has said: "Heaven and earth do not contain me, but the heart of my faithful servant does." Also see vv. 130, 448, 451.

151: Since the lover stands near the Kaʿbah, which is the *qiblah*, or direction for the five daily Muslim prayers, all prayers, pious acts, and pilgrimages face toward him.

152: Abraham's Station *(maqām Ibrāhīm)* is located near the corner of the Kaʿbah containing the Black Stone. The site is believed to contain the footprint of Abraham, whom Muslim tradition credits with building the first Kaʿbah. Pilgrims pray a short prayer there.

153–54: In union *(jamʿ)* the lover and beloved pray as one worshiper, finding oneness to be "his reality" *(ḥaqīqatihi)*. In many Sufi lexicons, *al-ḥaqīqah* ("reality") represents the culmination of the mystical quest. Also see vv. 218, 321, 441, 578.

And with her mention, my eye
longs to share my ear's good fortune,
while what remains of me envies
what she has caused to pass away.

In truth, I led my prayer leader in prayer
with all of humanity behind me;
wherever I turned
was my way,

And my eye saw her before me
in my prayer,
my heart witnessing me
leading all my leaders.

It is no wonder *150*
the prayer leader prayed toward me
since she had settled in my heart
as niche of my prayer niche.

All six directions faced me
with all there was
of piety and pilgrimage
both great and small.

To her I prayed my prayers
at Abraham's Station,
and I witnessed in them
her prayer to me,

Both of us one worshiper
bowing to his reality
in union
in every prostration.

155: The bond of allegiance *(ʿaqd bayʿatī),* whether to a beloved, to God, or to His prophets, requires duality, which has been lost in union.

156: As in vv. 68–69, the "bond" of allegiance is paired with the "pact" *(ʿahd),* which is clearly the Primordial Covenant. The lover claims that his loyalty and friendship with his beloved were granted to him in a primal state preceding even the Covenant, perhaps alluding to an earlier existence as an idea in the mind of God and/or the creative Light of Muḥhammad, as will become clear later in the poem. See the Introduction, vv. 50, 68–69, 256–59, 430–41, 456–57, 495–509, 549–52.

157: The lover's passion for the beloved was given him prior to the Primordial Covenant and the subsequent creation of his body, so his love is not the product of the senses, natural drives, or a fated acquisition.

158: According to Muslim tradition, the World of the Command *(ʿālam al-amr)* is where God initiates creation with the command "Be!" It is there, but before the command is given, that the lover claims to have been first intoxicated by love; see v. 1, and v. 1 of the *Wine Ode*. The lover's claim reflects the notion that the spirits of humans existed prior to creation, based, in part, on Qur'ān 17:85: "Say: the spirit is from the command of the Lord." See vv. 473–74, 543–44, 637–38.

159: Ibn al-Fāriḍ plays on the Sufi technical pair of *fanā'*, the mystic's "passing away" from the transient world, and *baqā'*, one's "abiding" in God or His will. The spiritual quality of this unitive experience is further underscored as it restores the lover to his preexistent state of union with his beloved. Also see v. 345.

160–62: From the perspective of union, the rapt lover now discovers his old world anew. Freed from self-love, he contemplates things from the beloved's perspective and so bears witness to their union. Ibn al-Fāriḍ alludes here to the tradition in which God says: "My servant continues drawing nearer to Me through supererogatory acts until I love him, and when I love him, I become his ear with which he hears, his eye with which he sees, his hand with which he grasps, and the foot with which he walks." See the Introduction and below, vv. 192–94, 313–14, 381–87, 545–48; 579–87, 639–42, 719–21.

For no one prayed to me but I
nor were my prayers performed
to other than me
in each genuflection.

How long must I be brother to the veil? *155*
I have rent it,
and its clasps were loosened
in the bond of my pledge!

I was given her protection
on a day not a day
in my priority
before she appeared to take the pact.

So I gained love of her,
but not by sound or sight,
not by fated acquisition,
or tugging disposition,

And I burned with thirst for her
in the World of the Command
where nothing was manifest,
drunk before my creation.

Passion annihilated
the attributes here between us
that had never abided there,
so they passed away,

And I found *160*
what I had cast away
emerging to me, returning from me
in abundance.

163: A popular tradition ascribed to Muḥammad states: "He who knows himself *[nafsahu]*, knows his Lord." The verb *ʿarafa* ("to recognize," "to know") contains the same root as *maʿrafah*, a popular Sufi term for "gnosis."

164: The poetic persona returns to the present in order to explain his earlier words inspired by a state of exhilaration *(basṭ)*, a common Sufi term designating a manic mystical state. Also see vv. 5, 269, 646–48.

166: The slanderer and blamer are now identified as aids to the lover; also see vv. 50–52, 366–67, 389–90, 397–402.

167–73: Ibn al-Fāriḍ plays on a number of economic terms and concepts in this discussion of spiritual poverty.

In my contemplation,
I saw my soul with the attributes
that had veiled me from myself
in my concealment;

I was her, my love
absolutely,
as my soul passed me on
to me for her.

For my soul had burned for her unaware,
but in my witnessing
it was not ignorant
of the soul of the affair.

Now it is time for me to expand
on what I have said in sum,
and summarize what I have said
expansively in my expanded state.

My taking her love *165*
bestowed on our union
rare gifts strange
to the ways of lovers:

The one slandering me before her
does so on my behalf,
while one blaming me for her sake
is her advisor to me.

So I pay her thanks,
for she never advanced me hatred,
but grants beneficence
for true love.

170: Poverty is not to be his mount or "beast of burden," that is, a means to gain further reward. The lover would rather sacrifice it and himself instead. Ibn al-Fāriḍ may be referring to a tradition of the prophet Muḥammad that says: "Respect your animals to be sacrificed, for they will be your mounts across al-Ṣirāṭ!" Al-Ṣirāṭ is the "path" or bridge passing over hell into paradise.

174: Having sacrificed himself for the beloved, the lover can now guide others to her, but only if she wills it.

I tried to draw near
giving up my soul, satisfied with her,
not hoping for reward from her;
then she drew close.

Quickly, I offered up
what I had earned for heaven
and all that she might still bestow
upon me.

I left behind *170*
any thought of recompense,
unwilling that it be
my beast of burden.

I aimed for her in poverty,
but this then made me rich,
so I threw away
both wealth and need.

Yet giving up
my poverty and fortune
secured the merit of my quest,
so I tossed all merit aside.

But as I cast away,
prosperity appeared,
and my reward was her alone,
my rewarder.

So I began to guide
one astray from the path of guidance,
to her, by her—not by me—
for she was guiding really:

175–84: The poet assumes the role of guide and teacher, issuing instructions to his student on how to undertake the holy war against his selfishness. A tradition of Muḥammad declares: "[The greater holy war] is the struggle against one's self *[nafs]*." Similarly, another tradition states: "The holy warrior is he who strives against himself *[nafsahu]*." See vv. 195–210.

Leave to her, my friend, *175*
your will and desire;
hand her your halter
with a soul at peace with her.

Be free of your selfish lot,
rise up from your low estate,
then plant yourself firm
and flourish.

Set yourself toward her,
draw near and obey,
return and reply to her
humbled in repentance.

Come back quickly
and answer her call; do not say:
"Tomorrow, I'll make ready
and strive to take a stand."

Be sharp and hard as time itself,
for hate is the fate of "maybe,"
and beware of "perhaps,"
a most dangerous disease.

Stand straight, try to please her; *180*
push yourself hard, do not waver,
and never give in
to a sudden passing weakness.

Though crippled, walk; arise, though broken—
you are a lazy lot,
so do not defer your firm resolve
in hopes of better health.

182: In contrast to the aspiring lover who has prepared himself and gone out to battle are those who choose to sit idly by. Ibn al-Fāriḍ may allude here to the Qur'ān's condemnation of those able-bodied Muslims who refused initially to fight alongside Muḥammad but later wished to take part when they saw the war booty. Qur'ān 9:83 rebuked them and commanded Muḥammad to say: "You were content to sit the first time, so sit [again] with those who are left behind!"

183: Qur'ān 4:95 declares: "Those believers who stay sitting behind...are not equal to those who fight in the way of God with their wealth and souls."

186: In context of Ibn al-Fāriḍ's holy war analogy, passion's "folk" or "troop" are suggestive of those who fought and died beside Muḥammad, especially at the crucial Battle of Badr in 624, and Uḥud in 625; see Qur'ān 7:86–87, 8:38–44, and 3:152–69, and vv. 460–61.

Lead the way, charge ahead,
for you prepared for this
with those left behind;
break the chains of distraction.

Slash with the sword of determination
any talk of future;
if you are fast, you will find freedom,
for the sacrificing soul strives on!

Turn and approach her
bankrupt and broke,
though you are heir to my advice
if you receive my bequest.

A rich man never draws near her *185*
however hard he tries,
while one choosing hardship,
will not be far from her.

Just so were terms of passion
met by love's folk,
and by a troop who kept the pact
and paid its pledge in full.

When fidelity's gale blows hard,
it snaps the rich in half,
but had the wind brushed poverty,
it would have raised him up,

And when a right hand
left soft and smooth by easy life
reaches out for love's union,
its share is long blades slashing.

192–94: Again invoking the tradition regarding God's assumption of His lover's faculties, the lover/guide urges his ward to stop babbling about love; what can be said of love has already been better said by true lovers of long ago. Instead of talking, the aspirant must strive to personally experience love, since that is the only way to know it. See vv. 160–62, 192–94, 313–14, 381–87, 545–48, 639–42, 719–21.

195–96: In Qur'ān 12:53, Joseph declares: "The selfish soul *[nafs]* incites to evil, unless my Lord is merciful!" Unless selfishness is reined in, lust not love will result; see vv. 41, 108, 176, 400–401, 415–42, 458–64, 656–715. The strongest shield probably refers to God, as the Qur'ān urges believers to seek refuge with Him; e.g., Qur'ān 113, 114.

Devote to her
  pure deeds of piety,
    and so be saved from slacking off
      in your poverty.

Resist the calls of wrangling talk, *190*
  and save yourself
    from false claims and their assaults,
      which truly aim only to be heard.

For the tongues of those called
  "gnostics most eloquent"
    said all that could be said,
      then fell silent.

You are intimate, akin to what
  you do not say, but speak of it
    and you are a stranger,
      so, shut up!

In silence is nobility,
  a place of strong and sound restraint,
    but he is slave to dignity
      who is silent for thought of rank.

So be sight and see,
  be an ear and hear,
    be a tongue and speak,
      for union is the truest way.

Do not follow one *195*
  seduced by his selfish soul,
    which incites him on
      and will not let go.

197: The past tense returns as the lover relates his story of how he broke and tamed his selfish nature in his quest for union with his beloved. The "blaming soul" *(al-nafs al-lawwāmah)* is mentioned in Qur'ān 75:2.

200: Qur'ān 4:84 states: "Fight in the way of God, impose this only on yourself/soul." Further, in several passages outlining God's rules and regulations for the Muslim community, the Qur'ān adds a phrase such as "God does not impose upon a soul more than it can bear" (2:286; also see 6:152, 7:42, 65:7), the idea being that God's commands are to guide and help believers without undue burden. The object is to tame one's selfish nature, not to commit suicide.

201: Qur'ān 89:27–30 says to the believer who has controlled his selfishness: "O tranquil soul, return to your Lord, contented and pleasing. Enter among My servants and enter My garden." Also see v. 555.

Stop her assailant,
attack her enemy, your soul,
and seek refuge
in the strongest shield.

Once my soul, too, blamed and criticized;
when I obeyed, it rebelled,
but when I rebelled,
it submitted to me.

So I led it to drink
what was far worse than death,
and rode and broke it
to give myself relief.

It grew used to bearing
the burdens I placed upon it,
so if I lightened the loads,
it suffered.

I imposed on it and made sure *200*
it carried out its charge
until it became attached
to my demands.

I took away all pleasure
to break my soul
driving it far from its habits,
so it grew tame.

I rode straight at any terror
standing there before it
so long as I saw my soul
mixed with fear.

204: Having given up all selfish desires in servitude to the beloved, the lover finds himself to be the object of her affection. Qur'ān 3:159 states: "God loves those who depend on Him completely."

205: Ibn al-Fāriḍ refers back to v. 98 to contrast the lover's selfless love in union with the beloved to his earlier imperfect phase.

206: Though the lover may strive for union, only the beloved can give it. Hence, Ibn al-Fāriḍ's use of the passive voice in vv. 208–9.

209–12: Ibn al-Fāriḍ makes yet another reference to the poem's opening scene to highlight the lover's realized union as compared with his earlier bungling attempts to achieve it. Ibn al-Fāriḍ has transposed the terms *jalwah* ("bridal chamber," "unveiling of the bride") and *khalwah* ("seclusion," "solitary retreat") of v. 8, suggesting that the beloved was encountered during the ascetic practices and introspection undertaken in spiritual retreat. Also see vv. 559–64.

Every station I passed on my way
was for service,
and I fulfilled them all
with devotion.

I was infatuated with her,
but when I gave up my desire,
she desired me
and loved me for herself.

So, I became a beloved, *205*
indeed, one loving himself,
but not like was said before:
"My beloved is myself."

By her, I departed to her
from me, never to return;
one like me never speaks
of coming back.

Kindly I secluded my soul
away from my departure;
never again did I allow it
to be my companion.

Then I was made to disappear
from where my soul stood apart,
that no attribute could appear
to crowd me in my presence,

And I was made to witness
my absence when she appeared,
so I found me, her there,
in the bridal chamber of my seclusion.

210: In the opening scene, a glance at the beloved intoxicated the lover who, in a manic drunken state, tried to possess her. But in union, the lover's former existence *(wujūd)* is lost in his contemplation or witnessing *(shuhūd)* of the beloved. See vv. 1–7, 230–38, 405–6, 649–50, 714.

211: Within the Sufi tradition, ecstatic intoxication *(sukr/sakrah)* is followed by a superior enlightened sobriety *(ṣaḥw)*. See the Introduction, and vv. 234–38, 310–12, 480–85, 573–75.

215: Compare v. 99.

216–17: Several Arabic terms in both verses have distinctive religious undertones. In v. 216, "calls" *(daʿā)* can mean "to pray," while "obeys" *(labbā)* is part of the expression *labbayka*, "At thy service, Lord!," which is to be repeated by all pilgrims at various stages of the Hajj. In v. 217, "whispers" recalls the well-known *munājāt*, the "whisperings" or intimate conversations between a mystic and God, while *ḥadīth* ("tale") may refer to a tradition of the prophet Muḥammad. Ibn al-Fāriḍ may be alluding here to al-Junayd's teaching that God answered His own question that He posed to the primordial spirits on the Day of the Covenant. See the Introduction, and vv. 495–96.

In my witnessing, my existence *210*
was cast off, and I was far
from the existence of my witnessing,
effacing, not transfixing.

I embraced what I witnessed
by bearing witness to it
in the effacement of my witness,
now sober after my drunkenness.

In the sobriety after effacement,
I was none other than her,
my essence adorned my essence
when she removed her veil.

Now I will make clear
my beginning in uniting,
and bring to an end my end
in abasing exaltation:

Unveiling herself revealed
existence to my eye,
so in everything seen
I perceived her.

My attribute is hers *215*
since we are not called two;
her shape is mine
since we are one.

If she is called,
it is I who answers;
when I am summoned, she replies
and obeys the one who calls me.

218: In Arabic, the letter *t* can mark a past tense verb as the second person singular masculine *(ta)* or feminine *(ti)*. In union, however, the second person is subsumed into the first person *(tu)*, namely, "I." Also see vv. 154–55, 321, 441, 578.

223: Concerning possession by the jinn, see v. 127.

If she speaks,
it is I who whispers;
when I tell a tale
she is the one who tells it.

For the second person's sign
became the first between us,
and so my rank is high above
all who cling to difference.

Now, if your wit
will not permit or recognize
seeing two as one
due to prudent circumspection,

Then I will reveal to you *220*
its hidden signs
as words and phrases
you obviously know.

This is no time to be obscure;
I will speak it clearly
in two strange examples:
one from hearing, one from sight.

I will support my words
with solid proof,
striking a sound parable—
and truth is my support—

About a woman possessed by the jinn;
when she is struck down, touched by madness,
another speaks to you through her mouth
of things to come,

ʿUMAR IBN AL-FĀRIḌ

And from this language
uttered by another with her tongue,
proofs of the signs
prove true.

Truly the one uttering *225*
those strange things you heard
was other than her,
although she spoke in a sense.

Had you been one, not two,
you would right away have sensed
and found what I said
a fact.

But could you know,
you are bent on a secret idolatry
with a soul that has strayed away
from the guidance of truth.

In love, one who scorns
to be one with his love
is cut off from her by infidelity
and roasted in the fire of estrangement.

Nothing marred this great affair of yours
other than otherness!
Cancel its claim against you in full
and so prove true.

I was like that for a time, *230*
before the veil
was raised from confusion,
still not parted from duality:

231–35: In a passage replete with Sufi technical terms and paradox, Ibn al-Fāriḍ recounts the lover's wanderings in ecstasy and trance, and final arrival at a more permanent union.

233: In this verse, Ibn al-Fāriḍ refers to Qur'ān 53:1–18, which is an account of profound spiritual encounters experienced by Muḥammad. Traditionally regarded as the prophet's Night Journey and ascent to heaven with Gabriel, the spirit of revelation, some of the events occurred "near the lote tree at the end point where the Garden of the Abode is, when there enveloped the lote tree what enveloped it!" (53:13–16). Also see the Introduction, and vv. 312, 327–28, 569–70, 729.

235: Regarding intoxication and sobriety, see the Introduction, and vv. 210–11, 310–12, 480–85, 573–75.

POEM OF THE SUFI WAY

Lost in a trance,
I composed myself in contemplation;
finding rapture,
I scattered myself in existence.

My mind was dividing,
preserving my presence,
my trance uniting,
cutting loose in my absence.

I imagined sobriety
as my perigee, and intoxication
my ascent to her, with effacement
my lote tree's end in space.

But when I cleared the clouds away,
I found myself up and awake,
while my inner spring
refreshed my eyes,

And from my drunken poverty *235*
I recovered, grew rich
in my second separation,
union like oneness to me.

So fight on!
Witness in you, from you,
a silence beyond description
when peace is found.

For after I fought, I witnessed
that he who made me see,
my guide to me, was me—
me, my own example.

238: The "Standing" occurs at ʿArafāt on the second day of the Hajj pilgrimage; it is the central event during which pilgrims humbly pray to God for His forgiveness of their sins. See v. 357.

243: These are the names of legendary Arab lovers whose love was without consummation due to familial disapproval of their relationships.

With me was my Standing;
  indeed, I turned to me;
    to me I prayed,
      and from me was my Kaʿbah.

So do not be seduced by your senses
  or enamored of your self,
    stuck on confusion
      and recklessness.

Leave the wrong way of separation, *240*
  for union follows the right road of troops
    who pushed each other on
      in oneness.

Declare beauty absolute!
  Do not profess to bind it
    by being drawn
      to ornaments and tinsel.

Every charming man,
  every pretty girl,
    their loveliness is lent to them
      from her beauty.

For her, Qays was mad for Lubnā,
  and just so all the other lovers
    like Laylā and Majnūn,
      ʿAzzah and Kuthayyir.

Each of them desired the quality
  she had wrapped
    in a form of loveliness shining forth
      in a loveliness of form.

246: Ibn al-Fāriḍ combines early Islamic descriptions of the fickle mistress as a ghoul who shifts her form with later notions of the beloved's incomparable and ideal beauty.

249: The "one against them" is Satan, who brings about their fall from Eden; see Qur'ān 2:35–38.

Because she appeared *245*
in outward forms they supposed
were someone else,
though she revealed herself there.

In veils she came forth,
hidden by external guise,
each showing shaded
with shape shifting:

At the first creation,
she showed herself to Adam
in the guise of Eve,
while mothering was yet to be,

And he longed for her
that by her he might be a father,
and so the pair made plain
the secret of childhood.

Thus began the outward forms
and their love for one another,
without one against them
to oppose with hate,

And for a reason, she continued *250*
to appear and disappear
in every age
according to the times,

Coming forth to lovers
in every form of disguise,
in shapes
rare and lovely.

253: The Qur'ān 6:163 speaks of God as one "who has no peer."

256–59: The lover's claim to primordial priority in love and his subsequent manifestations as various lovers resonate with the popular Sufi doctrine of the *al-Ḥaqīqah al-Muḥammadīyah*, the Reality of Muḥammad, or the *al-Nūr al-Muḥammadī*, the Light of Muḥammad, a kind of logos principle through which God was believed to have brought about creation. Further, this prophetic principle is manifest in the various prophets, culminating in the historical Muḥammad of Arabia. In a famous tradition, Muḥammad says: "I was a prophet when Adam was still between water and clay," which is to say, before Adam's creation; see the Introduction, and vv. 153–69, 456–57, 475–505, 594–99, 615–50, 730–61.

So one time as Lubnā,
and another as Buthaynah,
then as ʿAzzah,
that fawn-like dear.

They are not other than her,
no, they never were,
for in beauty
she has no peer.

By the force of uniting
with her loveliness
as she appeared
garbed as another,

I appeared to her *255*
in every lover enslaved
to every male and female
of rare beauty.

They were not other than me
nor prior to me in love,
because of my priority
in the pre-eternal nights,

And there are no lovers
but me in passion,
though I came forth to them
disguised in every form:

So one time as Qays
and another as Kuthayyir,
then appearing
as Buthaynah's Jamīl.

Boldly, I revealed myself among them;
within them, I lay hidden and veiled—
how wondrous an unveiling
by means of a veil.

The beloveds and the lovers— *260*
and this is not some feeble guess—
appear from us, to us, as we reveal
ourselves in love and splendor.

So every hero in love
am I and she
the beloved of every hero,
all names of a disguise,

Names that named me truly
as I self-appeared
through a self
that was hidden.

I was still her
and she still me,
no separation—
my being loved hers.

There was nothing with me
there in the world but me,
so "withness"
never crossed my mind.

I swear by this hand of mine *265*
that my soul feared only me;
it never hoped for reward
from another.

267–77: The realization of unity does not negate the need for righteous conduct, and Ibn al-Fāriḍ catalogs some of the many pious deeds undertaken by the lover following his recovery in the second sobriety. This renewed adherence to the letter of the law, however, is not motivated by fear of others' opinions. Rather, the lover aims to protect the high status of his saintly friends *(awliyā')* from charges of heresy or misconduct. Also see vv. 454–55, 464–66, 500–501, 557–58, 627–28, 743.

269: Also see vv. 5, 164, 646–48 regarding the mystical states of exhilaration *(basṭ)* and constriction *(qabḍ).*

271–72: Sufis often say a litany *(wird)* either alone in retreat, or in communal gatherings for recitation *(dhikr; samāʿ)*, as a means to induce ecstatic trance. Also see vv. 141–47, 407, 411, 420–41, 515–20, 528–29, 560, 731, 759.

My reputation's decline and fall
were never my soul's concern,
nor did it ever aim for high regard
or appreciation.

But with all my strength
to turn back the enemy
laying siege
to my courageous friends,

I returned, as before,
to acts of worship,
and equipped myself
with states of discipline.

I came to my ascetic ways
after my exposure and disgrace,
and from exhilaration's wild release
I returned to the grip of self-restraint.

I fasted all day *270*
desiring heavenly reward;
I stayed awake to pray all night
fearing divine chastisement.

I filled my moments reciting litanies
alone in proper silence
and reverent prayer
awaiting the arrival of rapture.

I left familiar places
far behind, cutting
the unbroken bond of brotherhood,
choosing my secluded retreat.

277: While adhering to union, the lover denounces *ḥulūl*, the belief in God becoming incarnate or dwelling within a human being; see the Introduction, and vv. 280–85.

279: *Al-Ḥaqq*, the "True" (or the "Real"), is one of God's ninety-nine names, and a favorite among Muslim mystics to designate God as the absolute or ultimate reality.

I thought to dissect and inspect
what was lawful to abstinence,
and to guard my strength,
restricting the food I ate.

I gave away the wealth
of a contented life,
satisfied with bare necessities
in this world below,

And I drilled my soul *275*
with disciplined devotions,
driving on to reveal
what veils of habit had covered.

I laid bare my resolve
alone in an ascetic life,
preferring my austerities
and an answer to my prayer.

When did I ever shift away
from my saying: "I am her"
or say—how wrong indeed!—
"She dwells in me"?

I do not mean to turn you
to something obscure;
no, nor toward absurdity
beyond all reason.

But how can I fear
rumors of error
when my certain truth remains
with the name: the True?

280–85: To distinguish his notion of union from that of incarnation, Ibn al-Fāriḍ cites the *ḥadīth* story of the archangel Gabriel, who was said to have appeared once to Muḥammad in the form of a handsome youth named Diḥyah al-Kalbī. While Muḥammad saw Gabriel, the Prophet's companions saw only Diḥyah. Gabriel, however, was not dwelling within a living person; rather he was clothed or disguised *(labasa)* by an attractive form, which could be penetrated only by the spiritual vision of the prophet. In this context, the "Trusted One" is a clear reference to Gabriel, whom Qur'ān 26:193 calls "the Trusted Spirit." Also see vv. 130, 751–53.

285: Ibn al-Fāriḍ explicitly cites *ḥadīth* and the Qur'ān in support of his view of union, which he claims to be within the bounds of true religion. In refuting unbelievers who will not accept Muḥammad as God's prophet, Qur'ān 6:9 reads: "Had We made an angel [as Our messenger], We would have made him as a man and disguised [the truth] from them as they disguise it now."

286–94: The lover's persona expands to praise his own high station in gnosis, which is far beyond the reach of scholars, ascetics, and mystics. Ibn al-Fāriḍ appears to be alluding to Muḥammad or his Prophetic Light, as was earlier the case in vv. 254–64; also see vv. 286–94, 448–60, 475–505, 545–48, 565–74, 594–99, 615–50, 716–61. He uses the term *sharīʿah* ("way," "law"), which usually refers to the divine law established by Muḥammad to be followed by believers.

Now take note of Diḥyah: *280*
in this form, the Trusted One
came to our Prophet
as revelation began.

Tell me, then,
when Gabriel appeared in human form
to the right and true guide,
was he Diḥyah?

Of all those present there,
the Prophet alone
knew without doubt
the true apparition.

He saw an angel
sent to inspire him;
others saw only a man,
a respected companion.

So in the clearer of two visions
I have a sign
that keeps my creed free
of any incarnation.

And in the Qur'ān, undeniably, *285*
there is mention of "disguise";
I have not transgressed the two truths:
the Book, and traditions of our prophet.

I have granted you knowledge;
if you want it unveiled,
then enter my path
and follow my course.

287: Ṣaddā' is the name of a spring proverbial for its sweetness among the ancient Arabs.

289: Ibn al-Fāriḍ quotes the Qur'ānic injunction 6:152, "and do not approach the wealth of the orphan," as an indication of the lover's high and unapproachable mystical station. This may be yet another allusion to Muḥammad who was an orphan and, according to Islamic tradition, the final and greatest prophet; see Qur'ān 93:6, and vv. 308–9.

290: If the lover of this section represents Muḥammad or the gnostic in union with his Prophetic Light, the brave warrior would likely designate the Prophet's cousin and son-in-law ʿAlī ibn Abī Ṭālib (d. 660), who many Muslims believe received a unique esoteric teaching from Muḥammad; see al-Qayṣarī's commentary to v. 1 of the *Wine Ode*, and vv. 464–68, 625.

291: "My journey" is a translation of *sayrī*, which is of the same root as *al-sīrah*, the word most often used to refer to a biography of the prophet Muḥammad.

For Ṣaddā's stream springs
  from a source near me;
    do not tell me of a mirage
      in the lowlands.

Before you is an ocean!
  I entered in
    while the ancients stood on shore
      guarding the place of my sanctity,

"And do not approach the wealth of the orphan!"
  points to an outstretched hand
    shunted aside
      when it reached for this sea.

No one but I drew from this deep, *290*
  save a young warrior determined
    to follow my steps
      in good times and bad.

So do not turn away blind in the night
  to the traces of my journey,
    but set out on my very path fearing
      the dark clouds of choosing other than me.

Because, my pure-heart friend,
  the valley of her friendship
    runs through the realm of my rule
      and under my command;

The domain of passion's high places
  is my dominion,
    deep meanings, my army,
      all lovers, my flock.

295: Muḥammad's spiritual ascent to heaven *(miʿrāj)* is invoked as the lover tells of his ascending in oneness beyond even love. Also see vv. 326, 361, 454–55.

299: "The legacy of the highest gnostic" probably designates the life and teachings of Muḥammad; see vv. 551–52, 595–99, 751.

O hero of love,
   see how I was parted from love
      by one judging it a veil,
         all desire beneath my station.

I pushed beyond passion's limit, *295*
   so love is like hate,
      as my trek sets out from the summit
         of my ascension to oneness.

But content yourself with loving desire,
   for you have led
      the cherished souls of worshipers
         serving every faith.

Attain nobility and rise above
   the ascetic praised
      for a pure soul
         and open acts of piety,

And pass beyond one heavy and slow,
   bound to haul rules, shackled by wisdom,
      though were his load lightened
         he would be of little weight.

Claim by kinship
   the legacy of the highest gnostic,
      who took great care
         that his aim made its mark;

Stride among the clouds *300*
   sweeping the skirts
      of a lover in union
         over tops of the Milky Way,

303: Ibn al-Fāriḍ uses the term *ummah* ("community" or "people"), and in Arabic this term often designates the Muslim community, which holds God's oneness as a major tenet.

And race free
 in the ranks of oneness;
  do not be tied to those
   passing life away nowhere.

For one of oneness
 is a vigilant host while all others
  are a rag-tag gang
   cut down by keen-edged proof.

So seek out the meaning of oneness
 and live there, or die its captive;
  go, follow a people
   who showed the way to oneness.

You deserve this glory
 more than one who struggles
  and labors hard
   from hope and fear.

No wonder you laugh *305*
 before him there
  in delicious joy
   and great delight.

How many have been chosen,
 raised up from oblivion
  by the names and attributes
   traced back to oneness.

Yet for all you have,
 you fall far short of me
  just as earth is distant still
   from the Pleiades.

308: Following long-standing Sufi tradition, Ibn al-Fāriḍ likens the intoxicated mystic to Moses, who swooned when confronted with God's splendor at Sinai; see Qur'ān 7:142–43, and vv. 9–11.

309: This verse may allude to Moses and his encounter with God in the form of the Burning Bush, as the lover warns the aspirant against coming too close to the consuming fire of union; see Qur'ān 20:10–24, and vv. 312, 326–27, 332.

310–12: The aspirant's state of intoxication is inferior to that of the lover/guide, who claims to possess alone union's sobriety. Similarly within Sufi tradition, Moses' swooning at Sinai is considered inferior to Muḥammad's sober state during his spiritual encounters. Though Moses spoke with God, he did not see Him, whereas Qur'ān 53:17–18 notes that during Muḥammad's visionary experience at the lote tree "[Muḥammad's] eye did not waver or transgress. Truly, he saw some of the greatest signs of his Lord." Also see the Introduction, and vv. 210–11, 233–35, 310–12, 478–85, 729.

313–14: Ibn al-Fāriḍ again alludes to traditions regarding God's assumption of His servant's senses, and to those asserting Muḥammad's Light as the source of prophecy. The gnostic's ear is that of Moses, who heard God speak through the Burning Bush; his heart is inspired by the most praiseworthy vision from an eye of Muḥammad. The lover's spirit is the spirit of all spirits, while every lovely thing in existence is from the emanation of his clay; see vv. 160–62, 192–94, 254–64, 381–87, 403–405, 545–48, 565–74, 639–42, 719–21.

Though you were brought to your Sinai
and reached beyond your bounds
a place the soul
had never dreamed,

This is your limit, stop there.
If you step forward
you will be seared
by a flaming brand.

My power is far beyond *310*
the grasp of lesser men,
and beyond your means, too,
is my beatitude:

All men are Adam's sons,
but of my brothers
only I have crossed over
to the sobriety of union.

Now I have the ear of Moses
who heard God's word,
and my heart knows that glorious sight
held by Muḥammad's eye.

My spirit is the spirit
of all that spirits are,
while all beauty you see in creation
flows from my clay.

So leave to me what I knew alone
before existence was manifest,
when my companions in the seed
did not know me.

315: In this verse, Ibn al-Fāriḍ uses the well-known Sufi pair: *murīd* ("aspirant," "novice") and *murād* ("guide," "master"). Superior to both of them is the lover and his "protection." According to Islamic tradition, the prophet Muḥammad had God's *ʿiṣmah* ("protection") from committing sins, which, in turn, made him the most reliable guide in matters of life and religion.

317: Qur'ān 49:11 reads: "Do not slander each other, nor call each other names."

321: *Muqarrab* ("one brought near") is found in several passages of the Qur'ān (e.g., 56:10–11; 83:21) to designate the most favored believers in paradise. Yet even this term of great honor implies distance and separation, which is annulled in union. Also see al-Qayṣarī's commentary on v. 1 of the *Wine Ode*, and vv. 154–55, 218, 441, 578.

Do not name me a novice in that group *315*
when one called a master—
one desired and drawn to her—
needs my protection.

Let all names and allusions fall from me,
stop stammering such nonsense;
they are only marks
of the shape I fashioned.

Take back my title of gnostic,
for as the Qur'ān reminds,
if you think name-calling is due,
you will be hated and despised.

To the least of my followers—
to the eye of his heart—
the virgin brides of gnosis
were led in marriage,

And he plucked the fruit of mystic lore
from the branch of sagacity,
and flourished by following me,
rooted in my holy nature.

So if he is asked of spiritual truths, *320*
he replies with secrets strange
beyond the scope of comprehension,
indeed, too fine for imagination.

Yet never qualify me
as a companion near,
which I regard an outrageous crime
severing the rule of union.

326: References continue to Muḥammad's heavenly ascension to God, "to Whom all things return," as asserted in many passages of the Qur'ān including 96:8 and 10:4. Also see vv. 295, 326, 361, 454–55.

327: This verse is patterned on Qur'ān 20:14 and the story of Moses before the Burning Bush, which declares: "I am I, God, there is no god but Me, so worship Me and begin/establish prayer to remember Me!" Also see vv. 754–56. Similarly, the *daʿwah* or "call" may refer to prayer, but also to Muḥammad's prophetic call to believe in God's oneness and do good works, perhaps corresponding to the "inner spiritual wisdom" underlying the "outer religious laws;" e.g., Qur'ān 40:41–43; 14:44; 13:14; 2:151. Regarding these inward and outward dimensions, see the Introduction.

328: After swooning, Moses "turned back" to God in repentance. Muḥammad, however, advanced to the lote tree at the "end-point." See Qur'ān 7:143 and 53:16, and vv. 9–11, 308–14, 729.

For my arrival is my parting,
my nearness, being far;
my loving, my loathing,
my beginning, my end.

By "her" I alluded to myself—
and I meant none but me;
for her sake I stripped off
my name, namesake, and fame,

And set out far beyond
where those before stood still,
where minds went astray on accustomed paths,
died and disappeared.

I have no attribute; *325*
that is a stamp, as a name is a brand,
but if you must, speak of me
allusively or with metaphor.

I ascended from "I am she"
to where there is no "to,"
sweetening my existence
by my return

From "I am I,"
for an inner wisdom
and outer laws
to begin my call.

Before I turned back,
I passed the furthest goal
of my devotee by her possessed,
and crossed the end-point of his masters.

331: Qur'ān 17:44 says of God: "There is nothing that does not praise Him." While Ibn al-Fāriḍ uses the term *midḥah* for "praise" in this verse, another root relating to praise is *ḥ*m*d*, which is the root for the name Muḥammad, "one worthy of praise."

332: The lover holds fast to "Ṭā Hā" with "the surest grasp." "Ṭā Hā" is the name for chapter 20 of the Qur'ān, which asserts God's oneness in words echoing the first half of the witness of faith: "There is no god but God"; see 20:8, 14. In addition, Qur'ān 2:256 declares: "One who rejects false deities and believes in God holds fast to the firmest bond"; also see Qur'ān 31:22. *Sūrah* 20 begins with the letters "Ṭā Hā," and continues (1–2): "We did not send down the Qur'ān upon you to distress you, but as a reminder to one who fears!" Therefore, Muslims have taken the letters "Ṭā Hā" as an epithet for Muḥammad as well as a title for chapter itself.

For what those before me
supposed to be their summit
was only the foothills below
bearing tracks of my path,

While the final peak— *330*
out of sight, beyond allusion,
where there is no higher elevation—
was the site of my first step.

Anyone who knows,
knows of my grace;
anyone who speaks
praises me.

No wonder I am lord
over all who came before,
for I had held fast
to Ṭā Hā's surest grasp.

Metaphorically I greet her:
"Peace!" I say,
but in reality my greeting
is from myself to me.

The sweetest thing I found
when I began to love her—
and every alarm against her
had sounded loud and clear—

Was my appearing *335*
singing joyously of her,
and though I hid my state,
it was plain to see.

She appeared, and I saw
the firm resolve to end my penitence,
for with her, the reason for my trials
was reasonable enough.

She freely gave me
hope's security
to waste my body,
then she cut me off.

Yet sickness for her sake
restores the body's health,
while destruction of the soul
is the life of chivalry.

My death in rapture with her
will be a delicious life,
but if I do not die in love,
I will live choked by grief.

So my heart, melt *340*
in burning flowing love;
O my love pains, help me
to dissolve and fade away.

O fire raging in my breast,
with violent passion
straighten the twisting turns
in my crooked ribs;

O my lovely patience,
adorn yourself with self-restraint
content with her I love;
let fate be cross with me.

345: In this verse, Ibn al-Fāriḍ plays on the root *b*q*ā* ("to remain," "last," "to spare") and its meaning in the Sufi lexicon as "abiding" with God, "the Glorious," who exalts whom He wills and humbles whom He wills; see Qur'ān 3:6, 26; 35:10, and vv. 159–64, 491.

O my endurance, taut and hard,
in accord with loving her
bear up under great misfortune
untroubled by fatigue.

O my wasted body,
forget about a cure;
O my aching heart, who will keep you
from breaking?

O my disease, do not spare me *345*
one last breath;
I renounce what is left of life,
for glory everlasting.

And so my health,
our companionship is at an end;
come or go, it is all the same
to a dead man among the living.

O whatever wasting has left of me,
move on;
there is no shelter for you here
among my ruined bones.

O whatever part of me
I imagine to call out to, "O,"
I have grown wild
and far from you.

Whatever pleases her
pleases me—
though death is easier—
for love made it so.

353–75: The lover's union with the beloved whom he worshiped has sanctified his entire existence. The two holy feast days of Islam are the *ʿĪd al-Adhā*, the great Feast of Sacrifice occurring at the end of the Hajj, and the *ʿĪd al-Fiṭr*, the Feast of Breaking the Fast at the end of Ramaḍān.

356: *Laylat al-qadr*, or the Night of Power, is believed to refer to the beginning of the Qur'ānic revelation to Muḥammad, occurring on or near the end of Ramaḍān in the year 610. Qur'ān 97:1–5 reads: "Indeed, We sent it down on the Night of Power! What will convey to you what the Night of Power is? The Night of Power is better than a thousand months! The angels and the Spirit [of revelation] descend then with every decree by permission of their Lord. Peace there is until the rise of dawn!" Also see v. 371. Friday or *yawm al-jumʿah*—literally, the "day of reunion"—is the weekly Muslim holy day.

Broken in pain, *350*
  my soul had no regrets;
    no solace from me,
      had it complained.

One living as dead
  in any tribe
    wants to die,
      victim to her love.

The passions have gathered around her
  where you will see
    only a lover
      fixed on desire.

If she unveiled
  on a holy day,
    every tribe would flock to gaze
      on her loveliness.

For their spirits long
  for her deep beauty,
    and in her loveliness,
      their eyes find a garden.

Every day is my holy day *355*
  when I see
    with an eye refreshed
      the beauty of her face;

Every night is the Night of Power
  when she draws near,
    and every day we meet
      is one of union, holy Friday.

357: During the Hajj pilgrimage, the "running" between the hills of Ṣafā and Marwah is followed, the next day, by the "standing" at ʿArafāt; see vv. 238, 450.

359–61: In pre-Islamic times, a *ḥaram* might refer to any number of sacred precincts. After Islam, however, this term came to designate primarily the areas surrounding the Kaʿbah in Mecca, Muḥammad's mosque and tomb in Medina, and the Dome of the Rock and Farthest Mosque in Jerusalem.

361: Qur'ān 17:1, mentions the *al-Masjid al-Aqṣā* ("Farthest Mosque") as site for one of Muḥammad's revelations: "Praised be He who made His servant travel by night from the Sacred Mosque to the Farthest Mosque, whose surroundings We have blessed, that We might show him some of Our signs." According to Muslim tradition, this was the beginning of Muḥammad's miraculous Night Journey *(isrā')* from Mecca to Jerusalem from where he ascended to heaven *(miʿrāj)*. Also see the Introduction, and vv. 295, 326, 454–55, 569–70.

My running to her
is a pilgrimage;
every standing at her door,
the Standing.

And so wherever she alights
among God's many lands,
though it cool my eye,
I see it not, but Mecca.

Any place that holds her
is a precinct holy;
every house where she resides
is Medina.

Wherever she dwells *360*
is Jerusalem, most sacred,
whose soothing sight
cools my burning heart,

And my Farthest Mosque
is where she trails her robe;
my musk, the moist earth
where she walked.

The dwellings of my joy,
the tower of my desire,
the limits of my longings,
and refuge from my fear,

Were abodes where fate
never entered between us,
nor did shifty time
ensnare us with separation.

366–67: For these protagonists see vv. 6, 20, 50–52, 135, 166, 366–67, 389–90, 397–402, 408.

The days did not seek
  to scatter our union,
    nor did the nights
      judge between us cruelly.

The turns of fate *365*
  did not greet us rudely in the morn
    nor did the changing times
      speak to us of misfortune.

The slanderer did not spread
  lies of scorn,
    nor did the abuser stir up trouble
      with rumors of discord and diversion.

The eye of the watcher never woke,
  while my eye
    in love with her
      watched me constantly.

No time was favored
  over another in pleasure;
    with her, all my moments
      are sweet seasons:

My whole day is vesper time
  if its first hours
    spread her fragrant reply
      to my greetings,

And my whole night there *370*
  is an enchanting dawn
    if a sweet-scented breeze
      arises from her to me.

371: For the Night of Power, see v. 356.

377: In the Sufi lexicon, *qurb* ("proximity," "being near") is an advanced spiritual state signifying the mystic's obedience to God as commanded in the Qur'ān 96:19: "Prostrate yourself and draw near [your Lord]!" See vv. 321, 571–72, 627, 646–48.

For if she comes at night,
my month by her becomes
the Night of Power, radiant,
as she visits me,

And if she draws near my home,
my year becomes
the spring season
luxuriant amid meadows.

For if she is pleased with me
my whole life will be
the pleasant time of childhood
and the age of youth.

Truly if she unites
the sum of beauties in a single shape,
then I shall see there
every subtle secret sense.

For my heart has drawn together *375*
all love and pain for her,
revealing to you
every desire.

How can I not outshine
any who claim to love her,
or not be glorified
in my place of favor?

She allowed me
to come near her,
closer than I expected
or even hoped for,

380: In Islamic tradition, the prophet Joseph is noted for his angelic beauty; see Qur'ān 12, especially 12:31.

381: Regarding those who risk their lives and property struggling for the way of God, Qur'ān 57:11 promises: "Who is it who will lend God a handsome loan, so that He will double it for him? And he will have a great reward!" In the same way the lover who gives up everything for his beloved is rewarded with union. Also see vv. 175–86, 460–61.

382–87: In line with the tradition of God assuming the senses of His devoted worshiper, the lover in union has assumed all of the senses of those worshiping the beloved; see vv. 160–62, 192–94, 313–14, 381–87, 545–48, 639–42, 719–21.

And her gentle kindness
pushed aside separation,
and gathered me in
beyond any grace.

I passed evening and morn
taxed by love of her
who left lovely in the morning
and returned the same at eve.

Had she bestowed *380*
a portion of her loveliness
on all the human race save Joseph,
he would not surpass their charm.

I spent all of me
for the hand of her beauty
so her beneficence
doubled my every union,

Every atom of me
witnessing her loveliness
with every glance
of every shining eye,

All my subtle words
adoring her
with every tongue
profuse with praise,

Smelling her sweet scent
with every fiber
of every nose breathing in
the rising air,

385: Qur'ān 7:204: "When the Qur'ān is recited, listen and give ear, perhaps you will receive mercy."

389–90: Concerning these rivals and their transformation see vv. 6, 20, 50–52, 135, 166, 366–67, 389–90, 397–402, 408.

Every bit of me *385*
hearing her word
with the ear
of all hoping to hear,

Every part of me
kissing her veil
with every mouth
in each touching kiss.

Had she unrolled my body,
she would have seen
every essence with every heart
holding every love.

What I found so beautiful in her,
bestowed on me by enlightenment,
was an unveiling
driving out every doubt:

With the eye of union,
I witnessed every rival
as a dear ally,
his scorn, as affection.

The one blaming me, loved me, *390*
abusing me from jealousy,
while mad with love of her,
the spying slanderer oppressed me.

So I thank both of them,
since their jealous blame
brings her mercy,
all traces of my grace.

397–402: See vv. 6, 20, 50–52, 135, 166, 366–67, 389–90, 408.

Yet others praise others—not I—
    as they turn themselves
        toward another—not me—
            for a favor.

My thanks are due to me;
    from me, I bring mercy to myself
        since my soul
            took hold of union.

There are affairs
    whose secrets were shown to me at last
        by recovering sobriety,
            though still concealed from others.

No one may reveal them *395*
    without risking his blood,
        but in allusion there is meaning
            that clear speech covers and conceals.

A connoisseur perceives
    my elusive signs
        free from the obvious
            a blockhead needs.

Revelation of these affairs
    begins with those two
        who clamored for me to leave,
            but union said no.

Both are one with us
    in inner union,
        though we count as four
            in outer distinction.

400–402: Regarding the workings of the spirit and the soul, see vv. 41, 108, 145, 197, 208–10, 313–14, 415–42, 458–64.

403–5: The lover's essence *(dhāt)* pervades a universe in union, and its emanation *(fayḍ)* freely nourishes the bodies and spirits in all of existence. The various levels of the universe, however, do not have the capacity to acquire and hold this emanation until the essence bestows upon them that ability as well. Also see vv. 313–14, 565–74, 639–42.

She and I are in essence one;
he who slandered me against her
and the one who turned away from her,
only appeared as attributes:

The slanderer displays the spirit *400*
that guides you to its high horizon
with a witnessing
beginning in an ideal form,

While the blamer divulges the soul
that drives you down to its cronies
with an existence
ending in a formal mold.

One, like me, familiar with these figures,
is not mixed up with duality's lot
when he lifts away
the ambiguity of doubt.

So my essence favored and embraced
the sum of my worlds
with sweet and delicate delights
as sustenance for union,

And it poured forth—
though there was nothing to accept it—
and before the worlds were ready to receive,
my essence was set to overflow.

The forms of existence *405*
took pleasure in the soul,
as the spirits of contemplation
were nourished by the spirit.

407–441: *Samāʿ*, or the "audition" of scripture, verse, or song, is a central Sufi ritual that aims to induce ecstatic trance. Many Muslims, including Ibn al-Fāriḍ, have believed that such audition could briefly return the participant's spirit to its pre-eternal state where it bears witnesses to God's oneness and so professes its dependence on and obedience to Him. This original state occurs prior to the spirit's being bound to the selfish soul and the body in earthly existence, which in turn causes the spirit to forget its divine origins. See the Introduction and vv. 141–47, 271–72, 515–20, 560, 731, 759.

408: Just as one love produces the slanderer and blamer, so too does one reality unite sense and spirit, form and idea.

410: Some Sufis have used beautiful objects or people as the focus for meditation, though Qur'ānic passages and God's divine names have been more common means.

411: In audition, the lover inwardly grasps the oneness underlying outward plurality. However, this demands a mental shift induced by his *dhikr*, his "memory" or recollection of the beloved and their pre-eternal union. Also see vv. 141–47, 271–72, 407, 420–41, 515–22, 528–29, 560, 731, 759.

My state of contemplation
between one ascending to his heights above
and a blamer inclining to his friends
with guidance and good advice,

Bears witness to my state in audition
as I am pulled between
where my fate was fixed
and where I pass my sentence.

These two examples
correspond to confirm
the passing of obscurity
caused by five distinct senses.

So here you are before my goal,
the secret of what the soul
secretly received from the senses,
then passed it on:

When the subtle sense of loveliness *410*
appears in any form,
or when one distressed by grief
moans at hearing the Qur'ān,

My thought sees her
with my inspiration's eye,
while my memory hears her
with the ear of my mind.

My imagination presents her
as an image to the soul;
my understanding reckons her
my close confidant in sense.

413: Compare vv. 1 and 26 of Ibn al-Fāriḍ's *Wine Ode*.

415–17: Now disciplined, the lover's soul no longer views existence in terms of its own selfish desires. Rather, it helps the lover to discover his beloved in all things. Also see vv. 201–9, 415–17, 676, 748.

I am amazed by this drunkenness of mine,
one without wine,
as I am moved within my hidden heart
by rapture arising from me.

So my heart dances,
and my trembling limbs clap like a chanter,
with my spirit
as my singing girl.

My soul continued *415*
to be nourished by desires
as it effaced the frail faculties
and grew in strength.

I found all existing things
allied to help there,
though, in fact, the aid
was my own assistance from me,

That every member might
unite all of me to her,
that every root of hair
could contain my union,

That any guise of estrangement
might be stripped away between us,
though I never found it to be
other than my intimacy.

Now push aside your studies and note
how the senses convey to the soul
by the inspiration of intuition
what she has brought to light:

420–23: The five senses, which had previously veiled the lover from creation's inner unity, now lead him to discover his beloved's handiwork manifest throughout time and space. Also see vv. 677–78.

424: Ibn al-Fāriḍ appears to allude yet again to the Divine Saying of Willing Devotions as the lover's heart *(qalb)* perceives the inner spiritual reality *(bāṭin)* hidden beneath external appearance *(ẓāhir)*.

425: In Sufi gatherings for audition, God's names are chanted to induce trance and return the mystic temporarily to the Divine Presence; see vv. 141–47, 407.

426: Describing Adam's creation in Qur'ān 15:29, God says: "I harmoniously shaped him and breathed into Him of My spirit." Also see vv. 476–77.

The north wind guides *420*
her memory to my spirit
whenever it comes from her by night
rising up at dawn,

And my ear is pleased
when her memory is roused at noon
by dusky doves on branches
warbling and gently cooing.

My eye is blessed
when a lightning flash
relays to it from her
thought of her in the evening,

And I taste and touch
her memory in vessels of wine
when, at night,
they come round to me.

Thus my heart reveals to me
her memory within
by what the sense-messengers
delivered from without.

One who chants her name brings me *425*
to the gathering of union
where by listening, I witness her
with my all.

Then my spirit soars toward heaven
where it was breathed into my outward form,
while this created body turns back
toward my earthly friends with affection.

430–41: Ibn al-Fāriḍ defends the Sufi practice of audition *(samāʿ)* against its critics by drawing a parallel between a tightly swaddled baby and the divine spirit bound to a corporeal body. Just as the baby struggling against his wrap is comforted by lullabies, the spirit distressed by its fleshy bonds is momentarily calmed by the melodious voice of the Qur'ān chanter, who leads the spiritually attuned to recollect their Pre-eternal Covenant with God. Also see the Introduction, and vv. 668–71, 748, 759.

433: Ibn al-Fāriḍ refers to the Primordial Covenant with the phrase *najwā ʿuhūdin qadīmati*, which may also be translated as "a secret whisper of pre-eternal covenants." Also see vv. 50, 68–69, 156–58, 495–96, 503, 549–52.

So part of me is drawn to her
as another part draws to me,
the throes of death
in every pull.

Yet this was nothing
but my soul recalling
its true nature within
when she revealed herself.

So in this earthly interval, my soul
longed for the eternal call alone,
though earth, as well as heaven,
were tugging on my reins.

A child—though he may grow *430*
into a man dull and slow—
will reveal my state to you
by instinct and intuition:

When the infant moans
from the tight swaddling wrap
and restlessly yearns
for relief from distress,

He is soothed by lullabies and lays aside
the burden that covered him;
he listens silently
to one who soothes him.

The sweet speech makes him
forget his bitter state
and remember a secret whisper
of ancient ages.

434–36: Just as the baby is calmed by the rocking of his cradle, the entranced Sufi finds relief in the swaying movements of dance.

His state makes clear
the conditions of audition
and confirms the dance
to be free of error.

For when he burns with desire 435
from lullabies,
anxious to fly
to his first abodes,

He is calmed
by his rocking cradle
as the hands of his nurse
gently sway it.

I have found in gripping rapture
when she is recalled
in the chanter's tones
and the singer's tunes,

What a suffering man feels
when he gives up his soul,
when the messengers of death
come to take him.

One finding pain
in being driven asunder
is like one pained in rapture
longing for friends.

The soul pitied the body 440
where it first appeared,
and my spirit rose
to its high beginnings.

441: The selfless lover is now beyond any notion of duality, even that implied by a union between lover and beloved. Also see vv. 154–55, 218, 321, 578.

443: The ascetic may succeed in avoiding the pains of hell while gaining the rewards of heaven, but these are, ultimately, selfish desires that will veil him from the beloved; see vv. 82, 304, 324.

My spirit soared past the gate
opening to beyond my union
where there is no veil
in communion.

One who follows after me
choosing this gate as his goal like me,
let him ride for it
with a true resolve,

For into how many dark depths
did I dive before I passed through,
where the poor ascetic seeking fortune
never even wet his lips.

In the mirror of my words, I will show you
the door if you are determined,
so attend to what I bestow
upon the ear of insight.

Out of jealousy, I cast out: *445*
my words from all statements,
my share
of every act and action,

My regard for the fine reward of works,
and my guarding mystic states
from the disgrace
of ostentation,

My preaching with sincere intent
the devotee's denial and abstinence,
and my casting out of all concern
for every casting out.

448–51: Ibn al-Fāriḍ follows Sufi tradition as he likens the lover's heart to the Kaʿbah, God's "holy house"; see vv. 130, 150–51, 451, and Qur'ān, 5:97; 14:37. Just as the *kiswah* ("brocade covering") enfolds and outlines the sacred Kaʿbah, so too do the lover's attributes hide yet suggest his underlying divine essence. Also see 545–48.

449: One corner of the Kaʿbah holds the Black Stone, which is kissed by pilgrims. This corner is right of the prayer niche and so, according to a *ḥadīth,* it is called "God's right hand."

450: The circumambulation of the Kaʿbah is among the rituals of the Hajj pilgrimage, as is the running between Ṣafā and Marwah; see v. 357.

451: Referring to the sacred precinct enclosing the Kaʿbah as a place of safety among the warring tribes, Qur'ān 29:67 says: "Don't they realize that We have made a sanctuary safe, while all around them, people are being snatched away?" Also see vv. 150–51, 359.

452–60: Not only does the lover hold the Kaʿbah in his heart, but he has internalized all required religious acts as well.

453: This verse alludes to the genuflections of Muslim daily prayers, as well as to the profession of faith, the "witnessing" to God's oneness, and the apostleship of Muḥammad.

454–55: Although the lover has experienced union, he still fulfills the requirements of religious laws and the laws of nature. See vv. 267–68, 557–58, 743.

So my heart is a holy house
in which I dwell;
before it, rising out of it,
my attributes appear from my veiling.

My right hand is a corner there
kissed within me, and by wise decree,
my kiss comes to my mouth
from my niche for prayer.

Mysteriously my turning *450*
is really around me,
and I run toward myself
from my Ṣafā to my Marwah.

In a sanctuary within,
my appearance is safe,
but around it my neighbors
risk being snatched away.

By fasting, my soul alone
from all others was purified
and gave as alms
the grace flowing from me,

And my existence,
bent double in my witnessing,
became straight and single in my union
as I awoke from sleep.

The night journey of my inner heart
from privileged truth to me
is like my course
among the common cares of law;

456–80: The lover claims to be the source of both the Pre-eternal Covenant and religious laws that he, in the form of an apostle, brought to himself. This, combined with the reference in vv. 454–55 to Muḥammad's ascension, strongly suggests that the poetic persona of this section is once again the Light of Muḥammad, whose most beautiful material form was the historical Muḥammad, "the apostle of God"; see vv. 254–64, 286–95, 361, 475–505, 565–74, 594–99, 615–50, 716–61.

461–62: Regarding martyrs, Qur'ān 9:111 says: "Indeed, God has purchased from believers their souls and property in exchange for their having the Garden; they fight in the path of God, and kill and are killed. This is a promise incumbent upon Him." Also see vv. 175–95.

Divinity did not distract me *455*
from the rules of my appearance,
nor did human nature lead me to forget
where my wisdom was manifest.

So from me the covenants
were bound to the soul,
and from me the limits
were set upon the senses.

For an apostle had come
to me from myself,
troubled by my wanton ways,
caring and compassionate toward me.

Thus from myself
I passed my decree upon my soul;
when it took charge of affairs
it never turned back.

From the age of my covenant
before the era of my elements,
before my mission
warning of resurrection time,

I was a messenger *460*
sent to me, from me,
and by my signs,
my being was led to me.

By right of its purchase,
I transferred the soul
from its earthly possession
to the Garden's dominion.

463: Qur'ān 2:30 refers to Adam as God's *khalīfah*—His "deputy" or "trustee"—on earth. In a famous tradition regarding the priority of the Light of Muḥammad to creation, Muḥammad declares, "I was a prophet when Adam was still between water and clay"; see vv. 475–77.

464–66: The Light of Muḥammad has dominion over the creative process and its preservation, while being the source of spiritual inspiration and guidance, as well. The "keepers *[awliyā']* of my kingdom" may allude to the Muslim saints *(awliyā')* who are believed to assist in maintaining world order, while the "followers" *(atbāʿ)* is a probable reference to the pious Muslims of the first generation after the historical Muḥammad. Further, the term "partisans" *(shīʿah)* strongly suggests the supporters or party *(shīʿah)* of ʿAlī and his male descendants with regard to their claims to political and religious authority. Here, too, the Light is their source of power. Also see vv. 267, 290, 500–501, 620–21, 625–28.

For my soul had fought hard
and died a martyr on its path;
it gained glad tidings
when it paid its price in full.

Then, due to my union, my soul soared with me
beyond the eternal life of its heaven,
as I was not inclined to linger
on the earth of my deputy.

How could I fall under the reign
of those over whom I rule:
the keepers of my kingdom,
my followers, my troop, and partisans?

For there is no heavenly sphere *465*
without an angel within
giving guidance by my will
from the light of my inner being,

And there is no earthly clime
without a drop falling there
causing clouds to flow with rain
from the flow of my outer form.

Compared to my dawn,
the long day's light is like a flash;
next to my drinking place,
the wide ocean is a drop.

So the whole of me
faces and seeks my all,
while part of me with bridle and reins
draws my other part.

469: Though the Light may be the instrument of creation, God is its ultimate creator. Qur'ān 2:115 declares: "To God belongs the east and the west! Wherever you turn, there is the countenance of God."

470: Describing God's creation of the universe, Qur'ān 21:30 states: "The heavens and the earth were closed up, then We split them, and We made from water every living thing." Ibn al-Fāriḍ also uses the phrase *ẓāhir sunnatī* ("my obvious way"), which could be translated as "the literal meaning of my custom," referring specifically to Muḥammad's sayings and actions. This again suggests that Muḥammad's Prophetic Light is the mediator of this creative process.

473: This verse resonates with Qur'ān 2:21–22, which warns against polytheism: "O people, worship your Lord who created you and those before you, perhaps you will fear God, who made the earth a couch for you and the sky a canopy. He caused water to come down from the sky to bring forth fruits for your sustenance. So do not set up equals to God." Regarding the "command" *(amr)*, which initiates creation, see vv. 158, 543–44, 637–38.

474: Concerning God's creation, Qur'ān 67:1–3 says: "Blessed be He in whose hand is sovereignty, holding power over everything, who created death and life that He may test you, which of you is best in deed. He is the mighty, the forgiving, who created the seven heavens in ordered harmony. Do you see disparity in the Merciful's creation?"

One who was above below—
while above was below him—
every direction submitted
to his guiding countenance.

Thus earth's below is ether's above *470*
because what I split is closed,
though splitting the closure
is my obvious way.

There is no ambiguity—
union is the source of certainty;
there is no where
as space only separates;

There is no number,
for counting cuts like the blade edge,
nor is there time since limit
is a timekeeper's idolatry;

There is no equal in this world or the next,
who could decree to raze what I raised up
or command to carry out
the decree of my command.

There is no rival in either place,
and due to harmony,
you will not see disparity
in humanity's creation.

From me, there appeared to me *475*
what I donned as my disguise from me,
and I returned to me
my wandering apparitions.

476–77: Ibn al-Fāriḍ refers here to God's creation of the human being and His command for the angels to prostrate themselves before Adam. In Qur'ān 15:29–30, God says: "When I have harmoniously shaped him, and breathed into him of My spirit, then fall down, prostrating to him. So the angels bowed to him in unison." Also see v. 426. That the poetic persona of this passage witnesses these events points, once again, to its identity with Muḥammad's Prophetic Light, which precedes the existence of Adam; see vv. 256–59.

478–79: Moving from the angelic sphere to the earth below, Ibn al-Fāriḍ alludes to Muḥammad's revelatory experience at "the highest horizon, and then He/he drew near..." as well as to Moses' swoon at Sinai; see Qur'ān 53:7–8; 7:143 and vv. 9–11, 233–35, 308–14, 327–28.

480–85: Regarding intoxication and sobriety, see the Introduction and vv. 210–11, 233–35, 310–12, 573–75. Manuscripts and commentaries give several alternative readings for the "eye of the self/essence *[ʿayn al-ʿayn]* awoke" in the last line of v. 480, including: "the source of confusion *[ʿayn al-ghayn]* became clear," and "the clouds of confusion *[ghayn al-ghayn]* were cleared away." Whatever the case, the meaning remains largely the same.

In me, I witnessed those bowed down
to my manifest form,
and I realized that I was Adam
to whom I bowed,

And I saw with my own eyes
among angels of the highest heavens,
spiritual beings from earthly realms,
equal to my rank.

My fellow-travelers begged guidance
from my horizon close by,
while the union of my oneness
arose from my second separation.

In a swoon crushing the senses,
the soul reviving
fell prostrate to me,
before repenting as Moses did.

For there is no "where" after the source; *480*
I had recovered from my drunkenness,
and with sobriety
the eye of the self awoke.

The end of effacement
arriving before my end was sealed,
is like the start of sobriety;
both are stamped by a given time.

So I balanced the scales of one rapt
and effaced by extinction
with one severed and cut-off,
sober in sense.

485–86: Compare v. 32 and the lover's earlier fluctuation between states, which is a sign of spiritual instability and immaturity.

486–88: Compare v. 147 and the lingering selfish nature of the immature lover.

For the cloudy film was wiped away
from my sobriety,
so the waking eye of self
wiped out my effacement.

One losing in being sober
and finding in effacement
is unfit in his shifting
for the steady state of being near,

While the drunken and the sober *485*
are qualified the same,
bearing the mark of presence
or the brand of rejection.

They are not of my folk
upon whom fall one by one
qualities of ambiguity
or signs of selfish residue,

And one who does not inherit
perfection from me falls short,
turning from the right path
toward ruin.

Nothing in me leads me to disguise
a last residue of selfish life;
I have no shadow
demanding my return.

How much inspiration
can a heart meet?
How much can a tongue say
in the mold of speech?

491: See vv. 7, 159–64, 345, 495–96.

492: From the perspective of divine oneness, the beginning of creation is equal to its end, as stated in Qur'ān 39:67: "The earth, all of it, will be His handful on the Resurrection Day, and the heavens will be rolled up in the right hand of Him who is exalted and far above what they associate with Him!" Also see vv. 745–46.

493: The Qur'ān urges Muḥammad to be patient in his prophetic mission, and not act hastily out of anger as did Jonah (see 68:48–50). Despite Jonah's shortcomings, the Qur'ān does not make distinctions among the prophets, whose functions and messages are essentially the same; see Qur'ān 2:136; 2:285; 4:152. Further, according to a tradition related by the prophet Muḥammad, God said to him: "My servant [Muḥammad] should not say that he is better than Jonah."

495–509: Ibn al-Fāriḍ directly invokes the Primordial Covenant of Qur'ān 7:172 in this meditation on mystical union. Due to the unity underlying reality, God appears in pre-eternity to answer on His creation's behalf; also see the Introduction, and vv. 50, 68–69, 156–58, 216–18, 430–43, 456–57, 549–52.

The sides joined, embraced me, *490*
and the carpet of otherness
was evenly rolled up
by the rule of the equal.

As the duality of existence
passed away, my being
returned to bear witness
in abiding oneness.

So what is above the intellect's range,
a first emanation,
is as a last handful
beneath holy Sinai.

Thus the best of all creation—
though he does deserve it—
forbade us to prefer him
over Jonah of the whale.

I have signed and signified
with what clear expression gives,
while what was dark, I have brought to light
by means of a subtle word:

Yesterday's "Am I not?" is not *495*
other than what one will be tomorrow—
as my pitch dark became bright morn,
and my day, my night—

For the secret of "Indeed, Yes!"
is the mirror of God's unveiling,
and the meaning of union is confirmed
by the denial of "withness."

497: According to an *ḥadīth,* hell will say to every pious person who comes near it, "O true believer, pass on, for indeed your light has quenched my fire!"

499: Compare v. 61.

500–501: Traditionally, in the hierarchy of Muslim saints, the *quṭb* ("axis") is the greatest living saint and spiritual guide who is drawn from among the four *awtād* ("pegs") who, in turn, rise to their spiritual status from among the forty *abdāl* ("substitutes"). The lover, however, claims to supersede this earthly axis, implying, once again, that he is one with Muḥammad's Prophetic Light, through which the universe was brought into existence and subsequently sustained. See vv. 153–54, 254–67, 286–94, 456–57, 464–66, 475–98, 615–50, 716–61.

502: Like the beloved in v. 84, the enlightened guide exhorts his disciple to hold firm to the straight *(mustaqīm)* path, again evoking the first chapter of the Qur'ān and its prayer for God's grace and guidance.

503: In pre-eternity, the Light of Muḥammad appears in Adam, from whom God drew forth his progeny or seed *(dhurrīyah)*, that all spirits might bear witness to His oneness; see Qur'ān 7:172.

So there is no spreading gloom or darkness,
  there is no wrong to fear,
    as the grace of my light
      puts out the fire of my wrath,

And there is no time
  save where time does not count
    the existence of my being
      by the cycle of the moon.

Yet the captive of time's constraints
  will never see
    what is beyond his cell
      in the garden of forever.

The celestial spheres turn on me, *500*
  so marvel at the pole of their turning,
    a central point
      that circles them all.

There is no axis before me
  to succeed based on the three:
    the pole arises from the pegs
      fastened among my substitutes.

So do not cross my straight line
  for in the corners
    are hidden things;
      seize your best chance now!

From me, the seed of love
  appeared in me,
    and for me, the breast of union
      flowed from me with milk,

504: God breathed His spirit *(rūḥ)* into Adam, and later into Mary, which caused her to conceive of Jesus, who also received the Holy Spirit *(rūḥ al-qudus)* from God; see Qur'ān 9:32, 15:29, 21:91, 66:12, and 2:87, 5:110.

505: Again through direct reference to Qur'ān 7:172 and the call to witness, Ibn al-Fāriḍ equates the beloved with God on the Day of the Covenant.

And I witnessed a wondrous thing there,
   and it astonished me
      as the wonder of my heart
         arose from the Holy Spirit's breath.

For she had called me *505*
   to witness her loveliness,
      so my mind was dazed, my manner
         unsteady in confusion.

With her I so forgot myself
   that I thought myself another,
      and I did not seek
         the way back to me.

My amazement drove me mad for her,
   and I did not recover me,
      nor did I follow a whim
         to search for myself.

Crazed for her,
   I was absorbed in her;
      whoever she infatuates
         forgets himself.

Then I was distracted
   from my distraction from me,
      and had I perished for her sake,
         I would not have sensed my passing.

Among the elements of crazy rapture *510*
   in a passion confounding my reason,
      was a capture and plundering
         like a sudden, blind-side attack.

511–12: The lover's selfish desires blind him to the selfless love demanded by the beloved.

514: The quest for mystical enlightenment is often described in Sufi manuals as following a threefold path to certainty *(yaqīn)*, from the certainty of religious knowledge *(ʿilm al-yaqīn)*, to the certainty of hidden or esoteric knowledge *(ʿayn al-yaqīn)*, to the certainty of true gnosis *(ḥaqq al-yaqīn)*.

515–20: These verses may allude to the Sufi practice of *dhikr* as the aspiring mystic attempts to harness his outer and inner senses, often through dance (perhaps alluded to in v. 519) and breath control (v. 520), accompanied by the contemplation of a beautiful object (v. 517) or, more often, by recollection and repetition of one of God's divine names (v. 518). See the Introduction and vv. 141–47, 271–72, 407–41, 528–29, 560, 731, 759.

I would ask her of me
  whenever I encountered her;
    she gave guidance,
      but only led astray.

I sought her from myself,
  she was there all along;
    how strange that I
      had concealed her from me.

I kept going back and forth
  with her, within myself—
    my senses drunk,
      her beauties, my wine—

Setting out
  from certain knowledge
    to its source and truth,
      reality my quest,

Calling to myself from me *515*
  to guide me by my voice
    to that part of me
      lost in my search,

Me begging me
  to raise the screen
    by lifting up the veil,
      for I was my only means to me.

I was gazing
  into the mirror of my beauty
    to see the perfection of my being
      in my contemplation of my face,

521–22: The lover's meditative quest toward selflessness, delineated in vv. 513–20, leads to an illumination by means of an ineffable mystical union with the divine reality underpinning all existing things. Verses 524–32 underscore the successful culmination of this quest by using parallel structures and many of the same words and images found in vv. 513–20.

And mouthing my name, I listened
  and leaned toward me,
    looking to one who could make me hear
      mention of me in my voice,

Placing my hands
  upon my heart,
    hoping to hold me
      there in my embrace,

Rushing toward my breaths *520*
  pleading they would pass by me
    that I might find
      me there.

Until a flash appeared
  from me to my eye;
    the break of my dawn shone clear,
      my dark sky disappeared.

There, where reason recoils,
  I arrived,
    and my bond and union
      reached to me from myself.

Then I glowed in joy,
  as I attained to me
    with a certainty that spared me
      from my journey's hard ride.

I led myself to me
  after I called me back;
    my soul my means,
      my guide to me.

525–27: Just as the five senses point toward a self of experience, the names and attributes of things suggest an underlying essence or being *(dhāt)*, which the mystic seeks to uncover and so recover from within himself. Also see vv. 280–86, 415–18, 448–51, 459–63, 676–714, 748.

528–30: Once again, Ibn al-Fāriḍ pairs the term *dhikr* ("recollection") with *ism* ("name"), suggesting the Sufi practice of repeating and meditating on one of God's ninety-nine names. Through this and other practices, the mystic has wiped away his transient individuality and selfishness in preparation for a union with his hidden identity *(huwīyah)*, a union in which God assumes His servant's senses, seeing, listening, and acting on his behalf. Also see vv. 141–47, 271–72, 407, 411, 420–41, 515–20, 560, 731, 759.

When I pulled away *525*
the curtains of sensuous disguise
brought down
by the mysteries of my wisdom,

I raised the screen from my soul
by lifting up the veil,
and so it answered
my question.

I had rubbed the rust of my attributes
from the mirror of my being,
and it was encircled
with my beaming rays,

And I summoned me to witness me
since no other existed
in my witness
to rival me.

My mentioning my name
made me hear it in my recollection
as my soul, negating sense,
said my name and listened.

I hugged myself— *530*
but not by wrapping arms around my ribs—
that I might embrace
my identity.

I inhaled my spirit,
while the air of my breath
perfumed scattered ambergris
with fragrance,

533–36: Speaking from the perspective of an illuminative union, the lover once again assumes the persona of the Light of Muḥammad. While this Light initiates and manifests itself in creation through attributes, qualities, and names, these latter transient and superficial forms should not be allowed to obscure their transcendental source. Also see vv. 153–54, 254–64, 286–94, 456–57, 475–505, 545–48, 565–74, 716–19, 726–61.

537–74: Using parallel and recurring structural patterns Ibn al-Fāriḍ constructs a stunning rhetorical account of the divine names *(asmāʾ)* and attributes *(ṣifāt)*, their manifestation within the individual as the self's senses and deeper meanings (537–48), their relationship to religious experience and truth (548–65), and their emanation and effects throughout the levels of the cosmos (565–74). Also see vv. 313–14, 403–5.

537–38: The self/soul *(nafs)* is attached to outward sense and form, while the spirit *(rūḥ)* knows the underlying essence *(dhāt)*, which the names and attributes reveal to one with spiritual insight. Also see vv. 41, 108, 145, 400–401, 425–26.

All of me free
from the dual quality of sensation,
my freedom within,
I, one with my essence.

Praising me by my attributes
helps my praiser praise me,
but praising me for them
rebukes me.

For one who sees my quality in me
is my close companion, but one who sees me
by my attribute never enters my camp;
I am camouflaged and self-concealed.

Recalling my names through me *535*
is a vigilant waking vision,
but recalling me by them
is a dream of heedless sleep.

One who knows me by my acts
is ignorant of me,
while he who knows them through me
is a master of the truth.

So grasp
the marks of attributes
in outward signs,
from a soul that knows them well,

And understand from them
the names of the essence
in the inner worlds,
from a spirit that is well informed:

539–42: Attributes such as seeing and hearing appear to be the product of the outward body and sensate self, upon which humans base their individual identities. But just as written marks and words are symbols pointing to inner meanings, so too do the five senses and sensation indicate deeper inner levels of reality to be encountered through mystical experience. Also see vv. 525–27, 679–714.

543–44: All existing things depend on the divine names and attributes for their existence. God creates by commanding, "Be," and this mention *(dhikr)* leads to all of creation, which praises Him for granting existence. This praise for the mercy of creation is frequently noted in the Qur'ān: "He is God, the creator, maker, and fashioner, possessing the beautiful names. Whatever is in the heavens and the earth praises Him; He is the Mighty, the All-Powerful!" (59:24; also see 57:1; 59:1; 61:1). See vv. 158, 473–74, 637–38.

545–48: Creation serves as the site/sight of temporal manifestation for the Light of Muḥammad, which exists in pre-eternity prior to time. In reality, then, all sense and form depend upon this creative principle, while the names and attributes are instruments to fix and reveal the divine behind creation's guise. Also see vv. 448–51, 677–78. In a similar way, the five senses help to form and inform the self, which may return to its source in union when the mystic's senses are said to be assumed by God. See vv. 160–62, 192–94, 313–14, 381–87, 639–42, 719–21.

My attributes seeming to arise
from the names of my limbs
with which, for wisdom's sake,
my soul was named,

Are marks of learning and lore *540*
on the temples' curtains,
bringing to light
what underlies sensation in the soul,

While my essential names rising up
from the attributes within my ribs,
in which, for secret joys,
my spirit took delight,

Are hidden signs of treasures
found in the inner meanings of allusion,
surrounded by the mystery
of what the secret hearts conceal,

And their traces in all the worlds
together with knowledge of them—
and all existing things
are bound by and to them—

Is the existence of recollection
preserved by sovereign power,
bearing witness to a harvest of praise
for universal strength.

They are my manifest sights *545*
where I appeared,
though I was not hidden from myself
before the site of my epiphany,

549–50: Beginning with this verse, Ibn al-Fāriḍ describes the descent of the divine names and attributes from God to creation, their blessings to humanity, and their spheres of influence. The one who "preserves the covenant" is probably God, who "never tires of preserving heaven and earth," and who "watches over everything." Further, God has created angels to sing His praises and bring His blessings, while He has sent prophets to guide humanity to Him; see Qur'ān 2:255, 11:57. God's "soul" *(nafs)* or essence, then, is one of loving kindness and mercy, as He keeps His side of the Primordial Covenant despite human waywardness. See Qur'ān 6:12, 56; 5:116–20, the Introduction, and vv. 50, 68–69, 156–58, 430–33, 456–57, 495–509.

551–52: The one who "last confirms the covenant" is the historical Muḥammad, the "Seal of the Prophets," who brings "news from the unseen world," including the good news of God's mercy and fearful tidings of a destructive Judgment Day, which will arrive without warning; see Qur'ān 33:40; 3:44; 11:49; 12:102; 11:100, 120; 54:1–5; 77:1–7; 78:1–5. Also see vv. 595–99, 615–17.

And so speech—
I am all tongue speaking of me—
and sight—
I am all eyes gazing on me—

And hearing—
I am all ears hearing the call,
and all of me is a hand
firm in fending off destruction—

Are the qualities of attributes
that fixed what lay behind the guise,
and the names of an essence
spreading what the senses relayed.

They flow out from one
who first preserves the covenant,
with a soul watching over them
in loyal love,

As chanters of high praise, *550*
guides to vigilance,
purveyors of sweet joys,
clouds pouring what is desired.

They are set down by one
who last confirms the covenant,
with a soul scorning
arrogant pride,

As gems of prophecy,
luminaries of union,
manifest tidings,
chargers of a sudden assault.

553–56: The well-educated and dedicated religious scholars explain difficult passages of the Qur'ān, while providing prayers and laws for the community. The great mystics then probe deeper through meditation and spiritual contemplation leading to the sought after spiritual union. Ibn al-Fāriḍ alludes here to Qur'ān 89:27–28: "O tranquil soul, return to your Lord contented and pleasing to Him." See vv. 200–205.

557–64: Ibn al-Fāriḍ invokes the traditional Muslim steps toward true religion—*islām*, *īmān*, and *iḥsān* ("submission," "faith," and "sincerity/perfect charity")—to highlight the benefits derived by believers from the names and attributes.

557–58: The body and outer actions of professed Muslims are disciplined by ritual and laws, which help them to deepen and strengthen their faith. Also see vv. 267–68, 454–55, 743.

559–60: Muslims of sincere faith actively gain control over their senses through *dhikr* and other forms of meditation, whether carried out individually in spiritual retreat *(khalwah)* or performed communally in mosques, thus enabling them to rein in pride and arrogance. See vv. 1–6, 209–12, 141–47, 271–72, 407–41, 515–20, 528–29, 731, 759.

They are made known by one
visibly seeking resolution,
a soul whose nature
is generous with existence,

As deep intimations,
inner meanings of high intelligence,
abodes of enigma,
the bases for laws,

And they are exalted by one *555*
inwardly holding true resolve,
a penitent soul
content in contemplation,

As the choicest of signs,
wonders of pleasure,
the most desired of goals,
squadrons of courage.

From the names and attributes,
for the body
attached to the station of Islam
with its wise principles

Come thunderbolts of decrees,
delicacies of sagacity,
verities of proficiency,
subtleties of capacity.

From them,
for the senses
realized in the station of faith
with its active signs

561–64: Muslims of true sincerity who have purified their selfish souls *(nafs)* are graced with spiritual wisdom and reward to the extent that their faith embodies the prophetic ideal set down in the *ḥadīth* in which Muḥammad says: "Sincerity is that you worship God as if you see Him, and if you do not see Him, know that He sees you!" For these accomplished masters, the names and attributes bring the strength to strive for spiritual perfection and union. Also see vv. 200–212.

565–74: Ibn al-Fāriḍ turns to the emanation of the divine names and attributes from the Light of Muḥammad into four levels of existence with their respective benefits to creation. Also see vv. 403–5, 643–45.

565–66: Again, the progression begins with the material world of the senses *(ʿālam al-shahadāh)*, where God's care and blessings for His creation are attested to by the Qur'ān, whose sections and allusions have been elucidated by scholars. See vv. 553, 617.

Come cloisters for recollections, *560*
flashing lights for contemplation,
mosques for relics and impressions,
bridles to restrain presumption.

From them,
for the soul
forged in the station of sincerity
with its tidings of the Prophet

Come elegant reports,
generous gifts of grace,
sage scrolls of scholars,
rightful rulers of reward.

And for the totality,
arising from the vision verses
from the beginning: "As if you see Him,"
to the end: "If you do not, He sees you,"

Come showers of excitations,
envoys of transcendence,
the occurrence of unions,
brave lions of the regiment.

In the visible world of sense demands, *565*
the names and attributes return
in what the soul
senses from me

As chapters of explanations,
the arrival of salutation,
the attainment of allusions,
and sources of benefit.

567–68: In the unseen world of the spirit *(ʿālam al-ghayb)*, the names and attributes are blessings confirming the spiritual progress of sincere believers while admonishing them to strive to grasp the inner meanings of outward forms as in traditions, texts, and prayer. Also see vv. 618–19.

569–70: Proceeding to the higher world of the angels *(ʿālam al-malakūt)*, the names and attributes take the form of revelation and its mystical exegesis for, according to tradition, Muḥammad ascended to the angelic world during his Night Journey referred to in Qur'ān 17:1 and, perhaps, in 53:13–18. There, the prophet received revelations, and instruction regarding the five daily prayers. See vv. 233, 295, 361, 454–55.

571–72: The highest world is that of power and proximity to God's divine presence *(ʿālam al-jabarūt)*. Here in paradise, where God's unity reigns supreme, the names and attributes form God's throne and the angels, as described in Qur'ān 39:75: "You will see angels surrounding the throne singing their Lord's praise. He will judge [humanity] with truth, and it will be said: 'Praise be to God, Lord of the Worlds!'" Also see vv. 377, 627–28, 646–48.

573–75: "The soul enriched by recovery" appears to denote the mystic who has recovered from rapture's intoxication to an enlightened sobriety; see vv. 210–11, 231–35, 310–12, 480–85. Such an enlightened soul draws sustenance from the names and attributes and finds, perhaps in descending order through the four worlds mentioned above, spiritual inspiration, prosperity, beneficence, and grace. Though having attained union, this gnostic continues to follow the Sufi path *(ṭarīqah)* and the rules and regulations appropriate to each spiritual level.

In the unseen world,
they arise
in what I find to be ever-new
blessings from me, upon me,

As glad tidings of approval,
clear proofs of admonition,
the secrets of traditions,
and treasures of prayer.

In the angelic world,
they settle down
where I alone among my folk
traveled by night,

As academies of revelation, *570*
fortresses of bliss,
gardens of exegesis,
and knights invincible.

In the world of power,
they shine in the east
of a conquering enlightenment
dazzling to insightful eyes,

As thrones of divine unity,
powerful ranks of nobility,
ways of glory and praise,
and angels of victory.

In every world,
they well up and overflow
for the need of a soul
enriched by recovery,

576: As Ibn al-Fāriḍ detailed above, the divine names and attributes contribute to the process of creation, but only by introducing multiplicity into reality. However, by means of mystical union, the gnostic mends these divisions and returns to the undifferentiated unity underlying all of existence. Also see vv. 648–50, 154–55, 218, 321, 441.

577: All trace of selfish love has been eradicated. See v. 488.

578: In true union, there can be no separation because the distinction between lover and beloved has vanished; see vv. 153–54, 205–18, 231–35, 321, 441.

579–88: Normally, the human imagination can metaphorically use one sense on the basis of another (e.g., envisioning the hidden beloved's face upon hearing her voice), while in mystical union, the senses are fused into a whole, as they bear witness to the unity of God, who assumes their functions; compare vv. 381–87, 545–48.

As benefits of inspiration,
heralds of prosperity,
profits of beneficence,
tables spread with grace.

So all of me *575*
follows what the path provides
in the way required
by my reality.

When I repaired the rift,
and unity—ruptured by difference
caused by attribution—
was healed and made whole,

And nothing remained
to estrange me
from my firm tie
to intimate love,

I realized
we in truth are one,
as sober union confirmed
the passing of separation.

So the whole of me was
a tongue, an eye, an ear, a hand
to speak and see
and hear and grasp:

My eye spoke softly *580*
while the tongue beheld;
my ear was speaking
as my hand listened near.

My ear was an eye
observing what appeared;
my eye was an ear
listening silent as the folk chant,

My tongue a hand,
a support from me;
my hand a tongue for me
when I spoke and preached.

My hand was an eye
seeing all that came to light,
my eye a hand,
lashing out to strike,

My ear a tongue
in my talk with others,
my tongue an ear,
silent as it listened near.

So too the sense of smell, *585*
following closely by analogy,
had rules of exchange
in the fusion of my qualities.

No member was singled out
without the others
for a fixed quality,
like a "seeing" eye,

For despite their singularity,
each of my atoms
held the sum
of my sensing actions,

589–94: In union, the gnostic transcends time and space as he instantly embraces the divine unity beneath multiplicity. Compare vv. 381–87, 726.

594–99: Again, the lover/master clearly speaks as the gnostic in union with the Light of Muḥammad and/or as the Light itself, which is the source of all enlightenment, miracles, and power, whether spiritual or material; see vv. 254–64, 286–94, 456–57, 475–93, 500–505, 533–36, 545–48, 565–74, 615–50, 730–61.

Whispering, then listening close
from the vision of one
casting away his all, instantly,
out of an omnipotent hand.

Thus I read the knowledge of the scholars
in a single word,
and I reveal all the worlds to me
with a simple glance.

I hear the many voices *590*
of those who pray in every tongue
in a space of time
shorter than a flash,

And I bring before me
what before had been
too far away to bear,
in a blink of my eye.

I inhale the bouquet of gardens
and the sweet scents clinging to the skirts
of the four winds,
in a simple breath.

I survey the far horizons round me
in a momentary thought,
and cross the seven heavens
with a single step.

The phantom forms of those
without abiding residue of self
are like spirits, light,
embraced by my union.

600–601: Ibn al-Fāriḍ reiterates the central theme of this poem: the elimination of selfishness and self-regard leads to an empowering union. Indeed, the source of miracles is union and not, as was traditionally believed, a breach in time and space.

So those who spoke sovereignly, *595*
bestowed their grace, or stormed the walls,
acted with only the barest trace
of my support and strength,

While no one walked on water,
flew through the air,
or plunged into flames
without my resolve.

Those I have aided
with my slightest trace,
cast everything away
in an instant,

While one following my union
with all his being,
recited the Qur'ān
a thousand times an hour.

Had a gentle grace from me
arose in a dead man,
his soul would have returned
restored to him.

This is the soul: *600*
if it throws down its desire,
its faculties double and bestow
their power on each atom.

Union should suffice you,
not a breach in the planes
of limited space
and finite time.

602–3: For the story of Noah, see Qur'ān 71:1–28; 11:25–48; 23:23–41; 26:105–22. Also see v. 13.

604–5: According to the Qur'ān, Solomon had command of the winds, two armies—one of jinn and one of men—as well as an army of birds, whose speech he knew. Solomon also secured the conversion of the queen of Sheba (Sabā'), Bilqīs, to monotheism by having her throne instantly transported from the Yemen to his palace; see Qur'ān 21:81–82; 34:12–14; 27:15–44; 38:36–40.

606–7: Having accepted monotheism, Abraham smashed his family's idols and was thrown into a fire by an angry mob; God, however, cooled the fire, and Abraham emerged unharmed; see Qur'ān 21:51–71. Though Abraham is described in the Qur'ān as a model of faith (60:4), he, nevertheless, asked God for an example of resurrection. So God told him to take four birds and tame them. Then Abraham was to slaughter them, place pieces of each of the four on several mountains, and call to them, at which time they would become whole again and fly to him; just so, the dead will reassemble their bodies and return to their Lord; see Qur'ān 2:260. Also see v. 13.

608–9: In confrontation with Pharaoh's magicians, Moses threw down his staff, which became a serpent and swallowed up the serpents that the sorcerers had conjured; see Qur'ān 7:103–26; 26:34–51. For Moses and the miracle of the springs from stone, see Qur'ān 2:60; 7:160.

By union,
  Noah rose above the flood,
    and saved his folk
      who sought refuge in the ark.

The deluge receded
  in answer to his prayer,
    and he sailed straight to Mt. Jūdī,
      and the ark settled there.

With the wind's back
  bearing up his carpet,
    Solomon and his two armies, too,
      swept across the earth's expanse,

And before the blink of an eye *605*
  the throne of queen Bilqīs
    was brought to him easily
      from Sheba.

Abraham quelled the fire of his foe,
  and from his light,
    the flames became a meadow
      in a garden,

And when he summoned birds
  from each mountaintop,
    they came without complaint
      though they had been killed and quartered.

Moses threw down his staff,
  which swallowed up
    the terrors of sorcery
      preying on his soul,

610–11: In the Qur'ānic account of Joseph, Jacob goes blind as a result of crying over his lost son. Years later, a messenger comes from Egypt with the good news that Joseph still lives and prospers as his father had long suspected. As proof, the messenger brings Joseph's robe, which he throws over Jacob's face, miraculously restoring his sight; see Qur'ān 12:84–87, 93–96. See v. 15.

612–13: Qur'ān 5:110–15 recounts a number of miracles performed by Jesus, including curing the blind and the leper, and bringing clay birds to life. Further, when his apostles asked Jesus for confirmation that he was truly God's messenger, Jesus prayed to God, who sent down a table spread with a sumptuous feast as proof.

614: Ibn al-Fāriḍ suggests the miraculous nature of his poetry by drawing a parallel with Jesus. By God's permission, Jesus brought to life clay fashioned in the form of birds (Qur'ān 5:110), while Ibn al-Fāriḍ brings to light mystical truth within the forms of his finely crafted verse.

615–16: Qur'ān 33:40 declares the prophet Muḥammad to be "the apostle of God and the seal of the prophets." Thus, Muslim tradition regards the historical Muḥammad to be the culmination of all the previous prophets, while his primordial Prophetic Light emanates and illuminates the entire universe, in general, and the prophets, in particular, beginning with Adam until their fulfillment in the historical Muḥammad. Also see the Introduction and vv. 256–59, 286–94, 456–57, 551–52, 565–74, 594–99.

And from his striking a stone,
springs burst out
streaming continuously,
running to the sea.

When the messenger *610*
cast Joseph's shirt
over Jacob's face
with news of his son's return,

Jacob saw Joseph from afar
with eyes long blind
from weeping
longingly for him.

Among the people of Israel,
a table spread for the feast
came down from heaven
to Jesus.

He made the blind see,
restored the leaper's health,
and with a breath, he turned dead clay
into a breathing bird.

With God's permission,
my finely forged words
have revealed to you the secret
within actions without,

And the secrets of all of them before *615*
were brought and bestowed on us
by him who was their seal
in prophecy's due time.

617: Ibn al-Fāriḍ refers to a *ḥadīth* in which Muḥammad said: "The learned scholars *[ʿulamāʾ]* of my community are like the prophets of Israel." According to Islamic tradition, there will be no further prophets after Muḥammad. Yet, because he was the most recent and seal of the prophets, Islam is the best religion to the extent that pious Muslims may serve as substitutes to subsequent generations. Therefore, the legal scholar *(ʿālim)* clarifies the rituals and regulations of the community brought by the prophets, while Muslim missionaries follow the messengers' way of calling people to believe in the one God. Also see vv. 553, 565–66.

618–19: *Aḥmādī* ("most praised") traditionally refers to Muḥammad, most praiseworthy of the prophets. In his community, the true gnostics selflessly and patiently accept the will of God, Who grants them gnosis and, occasionally, a miraculous gift of grace *(karāmah)* to strengthen their faith or protect them. The gnostics, then, resemble the prophets who received revelation, and whose veracity was often affirmed by a public miracle *(muʿjizah)*. Also see vv. 567–68.

620–21: The Muslim community, indeed all of humanity, is heir to the historical Muḥammad and to his Prophetic Light, as embodied and passed on by his immediate family, his intimate companions *(aṣḥāb)*, and the next generation of believers known as the "followers" *(tābiʿūn)*. Also see vv. 464–66.

622: The first four caliphs of Islam were all relatives and close companions of Muḥammad, and Islamic tradition relates instances of their being graced by God. Among God's blessings to the first caliph, Abū Bakr (r. 11–13/632–34), was the latter's victory over Musaylimah, who opposed Islam on the grounds that he was the prophet of the formidable Ḥanīfah tribe.

Only by following after him
and by his leave
did any prophet ever call
his people to the truth.

So now our learned scholar
is like their prophets of long ago,
while any one of us calling to the truth
undertakes the acts of an apostle.

Our gnostic in this Aḥmadī time
is like those prophets
with firm resolve
holding to God's decree,

And what was once a miracle among them,
after him became a gracious gift of grace
given to a caliph
or one sincere and true.

Humanity no longer needs *620*
the Messenger;
they have his family and companions,
and his followers leading in the faith.

Their gracious gifts of grace
fell to them from him
as he bequeathed them
a share of every virtue:

After him,
Abū Bakr waged war
against Ḥanīfah's folk
defending the true faith.

623: According to tradition, the second caliph, ʿUmar (r. 13–23/634–44), was able to warn Sāriyah ibn Ḥiṣn to seek refuge in a mountain and so escape his enemy; at the time, Sāriyah was in Iran while ʿUmar was in the prophet's mosque in Medina.

624: ʿUthmān, the third caliph (r. 23–35/644–56), was assassinated by Muslims who viewed his caliphate as one of nepotism. One tradition, however, relates that ʿUthmān, trusting in God, calmly read the Qur'ān as his assassins took his life.

625: The fourth caliph was ʿAlī (r. 35–40/656–61), Muḥammad's cousin and son-in-law, and father of Muḥammad's grandsons, al-Ḥasan and al-Ḥusayn. Many Muslims, especially Sufis, hold that Muḥammad gave ʿAlī a secret wisdom and the ability to mystically interpret *(ta'wīl)* the Qur'ān. See vv. 290, 464–66, and al-Qayṣarī's commentary to v. 2 of the *Wine Ode*.

626: Ibn al-Fāriḍ refers to the *ḥadīth* in which Muḥammad is reported to have said: "My close companions are like stars, whichever one you have followed, you have been guided aright." See vv. 2 and 13 of the *Wine Ode*.

627–28: Ibn al-Fāriḍ probably refers here to a *ḥadīth* in which Muḥammad calls the saints *(awliyā')* his "brothers" for whom he longs. Though longing implies a distance or physical absence, the saints have attained spiritual proximity to the Light of Muḥammad, even though they were born after the death of the historical prophet. Also see vv. 267, 377, 464–66, 500–501, 571–72, 646–49.

629–31: Once again, the Light of Muḥammad speaks, declaring that all of the prophets—upon whom descended Gabriel, the spirit of revelation—drew their inspiration and carried out their prophetic missions in his name. Though the historical Muḥammad was a descendent of Adam in terms of material form, Muḥammad's Prophetic Light was the spiritual source of Adam's prophecy and that of all subsequent prophets. Also see vv. 455–60, 594–99, 730–61.

ʿUmar called Sāriyah
to shelter in the mountain,
though the caliph
was in a place far away.

ʿUthmān sat absorbed
reading the Qur'ān
though the band of men
had passed the cup of death to him,

And ʿAlī made clear *625*
problem passages
with mystical exegesis,
his legacy to knowledge.

The rest of the Prophet's companions
are like stars;
whoever set his course by one of them
was guided right by their counsel,

And the saints—
believing though they never saw him—
have been elected to be near,
close with the tie of brothers.

They are near him in spirit
as he longs for them in form;
marvel, then,
at the absent present!

Those who received the spirit
called others to my path in my name
as they overcame the renegades
with my proof,

632–33: The cosmic growth and development of the Prophetic Light represent a process of revelation or self-manifestation *(tajallī)*. The Light's earliest meditation is appropriately chapter 21 of the Qur'ān, entitled "The Prophets," which speaks of prophecy in general, and recounts stories of many of the individual prophets prior to Muḥammad. As the Light matures, its study tablet is the "Preserved Tablet," mentioned in 85:21–22 as containing the Qur'ān, while the Light's chosen Qur'ānic chapter or, perhaps, lesson, is "The Victory" (48), which predicts Muḥammad's ultimate victory over polytheism and idolatry. Also see vv. 245–64, 537–74.

634–36: Before leaving the primordial world to take material form, the Light sets down the indivisible law to be revealed by all prophets and followed by their communities. Thus, the past prophets drew their inspiration and success from the Light, as will their followers who continue to call others to the truth.

Yet in spirit, I precede them all, *630*
so they turn on my circle
or come to water
by my path.

For though I am
Adam's son in form,
his spirit within
proves me to be his father.

My soul left its simple state
and moved toward maturity,
so it was raised
on the lap of revelation;

In the cradle, my prayer was the "Prophets";
among the elements,
my tablet was the one "Preserved,"
with "The Victory," as my ṣūrah.

Before my weaning,
prior to my charge in visible form,
I sealed every code
with my clear law.

So the prophets *635*
and their followers in faith
are on my path
never leaving the track of my way.

Those who called to me before,
my right hand holds their happiness;
my left offers comfort
to those coming after.

637–38: The Light of Muḥammad is the source of spiritual authority. This "affair" *(amr)* may also refer to all of creation, which is brought into existence, regulated, and controlled by God's command *(amr)*; see, for example, Qur'ān 19:35; 22:65; 30:25; 36:82; 40:15, 68; 42:52; 97:4. The Light thus embodies this divine command and so is directly responsible for existence, revelation, and the pledging of the Primordial Covenant witnessing to the one God. Further, Ibn al-Fāriḍ probably alludes here to the Divine Saying in which God tells Muḥammad: "If not for you, I would not have created the heavens." See v. 158, 473–74, 543–44.

639–42: To this point in the poem, the senses of the passive lover have been assumed by the beloved in union. Now, as the Prophetic Light, the poetic persona takes the active role of assumption since, in fact, all existence is its emanation. Compare vv. 160–62, 192–94, 313–14, 381–87, 403–5, 545–48, 719–21.

643–45: The Light arises in progressively more ethereal manifestations moving from beauty in realm of the senses to abstract thought in the mind, and, finally, to mystical vision in the spirit's world, which is beyond thought and intellect. See vv. 73–75, 403–5, 565–74.

So do not reckon the affair
as outside of me;
no one ever attained dominion
save by serving me.

If not for me
existence and witness would not exist,
and covenants of protection
would have gone unpledged.

No one lives
unless his life is from mine;
obedient to my will
is every aspiring soul.

No one speaks *640*
unless his speech is from mine;
no one sees
but by the gaze of my eye.

No one listens
unless listening by my ear;
no one grasps
but by my might and strength.

No one
is speaking, seeing, hearing
in all of creation
but me!

In the composite world,
I appeared deep within
every shape and form
adorning them with beauty.

646–48: Ibn al-Fāriḍ plays on the traditional Sufi psychological states of exhilaration *(basṭ)* and constriction *(qabḍ)* to contrast the divine attributes of mercy and terrible power. By joining these opposing attributes and reversing the process of emanation, the mystical state of proximity to God *(qurbah)* ensues. See vv. 5, 71–73, 164, 269, 377, 571, 627.

649–50: Again, Ibn al-Fāriḍ invokes God's interactive attributes of majesty, beauty, and perfection as the Light returns to the primordial divine presence, bearing witness to God's lordship. Beyond time and space, beyond multiplicity, the Light beholds its existence in divine oneness and, so perhaps, becomes God's organ of self-contemplation. See vv. 71–73, and 154–55, 218, 321, 441, 574–78.

While in every subtle sense
not revealed by my visible guise,
I was conceived and formed
but without a body's shape.

Yet in what the spirit sees *645*
clairvoyantly,
I was rarified,
concealed from this subtle sense confined.

In the mercy of expansion,
all of me is a wish
expanding wide
the hopes of humanity,

While in the dread of contraction
all of me is awe;
wherever I cast my eye,
I am honored.

In joining both attributes
all of me is proximity;
come, draw near
my inner beauty.

For in the end-place of "in,"
I still found with me
my majesty of witness
arising from my perfect nature,

And where there is no "in," *650*
I still witnessed within me
the beauty of my existence
without an eye to see.

651–52: The Light and/or master exhorts the aspirant to seek spiritual union, and the oneness, which has been divided by the names and attributes, and obscured by the senses.

653–54: The master warns his disciple not to mistake the emanation of the one into a multiplicity of forms as the false belief in reincarnation or gross notions of transmigration within the nature.

655–59: To illustrate the underlying divine nature of the soul, indeed of all existence, Ibn al-Fāriḍ compares the human soul to Abū Zayd al-Sarūjī, a trickster popularized in the tales of al-Qāsim al-Ḥarīrī's (d. 516/1122) *al-Maqāmāt*. Just as Abū Zayd constantly changes his disguise to dupe others for his own selfish ends, so, too, does the soul *(nafs)* hide behind the senses and actions in order to create the fiction of a permanent self independent of its divine source. See vv. 41, 108, 145, 195–210, 415–42, 458–64, 537–38, 669–71, 710–15.

If you belong to me,
  rush to my union and erase
    the difference of my division;
      do not tend toward nature's dark side.

Before you are signs
  of inspired wisdom
    removing from you
      the delusions of sense.

So steer clear of one
  professing reincarnation,
    in man or beast;
      stay away from his beliefs.

Leave him and his claims of transmigration
  into plants or minerals in the ground,
    though were the latter true,
      it would surely suit him in every round!

Now, the parables I strike *655*
  time after time about my state
    are a blessing
      from me to you.

Ponder the trickster in the *Maqāmāt*,
  learn from his shifty ways,
    and you will be thankful
      for my advice;

Know that the self,
  whenever it appears without,
    in any shape and form,
      is obscured within by sensation.

664–67: Ibn al-Fāriḍ refers here to the widely held belief that in dreams, the soul *(nafs)* has access to knowledge of past and future events. Qur'ān 39:42 has been used to lend support to this notion: "God gathers the souls *[anfus]* at the time of their death, and those that do not die, when they sleep. Then he withholds those upon whom He has decreed death, and sends the others back for their appointed term. Indeed, in this are signs for a folk who reflect."

Though the *Maqāmāt* are fiction,
  truth draws a parable from them,
    for the self
      is unstable still.

Be perceptive,
  and with your sense
    consider impartially
      your self within your outward acts.

Contemplate what you see *660*
  clearly without question
    in the polished mirrors,
      if you seek to uncover your self.

Did other than you
  appear in them,
    or did you see yourself there
      in the rays' reflection?

Listen, as the voice
  that died away
    returns to you
      off the high fortress walls.

Was the one who whispered to you there
  other than you,
    or did you hear
      your own words echoed?

So tell me, who was it
  delivered his knowledge to you
    when your senses
      were still in slumber?

668–71: Detached from the material world, the soul enters a spiritual plane where it conceives of itself as both teacher and disciple of esoteric wisdom. This secret lore, however, has existed in the soul since the time of its creation just as Adam, humanity's father, knew the names of existing things in the beginning. Ibn al-Fāriḍ alludes to Qur'ān 2:31: "[God] taught Adam all of the names." This knowledge is not the partial one of reason and intellect, but whole, innate, and akin to revelation, since it was placed in the soul by God on the Day of the Covenant. See vv. 248–49, 430–41, 630–31, 759.

Before your dozing dream, *665*
you did not know
what happened yesterday
or what would be tomorrow.

But then you knew,
certain and proud,
reports of those gone by
and the secrets of those to come.

Do you reckon someone
other than yourself
brought you this glorious knowledge
in drowsy sleep?

No, it is none other
than the soul
busy in its world
away from human form.

In this unseen realm,
the soul revealed itself to itself
in the form of a sage guiding it
to grasp strange and secret meanings.

Long ago, the soul *670*
was stamped with knowledge
and taught the names,
inspired by the father,

Not by learning derived
from distinction through difference;
no, the soul slowly savored
what it said to itself.

673: Just as the soul returns to God during sleep, so too, will it return to Him on the day of resurrection.

674–76: Knowledge is not confined to what one derives by reason or through the study of tradition, for there is another more subtle form of knowledge taught by a spiritual master and found within one's soul. Also see vv. 415–41, 459–63, 747–48, 759.

677–78: Though gnosis and union may be found within the soul, the world of sense and form should not be ignored, since it is through both that divine manifestation occurs at all. Phenomena, too, are the product of the divine names and attributes, emanations from the Light, and so they may serve to guide the alert seeker toward truth. Also see vv. 420–23.

Had the soul broke free of the body
  before the dream,
    you would have witnessed it, as I do,
      with perfect eyes.

This breaking free in dreams
  confirms the soul's second separation
    in the life to come,
      so stand firm,

And do not be one of those
  confused by their lessons,
    agitated,
      and robbed of reason.

For beyond tradition, *675*
  there is a knowledge
    too subtle to be grasped
      by the farthest reach of sound minds;

I learned of it from me,
  and taught it to myself,
    as my soul endowed me
      with my gift.

But do not forget play completely,
  for the joy of diversion
    is the endeavor
      of an earnest soul.

Take care;
  do not avoid every gilded form
    or dismiss a case
      that appears impossible.

679–706: Ibn al-Fāriḍ describes a traditional shadow play to illustrate the soul's relationship to its actions and the five senses, as well as the relation of the Prophetic Light to creation. In shadow theater, a puppeteer manipulates wooden shapes whose silhouettes are projected onto a diaphanous screen illuminated from behind. The audience, then, sees the shadows move and act upon the screen, recounting wondrous tales of both good and bad from the worlds of animals, humans, and jinn.

For in illusion's drowsy dream
the phantom shadow
leads you to what shimmers
through the screens.

You see the shapes of things *680*
in every display
disclosed before you
from behind the veil's disguise,

And opposites were joined in them
for the sake of wisdom,
so their figures appear
in every form:

Silent, they seem to speak;
still, they seem to move,
shedding light
though dark,

While amazed you laugh,
giddy and full of cheer,
then cry bereaved like a mother
who lost her child.

You wail when they mourn
their plundered fortune,
and rejoice
when they sing a sweet tune.

In the branches *685*
you see birds cooing
and warbling sad songs
that stir you,

ʿUMAR IBN AL-FĀRIḌ

And you are awed by sounds
of their many voices,
for they clearly spoke
in foreign tongues.

On land,
camels cleave the desert night;
on sea,
ships race amid the heaving deep,

And you see two armies
on land, at times,
other times, at sea,
in great formations.

Courageous,
dressed in iron mail,
they stand their guard
with swords and spears.

The soldiers of land— *690*
knights on horse
or mainly
manly infantry—

And the heroes at sea—
riding the decks
or climbing
the lance-like masts—

Are striking wild
with shining sword,
thrusting the brown shaft
of a strong quivering spear,

ʿUMAR IBN AL-FĀRIḌ

Drowning in the fire
of striking arrows,
burning in the deluge
of piercing hot blades.

You see one charging headlong
giving up himself,
while another turns,
defeated and broken,

And you witness *695*
the catapult hoisted up,
then it fires to destroy
fortresses strong and forbidding.

You glimpse specters,
like disembodied souls,
lying in stealth within
their genie land;

Wild attire, savage nature
set them apart
from the humanity of humans,
for the jinn are not humane.

Into the river,
the hunter's hand
casts the net
and quickly draws out fish,

And cunningly,
he sets the traps,
and hungry birds
are snared for seed.

Ravenous serpents *700*
shatter ships at sea;
lions in the jungle
claw their prey,

And in the air
some birds snatch others,
while savage beasts
hunt in the badlands.

You will see other shapes
I have not mentioned,
but I will trust
in these choice few.

Consider and learn
what appeared to you
in that single span
without a long delay:

All that you witnessed
was the act of one
alone within
the cloistering veils.

But when he removes the screen *705*
you see none but him;
no doubt lingers
about the shapes and forms,

And you realize
when the truth is shown,
that by his light you were guided
to his actions in the shadows.

707–9: The Light of Muḥammad hides its unity behind its emanation into multiplicity, which ends in the material world. However, like the screen of the shadow play, creation glows with light to reveal the acts of the divine puppet master, who aims to bring the seeker full circle and back to the Light.

710–21: The master interprets for the aspirant the shadow play in terms of the quest for mystical union.

713–14: Leaving multiplicity behind, the mystic looks deep within himself to behold his unfettered soul and so bear witness to the Light illuminating all of existence. Also see vv. 525–27, 539–42.

Just so, I let fall the veil
    between me and myself,
        obscuring the soul
            in a light of darkness,

To appear by degrees
    time after time
        in creativity
            to delight the senses.

I matched that play
    with my earnest aim
        to bring your mind near the ends
            of my furthest desires.

For a semblance of scenes *710*
    joins us both—that puppeteer and I—
        though his case and mine
            are not the same.

His shapes on screen
    reveal his acts;
        when he appears,
            they turn and leave.

My soul resembles him
    in action;
        senses are the shapes,
            body, the screen.

As he had done,
    I raised the screen
        that the soul appear
            unveiled to me,

715: To underscore the mystical transformation from ignorance to gnosis, Ibn al-Fāriḍ draws on Qur'ān 18:65–82, which tells the story of Moses' encounter with a mysterious stranger, later identified by tradition as the prophet Khiḍr. On three occasions, Moses questions and criticizes his companion's outrageous actions, which include killing a youth, repairing a wall in an inhospitable village, and damaging a perfectly good boat. At last, the stranger informs Moses that these matters were not as they appeared to be. The slain youth would have grown up to disgrace his parents with his impiety; perhaps God would now bless them with a new, pious offspring. The repaired wall hid from the rude villagers a treasure belonging to two faithful orphans, who would later claim their inheritance. As for the boat, it was the property of poor people who depended on it for their livelihood. Yet a king was in the area confiscating good boats, so, by damaging the boat, the stranger enabled the owners to keep it for later repairs. The mysterious stranger's knowledge of hidden dimensions of reality is like the gnostic's grasp of the unity beneath plurality. Through union, the mystic finds that his individual self or soul *(nafs)* is not a permanent entity but a reflection of the Light. Thus the mystic annihilates his independent selfish existence and disciplines his body and physical desires by adhering to religious laws in order to preserve the treasure of the unitive life.

716–18: The naked brilliance of the Light of Muḥammad would consume all of its manifestations, hence the need for the veil of names and attributes. Ibn al-Fāriḍ is probably referring here to a *ḥadīth* in which Muḥammad says: "God has seventy thousand veils of light and darkness. Were He to remove them, the splendors of His countenance would consume everyone who saw it!"

719–21: Once again, Ibn al-Fāriḍ explicitly supports his doctrine of union with the tradition regarding God's assumption of the mystic's senses; see vv. 160–62, 192–94, 313–14, 381–87, 545–58, 639–42.

For the sun of witness had arisen,
and existence blazed,
so I severed
the ties that bind.

I killed my young soul *715*
and raised a wall
to guard my laws;
I wrecked my boat.

Again I spread my grace,
as acts required,
over every world
in every span of time.

But had the attributes not veiled me,
my blazing splendor
would have burned away
the showings of my being.

The tongues of all beings—
if you listen close—
witness with eloquence
to my unity,

While about my union
a tradition has come,
its transmission clear
without doubt,

Declaring true love *720*
for those who draw near Him
by willing devotions
or those decreed.

722–23: The master's mystical progression toward union begins with his own soul, which is an agent of cause and effect. If left untended, the soul will lead one astray in plurality and selfish existence. Yet, as an emanation of the Light, a soul disciplined by means of religious precepts and devotional exercises will assist the mystic's return to unity. Also see vv. 415–18, 459–63, 676, 748, 759.

724: All of the various laws, exercises, and other means to attain union must be given up in true unity, even the notion of union that implies the coming together of two things. Also see vv. 154–55, 218, 264, 321, 441, 574–78.

726–30: Viewing existing things from the perspective of the creative Light, the mystic senses the unity within all of them. Also see vv. 381–87, 419–25, 589–94.

The point of its teaching
  is clear
    as noonday light:
      "I am his ear..."

I worked hard for oneness
  till I found it,
    and the agent of causes
      was one of my guides,

And I joined my causes together
  till I lost them,
    for the bond of oneness
      was my best connection.

Then I freed my soul
  from the two of them,
    and it was one,
      alone as always.

I dove into the seas of union, *725*
  dove deeper still for solitude,
    and so recovered
      the pearl without equal,

That I could hear my acts
  with a seeing ear
    and witness my words
      with a hearing eye.

So when the nightingale mourns
  in the tangled brush,
    and birds in the trees
      warble in reply,

729: The *sidrah* or "lote" tree was the site of Muḥammad's great vision as described in Qur'ān 53:13–18: "When there covered the lote tree, what covered it" (53:16). See vv. 233, 310–12, 328, 478–79.

730–42: The Light is the source of all inspiration, creativity, and religion, whatever their imperfect earthly forms may be.

731: The "chanters" *(adhkār)* may be those who perform the Sufi *dhikr*, the chanting of God's names, whether aloud, or silently within their hearts, where, like an attentive reader, they grasp the meaning within the words. This insight, in turn, intoxicates the spiritual warriors with the wine of mystical love and gnosis; see vv. 1–4, 420–41, and the *Wine Ode*.

732: In medieval Muslim societies, non-Muslim monotheists were often required to wear objects, such as a sash, to distinguish them from Muslims. Removal of such objects implies conversion to Islam, which not only bears witness to one God but also acknowledges Muḥammad as His prophet.

Or when the flutist's notes
  quiver in accord
    with the strings plucked
      by a singing girl's hand

As she sings poetry
  whose every note
    moves hearts to fly
      to their lote tree,

Then I delight in my works of art *730*
  declaring my union
    and company free
      of the idolatry of difference.

By me the chanters' assembly
  is the ear of one who reads with care;
    for my sake, the open tavern
      is the eye of soldiers on patrol.

No hand but mine
  bound the non-Muslim's sash,
    but if it is loosed to acknowledge me
      my hand untied it.

So if the prayer niche in a mosque
  shines by the Qur'ān within,
    then a temple's altar is not disgraced
      by the gospel,

And the Torah's sacred books
  came from Moses to his people,
    so each night through scripture
      rabbis confide with God.

741: Qur'ān 3:83 declares: "Do they seek a different religion than God's? Whoever is in the heavens or the earth submits to Him, obediently or by force; to Him they shall return!"

When a devotee falls down *735*
before an idol temple's stones,
do not transgress
and censure from bigotry.

For many of those free
from the idol's shame
are bound secretly within
to worship cash and coin!

My warning has reached
those who heed,
and by me, absolution has arisen
for all who broke away:

The eyes of every faith
have never strayed,
nor did the thoughts of any creed
ever swerve aside.

One dazed in desire for the sun
is not deranged,
for it shines from the light
of my blazing splendor, unveiled.

And when the Magi worship the fire *740*
that, tradition tells,
has been burning bright
for a thousand years,

They aim only for me,
though they do not show
a firm resolve
as they seek another.

743: Though the gnostic may attain union with the Light of Muḥammad and so witness the oneness of existence, he is nevertheless still bound by the rules and laws that regulate him as a limited, if divine, manifestation. See vv. 267–68, 454–55, 557–58.

744: On creation, Qur'ān 23:115 states: "Do you reckon that We created you in jest, and that you will not return to Us?"

745–47: Creation is the product of the divine names and attributes, which determine the potentialities of all things according to God's decree. Some creatures will have good fortune, others bad, but God has sent them prophets and, ultimately, the Qur'ān as guidance for their lives in this world and the next. Ibn al-Fāriḍ refers to a Divine Saying in which God scoops up Adam's progeny in two handfuls, and says, "These are for the garden, and I don't care, and these are for the fire, and I don't care!" See vv. 492, 537–74.

748: For the soul's innate gnosis, also see vv. 430–41, 668–71, 759.

They saw the flash of my light, once,
and supposed it to be a fire,
so they went astray, misled
by shining rays.

If not for the veil of being
I would speak out,
yet respect for the laws of sense
keeps me silent.

This is no jest:
creatures were not created in vain,
though their actions
fall short of the mark.

Their affairs run the course *745*
marked by the names,
while the attribute of essence
drives them on to the divine decree:

"No and no!"—dispatching with dispassion
two handfuls of humans,
one for a pleasant life,
one for misfortune.

So it is; let the soul know it
or leave well enough alone,
though for the sake of the soul
the Qur'ān is recited every morn.

The gnosis of the soul is from itself,
and it told me
through the senses
all that I had hoped for.

749: While plurality exists in the realm of time and space, oneness is the essence of existence. Thus, the gnostic does not equate the soul with its senses, nor the one absolute God with His numerous limited manifestations; to do so would be like regarding a poet as identical to his poetry, when the latter is clearly the creation of the former. Also see vv. 679–717, 730.

751: The master claims kinship through union with the Light of Muḥammad, whose greeting foretells gnosis. For the Qur'ān speaks of the Muḥammad's visionary experience when an awesome being, identified by tradition as Gabriel, descended to the prophet at a distance of "two bows' lengths or nearer"; see Qur'ān 53:5–9. Also see vv. 130, 299, 478–79, 629–31.

752–53: Ibn al-Fāriḍ alludes to the Qur'ān's "Light Verse" (24:35); see the Introduction.

754–58: Ibn al-Fāriḍ refers here to Moses and his encounters with God. According to the Qur'ān (20:12), when Moses approached the Burning Bush a voice called out and said: "Indeed, I am I, your Lord, so take off your sandals for you are in the holy valley of Tuwā!" Since the Light of Muḥammad precedes and is the means of prophecy and creation, it may be said to have sanctified the holy ground on which Moses stood, as well as delivered and received the revelation at Sinai as it emanates and illuminates all levels of existence, from the earth below, through the spheres of the moon, sun, planets, and stars, to the realm of the angels who worship at God's throne. See vv. 9–11, 153–54, 254–64, 286–94, 308–14, 327–28, 456–57, 475–505, 478–79, 565–74, 594–99, 615–50.

Had I thought it all as one,
  I would have been a heretic,
    stripped of the signs of my union,
      taking my art as equal to me.

I am not to blame *750*
  if I spread my bounty
    and bestow my gracious gift
      on those who follow.

I have received the sign of kinship
  from one bringing news of union
    when he greeted me with
      "Or nearer!"

From his light,
  the niche of my essence enlightened me;
    by means of me,
      my nights blazed morning bright.

I made me witness my being there
  for I was he;
    I witnessed him as me,
      the light, my splendor.

By me the valley was made holy,
  and I flung my robe of honor—
    my "taking off of sandals"—
      on those summoned there.

I embraced my lights *755*
  and so was their guide;
    how wondrous a soul
      illuminating lights!

759: The soul possesses an innate knowledge of its primordial relationship with God, a knowledge recalled in dreams and invoked by the mystical practice of *dhikr*; see vv. 428–41, 515–22, 664–71.

I set firm my many Sinais
and there prayed to myself;
I attained every goal,
as my being spoke with me.

My full moon never waned;
my sun, it never set,
and all the blazing stars
followed my lead.

By my leave, in my realm
planets moved,
and angels bowed
to my dominion.

In the world of remembrance
the soul has her ancient lore;
my young disciples
seek it from me,

So hurry to my union old *760*
where I have found
the elders of the tribe
as newborn babes,

For my friends drink
what I left behind,
while those before me,
their fine qualities fall short of mine.

Saintly Life

Adorned Proem to the Dīwān

Memorial to a Grandfather

Perhaps the most important figure in the preservation and transmission of Ibn al-Fāriḍ's poetic and religious legacies was Abū al-Ḥasan Nūr al-Dīn ʿAlī al-Miṣrī. Later generations generally refer to ʿAlī as Ṣibt Ibn al-Fāriḍ, drawing attention to his direct descent from the poet as a grandson on his mother's side *(sibṭ)*. Other details of ʿAlī's life, however, are sketchy; we have yet to discover the dates of his birth and death, or his father's identity. ʿAlī was said to have been the shaykh of a mosque in Cairo and apparently a man of some importance, flourishing in the late seventh/thirteenth and early eighth/fourteenth centuries. At one point in his writings ʿAlī mentions the date 735/1334, so it is highly unlikely that he personally knew his famous grandfather, who had died a century earlier.[1] This may have been one of the reasons prompting ʿAlī to collect and edit a *dīwān* of his grandfather's poetry. ʿAlī gathered some verse passed down from Ibn al-Fāriḍ's companions, but he related most of the poems based on a collection compiled by one of Ibn al-Fāriḍ's sons, Kamāl al-Dīn Muḥammad (d. 689/1290). ʿAlī also cited this uncle as his primary source for most of the material that composes a preface to the poems. Known as the *Dībājah (Adorned Proem),* this substantial introduction contains valuable information regarding Ibn al-Fāriḍ's biography, the collection of his verse, and a brief defense of his religious beliefs. For the most part, however, this preface renders an account of Ibn al-Fāriḍ's spiritual life, with special emphasis on the poet's inspirational states and reported miracles.

In a tone of awe and humility, ʿAlī states that he had preserved this account of Ibn al-Fāriḍ's miracles and fine appearance so that his preface might serve as "a memorial to the glorious deeds of the fathers and grandfathers." ʿAlī's main purpose, then, was to compose a hagiography, and so he structured his *Proem* around a few central religious events involving his grandfather.

ʿAlī begins with Ibn al-Fāriḍ's spiritual restlessness as a young man and his subsequent mystical awakening at the hands of one of God's saints disguised as a seller of greens. Next ʿAlī mentions his grandfather's fifteen-year stay in Mecca, where he was befriended by a ferocious lion, and Ibn al-Fāriḍ's return to Cairo to bury his spiritual master amid miraculous events indicative of his master's saintly rank. This leads ʿAlī to relate a number of stories concerning his grandfather's mystical states, and his famous *Poem of the Sufi Way*, which factored in a religious and political controversy arising during ʿAlī's lifetime. Though ʿAlī gives some details of this dispute, his primary focus remains on Ibn al-Fāriḍ's piety and mystical insights. ʿAlī recounts various miracles featuring his grandfather in Cairo, while paying particular attention to Ibn al-Fāriḍ's vigilance against spiritual and artistic compromise as he actively avoided contact with Egypt's sultan and his royal court. Finally, ʿAlī gives two differing accounts of his grandfather's last hours and death, and a long description of his funeral, burial, and the extraordinary events surrounding this solemn occasion.

In his concluding statements, ʿAlī claims that he had transmitted his material from his uncle and other reliable individuals, some of whom he names. Further, the form and contents of ʿAlī's preface coincide with his assertion of direct transmission, for the *Proem* consists largely of what purport to be verbatim quotations from either Kamāl al-Dīn Muḥammad or Ibn al-Fāriḍ himself. ʿAlī weaves these extensive quotations together with his own comments written in a generally unadorned Arabic prose, which may have lent a factual quality to these amazing stories. Yet, while ʿAlī details numerous miracles occurring at the hands of his grandfather, he never explicitly declares Ibn al-Fāriḍ a saint *(walī)*, or claims that he was endowed with sainthood *(walāyah/wilāyah)*, perhaps fearing charges of self-interest or nepotism. Nevertheless, the *Proem*'s accounts of Ibn al-Fāriḍ's miracles, his dream encounters with the prophet Muḥammad, and meetings with other mystics create an unmistakable saintly aura around the poet, as ʿAlī stakes a claim for his grandfather's sainthood. Succeeding generations read the *Proem* prefacing Ibn al-Fāriḍ's highly celebrated *Dīwān*, and many later notices to Ibn al-Fāriḍ openly proclaim his sainthood. That most of these affirmations were based to some extent on the *Proem* attests to ʿAlī's successful attempt to number his grandfather among God's saintly friends.[2]

Text and Translation

The following translation of the *Adorned Proem* is based on the Arabic text in the Maḥmūd edition of Ibn al-Fāriḍ's *Dīwān* (19–44). However, I have made minor corrections and additions based on several of the oldest manuscripts containing the *Proem* and checked against al-Nābulusī's commentary; these sources are cited in the bibliography.

ʿAlī Sibṭ Ibn al-Fāriḍ
Adorned Proem to the Dīwān (Dībājat al-Dīwān)

In the name of God the Compassionate and the Merciful

Praise be to God who distinguished His most radiant lover Muḥammad with the station of "two bows' lengths or nearer," and linked his noble name to the most awesome of His beautiful names as I bear witness that there is no deity but God alone, absolutely without partner, the protector of His servants, the beloved of His worshipers, and that our master Muḥammad is His servant, His messenger, His beloved, and special friend![3] God bless him and his noble family, his supporting companions and caliphs, his brothers among the prophets and his followers among the saints with a blessing whose fragrant breaths will spread over their pure spirits and whose beneficence will shower liberally over them inwardly and without,[4] and may He give them peace!

So speaks this poor wretch confessing his sins and scooping water from the river of his Lord's bounty, ʿAlī, the maternal grandson of the shaykh Ibn al-Fāriḍ, in hopes of the overflowing generosity of his Lord, may God forgive this one's lapses and sins and overtake him with His mercy:

I examined copies of the *Dīwān* of our Shaykh Ibn al-Fāriḍ—may God bless and gladden his heart, and give him joy with a glance toward him!—and I noticed that the copyists were ignorant regarding some of its language, which they did not understand. Further, some of its word plays *[jinās]* were obscure to them, so they misread them, taking them out of context and failing to trace them back to their source. Therefore, I ask God's guidance and aid in editing this blessed copy in that I have correctly followed his words, relying on a copy in my possession that was accurately related from him, its pages free of alterations and misspellings. I received it from his son, my master, the shaykh Kamāl al-Dīn Muḥammad—may God join both of them together before Him in a seat of sincerity; how excellent is that seat! I recited it to him critically and faithfully, for I used to hear him quote it in the sweetest voice. He informed me that he had read it and heard it exactly like that from the Shaykh, his father, and that nothing was missing from it save one ode.

His father had composed this ode during a period of spiritual retreat in the Ḥijāz amid Mecca's mountains and valleys. The Meccans used to teach it to their children in the Qur'ān schools, and they would chant it before daybreak from the minarets. But it had not been recorded in a copy of his *Dīwān* because the Shaykh had composed the ode in the Ḥijāz, whereas he had dictated his *Dīwān* later in Cairo, where he resided after his spiritual retreat. His son said to me: "I took it upon myself to search for it for years, but I did not find it with even one of the Shaykh's companions. All I remember of it is this opening verse:

'Did lightning flash
from the sloping side of the valley
or did veils fall away
from Laylā's glowing face?'"

His son—may God have mercy upon him—made me promise to search diligently for it, so that I could gather all of it together with its sister poems in a properly collected edition. I made every effort to do just that, but I neither saw the ode in writing nor heard it recited, though I took it upon myself to search for it for forty years. In the meantime, I followed a good method for supplementing this verse in order to create a new poem; I contemplated the best verses in the Shaykh's odes and culled from them the loveliest of his beautiful motifs. But I beg the indulgence of any who come across my addition that they kindly be discreet, for how could I produce such creative poetry? Can a limping horse ever match a thoroughbred? So we ask God's indulgence, and that He guide us for love of the Shaykh to his proper words! But praise be to God most high that this addition did not deviate from the essence of this preserved verse. Yet, whenever I heard my version, I would recite: "If only my people knew."[5] For I had placed my improvised poem in this copy of the *Dīwān* after the Shaykh's completed odes, making it the last of them—though it could take pride of place—to serve as the seal to its sister poems, bringing rest and peace to the heart of one who heard it. Then I found the ode whose text was missing from the *Dīwān*; I have placed it at the end of this preferred edition, prefaced by the story of its return, and how, though it had set, this ode's splendor rose again to shine upon its spring encampments![6]

His son [Kamāl al-Dīn] informed me that he had compared his aforementioned copy of the *Dīwān* to one he had in the handwriting of the Shaykh—may God be satisfied with him. However, Ibn Shaykh al-Shuyūkh had borrowed the latter from him, swearing to return it, but he left on a journey without giving it back.[7] The shaykh Abū al-Qāsim al-

Manfalūṭī informed me when he came to Cairo from Manfalūṭ in the year 735/1334, that he had this missing copy with him in Cairo. This copy had been passed down to him by his ancestors who had received it from the shaykh Ṣafī al-Dīn Ibn Abī al-Manṣūr.[8] He promised me that he would bring it to me, but he left for al-Manfalūṭ without doing so. I have been told that this shaykh has a religious retreat and hostel *[zāwiyah]* in the Manfalūṭ region and that he is well known for his spiritual authority there.[9]

This copy that I have made, then, becomes the third one and the direct heir to these first two in terms of their authenticity, and God grants success to what is right and guides to upright conduct. I have also written down in its preface some of the Shaykh's most amazing and celebrated miracles and a description of his excellent appearance in the most handsome of forms created by God. One who understands the meaning of the Shaykh's words will be guided by his gnosis to his mystical station. For one chosen by God most high for His love and intimacy will recognize the lover among his own kind. God has made those who love Him the treasuries of His closely guarded secrets, and the treasure-troves of "He loves them, so they love Him!"[10]

So then, my master, his aforementioned son—may God's mercy be upon him—said to me:

> The Shaykh—may God be satisfied with him—was of medium build, with a very handsome face and a healthy reddish complexion. When he participated in an audition *[samāʿ]* and went into ecstasy as a mystical state overcame him, his face would increase in beauty and brightness, and sweat would pour from the rest of his body until it flowed beneath his feet onto the ground. I have not seen among Arabs or non-Arabs one as handsome of form, and I, of all people, resemble him the most in appearance.
>
> He had a light, a diffidence, a splendor, and a venerableness. When he attended a session, there would appear over the people there a dignified silence and tranquility. I saw attending his teaching session a group including respected jurisprudents, mendicants, and judges, and great men of state, including amirs, viziers, and the leaders of the people, and they treated him with the utmost respect and humbleness; when they addressed him,

it was as if they were addressing a great king. Further, when he walked in the city, people would crowd around him seeking from him spiritual blessings *[barakah]* and benedictions, while trying to kiss his hand. But he would not allow anyone to do that; rather he shook hands with them. His clothes were fine, and his scent was fragrant. He would spend amply on those who visited him, being very generous. He never demeaned himself by seeking to obtain anything from this world, and he never accepted anything from anyone. The sultan Muḥammad al-Malik al-Kāmil—may God have mercy upon him—sent 1,000 dinars to him, but he sent them back. The sultan asked if he could prepare a grave for him next to the tomb of the Sultan's mother in the domed shrine of al-Imām al-Shāfiʿī—may God be satisfied with him—but the Shaykh would not allow it. Then the Sultan asked his permission to build a shrine especially for him, but he was uneasy with that.[11]

I [ʿAlī] will recount all of that in its proper place. His son—may God have mercy upon him—said: "I heard the Shaykh—may God be satisfied with him—say:

'When I first began my spiritual retreat, I would ask my father's permission, and then go up to the Oasis of the Wretches *[Wādī al-Mustaḍʿafīn]* on the second mountain of Cairo's Muqaṭṭam range where I stayed, wandering around night and day. Then I would obediently return to my father in deference to him and his heart. At that time, my father was an assistant to the governor of Cairo and Fusṭāṭ, al-ʿAzīz al-Ḥanafī, and my father was among the great men in religious knowledge and acts.[12] He would be overjoyed by my return to him, and he would make me sit with him both in court and in teaching sessions. But then I would long for spiritual retreat, and so I would again ask his leave and return to wandering. I did this time and again until my father was asked to become the chief judge, but he declined the post and left the judiciary. He dropped out of public life and devoted himself to God most high at the Azhar mosque until his death—may God have mercy upon him.[13] Then, I returned to retreat and wandering, following the mystical path toward truth, but I was not enlightened in the least.

'One day I ceased wandering and returned to Cairo, where I entered the Suyūfīyah law school *[madrasah]*.[14] I found an old greengrocer there at the door of the law school doing ablutions out of order; he washed his hands, then his legs, then he wiped his head and washed his face. So I said to him, "O shaykh, you are this old, in the land of Islam, at the door of the law school, among the scholars of Muslim jurisprudence, yet you are doing the prayer ablutions out of the order prescribed by religion?" He looked at me and said, "ʿUmar! You will not be enlightened in Egypt. You will be enlightened only in the Ḥijāz, in Mecca—may God glorify it! So head for it, for the time of your enlightenment is near!"

'Then I knew that the man was among the saints of God most high and that he disguised himself with this lifestyle and by feigning ignorance of the order of ablutions. So I sat before him and said, "Oh, sir, I am here but Mecca is so far away, and I will not find a mount or a travel companion in the non-pilgrimage months." Then he looked at me, pointed and said, "Here is Mecca before you!" And I looked with him and saw Mecca—may God glorify it! So I left him and sought Mecca whose image remained before me until I entered it almost instantaneously. Then as I entered, enlightenment came to me wave after wave and never left."'

I [ʿAlī] say that the Shaykh—may God be satisfied with him—alluded to this enlightenment in his ode rhyming in *D* when he said:

O my night companion,
  refresh my spirit
    singing of Mecca
      if you wish to cheer me.

In her was my intimacy
and the ascent of my sanctity:
my station was Abraham's
and the enlightenment clear![15]

The Shaykh—may God be satisfied with him—said:

Then I began to wander in the valleys and mountains of Mecca, and I used to be on friendly terms with wild animals night and day.

I [ʿAlī] believe that he alluded to this in his *Ode in T Minor*:

My love for you led me
to hate joining with my tribe,
and drew me to love leaving them behind
as long as I live.

Now I am far from my spring encampments
having lost four things:
my youth and its pleasure,
wise reason and sound health.

So after dwelling with my people,
I now reside in a barren land,
intimate with beasts,
estranged from human company.[16]

The Shaykh—may God be satisfied with him—said:

I stayed in an oasis that was a hard ride of ten days from Mecca, but every day and night I would leave it to pray the five daily prayers at Mecca's Noble Sanctuary. A huge lion would accompany me, kneeling down to me like a camel and saying: "O my master, ride!" But I never rode him. Once a group of the great scholars residing at the Noble Sanctuary were discussing the provisions that should have been necessary for my mount to make that desert crossing when the lion appeared to them at the gate of the Noble Sanctuary. They saw him and heard him say: "O my master, ride!" They then asked God's forgiveness, removed their turbans, and apologized to me.[17]

Then after fifteen years I heard my shaykh the greengrocer calling to me, "ʿUmar, come to me in Cairo to attend my death and funeral, and to pray for me with others." So I quickly went to him and found him at the point of death. I greeted him, and he greeted me and bade me farewell. Then he gave me some gold dinars and said, "Prepare my funeral with this money and do what is required. Give one dinar to each man bearing my bier to the Qarāfah cemetery, and bury me in that spot." He pointed, and there appeared before me a plot located in the Qarāfah below the mosque known as al-ʿĀriḍ, by a flowing stream and near Moses' Place of Prostration at the foot of Mt. Muqaṭṭam.[18]

Finally the greengrocer said: "Wait for the arrival of a man who will come down to you from the mountain. Both of you should pray for me and then wait to see what God will do with me." Then he died—may God have mercy upon him—and I prepared his funeral as he had instructed, burying him in the blessed plot that he had requested. Then a man came down to me from the mountain, quickly descending like a bird, and I did not see his feet touch the ground! I recognized him as the man I used to see slapping himself on the back of his neck in the marketplace. He said to me: "Lead on, ʿUmar, and let us pray for the shaykh." So we went, and I led the prayer, and I saw praying with us rows of green and white birds filling the sky! I saw a great green bird descend from the flock and land at the shaykh's feet; he gobbled up the corpse, rose back up to the flock, and off they flew together joyously singing in praise of God until they were out of our sight!

I asked my companion about this, and he replied: "ʿUmar, haven't you heard that the spirits of martyrs are in the stomachs of green birds roaming where they will in paradise? They are the martyrs of war. As for the martyrs of love, all of

> them—their spirits and their bodies—are in the stomachs of green birds, and this man was one of them, ʿUmar![19] I, too, was once among them, but I made a slip and was banished from them. So now I slap myself on the neck in the marketplace in repentance and chastisement for that slip." Then the man rose up the mountain like a bird and disappeared!

The Shaykh's son [Kamāl al-Dīn Muḥammad] said:

> My father said to me, "Muḥammad, I have only told you this account so that you will desire to enter our mystical way *[ṭarīq]*, so don't mention it to anyone while I am alive." Therefore, I never recounted it until he passed away, may God be satisfied with him!

I [ʿAlī] want to add that the Shaykh Ibn al-Fāriḍ—may God be pleased with him—was also buried in this blessed spot according to his will. His tomb there is well known, and it has been mentioned by a distinguished man, Abū al-Ḥusayn al-Jazzār,[20] in an elegy for the Shaykh:

> The massive rain clouds linger
> for they must visit Ibn al-Fāriḍ.
> No wonder his earth stays moist till Judgment Day
> as his grave remains under al-ʿĀriḍ.

And I [ʿAlī] have said:

> Pass by the Qarāfah
> beneath the hem of al-ʿĀriḍ
> and say: "Peace be upon you,
> O Ibn al-Fāriḍ!"
>
> You made wonders appear
> in the "Poem of the Way,"
> and revealed a secret
> mysterious and guarded.

And from the same poem:

> You drank from the cup
> of love and affection
> and so were quenched
> by a vast, flowing sea.

His son—may God have mercy upon him—said:

> I saw the Shaykh sleeping on his back and saying: "I believe you, Messenger of God! I believe you, Messenger of God! I believe you, Messenger of God!" raising his voice and pointing with his right and left index fingers. Then he awoke still speaking and pointing as he had been doing in his sleep. I told him about what I had seen and heard from him, and I asked him about it. He replied: "My son, in a dream I saw Muḥammad, the Messenger of God—His blessings and peace be upon him. He said to me: 'ʿUmar, what is your lineage?' I answered: 'Messenger of God, I am a descendant from the Saʿd tribe, the tribe of Ḥalīmah, your wet nurse, O Messenger.' But he said: 'No, indeed, you are from me, and your lineage is connected to me!' I said: 'I believe you, Messenger of God, though I have learned of my lineage to the Saʿd tribe from my father and grandfather.' But then he said emphatically, 'No, indeed! You are from me, and your lineage is connected to me!' So I replied, 'I believe you, Messenger of God!' repeating that and pointing with my fingers just as you heard and saw."

I [ʿAlī] say, that I saw the Shaykh's son Kamāl al-Dīn Muḥammad standing with his fingers reaching to his knees, and he said:

> I saw my father the Shaykh standing just as I am with his fingers reaching to his knees, and he said to me, "This is among the characteristics of those directly descendent from the Prophet Muḥammad."

Now, this noble lineage is either descent by birth or by love. Love's lineage is more noble than that of paternity for it made Bilāl the Abyssinian,

Salmān the Persian, and Ṣuhayb the Greek members of the Prophet's household. But how much less was Abū Ṭālib, who was neither ennobled nor blessed by his being the Prophet's paternal uncle, though that is of the closest family ties, because he was veiled by the divine will from receiving spiritual guidance.[21] Likewise, the prophet and friend of God, Abraham, washed his hands of his own father "when it became clear to him that his father was God's enemy."[22] Similarly Noah, upon whom be peace, was told regarding his son: "Indeed, he is no longer in your family!"[23] Our Shaykh alluded to this noble lineage in his ode rhyming in *Y,* where he said:

In the law of passion
between us
is a bond
closer than paternity![24]

Once in a dream it was as if I [ʿAlī] were in the noble presence of Muḥammad, and before the Messenger of God—His blessings and peace be upon him—was a large gathering of the prophets and saints. Among them in that noble presence was the Prophet's descendent and their appointed leader in Egypt *[naqīb al-ashrāf]*, Shams al-Dīn Muḥammad ibn al-Sayyid al-Sharīf Shihāb al-Dīn al-Ḥusayn ibn al-Sayyid al-Sharīf Shams al-Dīn Muḥammad al-Armawī, the military judge of the Manṣūrah province of Egypt, may God sanctify his spirit.[25] I recognized no one else by sight. The Prophet—God's blessings and peace be upon him—ordered that the shaykh Ṣubayh the Abyssinian be registered as his descendent.[26] I saw a man who had a register with him that certified this lineage, and he was going around to those present at the gathering, taking down their written testimony in the register. Then he came to me and presented the register saying, "Write!" So I replied: "I never saw the shaykh Ṣubayh in person, for I was not his contemporary. I do not know his lineage, though I do know his sons who are among my companions." He shouted at me, filling me with dread: "Write what has been ordered by the Prophet—God's blessings and peace be upon him!" So I replied: "What should I write?" The man said: "Write: I bear witness that the Prophet—God's blessings and peace be upon him—is a direct ancestor to the shaykh

Ṣubayh!" So I wrote down what had been ordered by the Prophet—God's blessings and peace be upon him.

The shaykh Ibn al-Fāriḍ's son—may God have mercy upon him—said, "I heard the Shaykh—may God be satisfied with him—say:

> 'In a dream I saw the Messenger of God—His blessings and peace be upon him. And he said to me: "ʿUmar, what have you named your ode (rhyming in *T*)?" I answered: "Messenger of God, I have named it *Lawā'iḥ al-janān wa rawā'iḥ al-jinān [The Diaries of Hearts and the Gardens' Sweet Scents]*." But he said: "No, name it *Naẓm al-sulūk [Poem of the Sufi Way]*." So that is what I named it.'"

The Shaykh's son said:

> A certain man (and his son named him, but I have forgotten the name) attended the Shaykh's teaching session—may God be satisfied with him. The man was one of the great religious scholars of his day, and he asked the Shaykh's permission to write a commentary on the ode *Poem of the Sufi Way*. The Shaykh asked him, "How many volumes will your commentary fill?" The scholar replied, "Two volumes." The Shaykh—may God be satisfied with him—smiled and said, "If I wanted, I could compose a two-volume commentary on each verse!"

I [ʿAlī] say that the shaykh Shams al-Dīn al-Aykī, the chief shaykh *[shaykh al-shuyūkh]* of the Saʿīd al-Suʿadā' khānqāh, came to visit my master, the shaykh Kamāl al-Dīn Muḥammad, the son of the Shaykh—may God be satisfied with him. This was in the latter part of the reign of the sultan al-Manṣūr Qalā'ūn—may God shelter him with His grace. Accompanying the shaykh al-Aykī was the shaykh Nūr al-Dīn al-Naqshawānī and a group of the senior Sufis.[27] I heard the shaykh al-Aykī say to Kamāl al-Dīn Muḥammad, "My master, praise be to God that I have lived to see you, for it is like the day that I saw my master the shaykh Sharaf al-Dīn, your father! I follow the school of our master the shaykh Ṣadr al-Dīn al-Qūnawī in loving the Shaykh Ibn al-Fāriḍ, believing in his creed, and devoting oneself to his ode *Poem of the Sufi Way*."[28] Then the shaykh al-Aykī recited some of its verses, including this one:

> If not for the veil of being
> I would speak out,
> yet respect for the laws of sense
> keeps me silent.[29]

Then the shaykh al-Aykī began to comment on the meanings of these verses, saying:

> A group of scholars and students of religion would attend the teaching sessions of our shaykh Ṣadr al-Dīn al-Qūnawī, and he would discuss specific disciplines within the religious sciences. Then he would bring his discourse to a close by mentioning a verse from the ode *Poem of the Sufi Way*. He would discuss it in Persian, using rare and mystical terms, which were not understood save by those possessing mystical experience *[dhawq]* and desire. Then on the following day he would say, "Another meaning has come to me regarding the commentary of the verse about which we spoke yesterday," and he would say something even more amazing than the day before! Also, he used to say, "The Sufi should memorize this ode, and one who understands the ode should comment on it."

The shaykh al-Aykī—may God have mercy on him—added:

> The shaykh Saʿīd al-Dīn al-Farghānī devoted himself with determination to understanding what Ṣadr al-Dīn al-Qūnawī mentioned as commentary on this ode, and he wrote it down in his presence, first in Persian and then in Arabic. He made his famous commentary in two volumes, and that commentary is based on the inspired sayings of our shaykh Ṣadr al-Dīn al-Qūnawī—may God have mercy upon him.[30]

I [ʿAlī] continued to search for a copy of this commentary until I met the chief shaykh of the Ṣalāḥīyah khānqāh, Karīm al-Dīn, together with

ʿUmar al-Saʿūdī in a suite above the entrance to the latter's Sufi retreat and hostel *[zāwiyah]* in the Qarāfah cemetery.[31] The shaykh Karīm al-Dīn told me that he had the commentary, so I borrowed it and made a copy, which I now have. Al-Farghānī—may God have mercy upon him—distinguished himself with this commentary in which he has opened doors of meaning like no one else! I was also told by the judge Jamāl al-Dīn ʿAbd Allāh, the son of our master and lord, the shaykh Jalāl al-Dīn Muḥammad al-Qazwīnī, the chief judge of Syria, then of all Egypt, that his father the chief judge—may God guard his glory and protect his fine attributes and qualities—composed a multi-volume commentary on the ode.[32]

The Shaykh's son Kamāl al-Dīn Muḥammad said:

> The Shaykh—may God be satisfied with him—in most of his moments of inspiration *[awqāt]* was perplexed, eyes fixed, hearing no one who spoke, not even seeing them. Sometimes he would be standing, sometimes sitting, sometimes he would lie down on his side, and sometimes he would throw himself down on his back wrapped in a shroud like a dead man. Ten consecutive days—more or less—would pass while he was in this state, neither eating, drinking, speaking, nor moving, as has been said:
>
> See the lovers felled
> in their encampments,
> like the youths of the cave, not knowing
> how long they have lingered.
>
> By God, had the lovers sworn
> to go mad from love or die,
> they would not break
> their oath![33]
>
> Then he would regain consciousness and come to, and his first words would be a dictation of what God had enlightened him with of the ode *Poem of the Sufi Way*.

I [ʿAlī] carefully examined a collection of writings made by a worthy man in which I saw the ode known as the *Poem of the Sufi Way*. I found before it an introduction, which reads as follows:

> The trustworthy shaykh, Sharaf al-Dīn ʿUmar Ibn al-Fāriḍ—may God illuminate his resting place—recited this exciting and unique ode, the likes of which can neither be conceived nor created, for this ode is nearly beyond the capacity of human potential in both meaning and expression. He originally named it *Anfās al-jinān wa nafā'is al-janān [The Breaths of the Gardens and the Gems of the Hearts]*, then he named it *Lawā'iḥ al-janān wa rawā'iḥ al-jinān [The Diaries of Hearts and the Gardens' Sweet Scents]*. But then in a dream he saw the Prophet—God bless him and give him peace—who said, "Name it the *Naẓm al-sulūk! [Poem of the Sufi Way]*," which he did.
>
> A trustworthy group of Ibn al-Fāriḍ's companions and confidants have said that he did not compose this ode in the way that poets normally compose their verse. Rather, spiritual raptures *[jadhabāt]* would come to him, and he would be senseless for about a week to ten days. Then he would recover and dictate what God had inspired him to compose of the ode, about thirty, forty, or fifty verses. Then he would stop until this state returned to him. One who truly contemplates this ode knows that it bears great tidings, which God has concealed from those who are not worthy of them.

Then, after this introduction, the compiler of the collection wrote down the text of the ode.

During the reign of the sultan al-Malik al-Manṣūr Sayf al-Dīn Qalā'ūn al-Ṣāliḥī—may God make him one of the martyrs and elevate him in paradise to the abodes of the auspicious ones—the office of vizier was entrusted to the chief judge, Taqī al-Dīn ʿAbd al-Raḥmān Ibn Bint al-Aʿazz—may God sanctify his spirit and illuminate his grave. It has been related that Ibn Bint al-Aʿazz slandered the shaykh Shams al-Dīn al-Aykī during a session attended by dignitaries at the al-Ṣalāḥīyah khānqāh, saying, "You order the Sufis to study the *Poem of the Sufi Way*, though in this ode Ibn al-Fāriḍ is inclined toward the heresy of incarnation *[ḥulūl]*!" Ibn

Bint al-Aʿazz also verbally abused al-Aykī, who then cursed him saying, "May God humiliate you as you have done to me!"[34]

Shortly thereafter, at the end of Qalā'ūn's reign, Ibn Bint al-Aʿazz was removed at his own request from the office of vizier and then, during the reign of Qalā'ūn's son al-Ashraf, he was removed from the position of judge, his property confiscated, and he was humiliated and imprisoned for a time. He was charged with heresy, slander, and immorality, as an unscrupulous man bore false witness against him at the instigation of the lord Shams al-Dīn Ibn al-Salʿūs, may God forgive him.[35] Regarding the false accusations against Ibn Bint al-Aʿazz it has been said:

God save him
from lies forged against him,
for the angels
know of no evil from him.

Though the reins of high office
have slipped from his hands,
his wise rule is still praised
in many domains.

This chastisement was a requital for his slandering the spiritually elect. Ibn Bint al-Aʿazz used to send me in secret to those amirs and Sufi shaykhs who worked hard for his release, but when things looked bad for him he would say over and over, "Confound you, my crisis, and be dispelled!"[36] When God released him from this misfortune and relieved his torment, I paid him a visit accompanied by the shaykh Saʿd al-Dīn al-Ḥārithī al-Ḥanbalī, the *ḥadīth* scholar and one of Ibn Bint al-Aʿazz's dearest companions.[37] I heard Ibn Bint al-Aʿazz ask God's forgivenes; then he praised God and thanked Him for his safety and this felicitous end to the affair. Then I brought to his attention his previous argument with Shams al-Dīn al-Aykī, and his slandering of al-Aykī and our shaykh Ibn al-Fāriḍ, whom he had charged with the heresy of incarnation, of which both were innocent. I asked him, "How could anyone imagine that the Shaykh was inclined toward incarnation in his ode since he had exonerated his faith from such a thing when he said:

But how can I fear
rumors of error
when my certain truth remains
with the name: the True?

Now take note of Diḥyah:
in this form, the Trusted One
came to our Prophet
as revelation began.

Tell me, then,
when Gabriel appeared in human form
to the right and true guide,
was he Diḥyah?

Of all those present there,
the Prophet alone
knew without doubt
the true apparition.

He saw an angel
sent to inspire him;
others saw only a man,
a respected companion.

So in the clearer of two visions
I have a sign
that keeps my creed free
of any incarnation.

And in the Qur'ān, undeniably,
there is mention of "disguise";
I have not transgressed the two truths:
the Book, and traditions of our prophet."[38]

Ibn Bint al-Aʿazz replied, "I am one of the greatest lovers of the Shaykh's poetry, and I memorized his *Dīwān* when I was a youth to my great benefit. But it is as if I have just heard these verses for the very first time, and they have now dispelled from my mind any suspicion that the Shaykh was inclined in his ode toward the heresy of incarnation. I ask God's forgiveness for what I said against his good reputation!" Then I said to him, "And what of the reputation of the shaykh Shams al-Dīn al-Aykī?" He replied, "Yes, I remained anxious about his curse until this inquisition befell me, so may God forgive both of us. I turn in repentance to God most high for slandering the folk of the Sufi way, for because of them, I was afflicted, but now I am safe beseeching God most high for their blessings!"

Then Ibn Bint al-Aʿazz went on the pilgrimage, and he praised the Messenger of God—His blessings and peace be upon him—in an ode, which he humbly recited in the Noble Courtyard near the Prophet's tomb in Medina. He cried profusely, as did the people with him who cursed his enemies. Then the eunuch of the mother of al-Malik al-Saʿīd, who had a beautiful voice, read a section of the Qur'ān in which God the great and glorious has said: "God has promised those who believe and do good works among you that He will certainly appoint them vice-regents on earth as He has done with those before them. He makes them strong in their religion, which He has approved for them, and He will give them security after their fear!"[39]

Ibn Bint al-Aʿazz rejoiced at this good omen, as did the people with him, for they knew that God had accepted their prayer. When Ibn Bint al-Aʿazz returned to Cairo from the Ḥijāz, he found that among the enemies who had slandered him "some of them had perished as a clear sign!"[40] Then he was again entrusted with the position of judge until he passed away, may God have great mercy upon him and make his resting place in the meadows of paradise! After his death, I saw him in a dream; his face was as bright as the moon and a light shone upon him, but he was dressed in a filthy garment. So I asked him about this, and he replied, "This is the light of religious knowledge, while this is the garment of administering justice!" Once again I saw him in a dream in which he was giving the Friday sermon from the preacher's platform *[minbar]* at the Azhar congregational mosque. I remember he said, "Our standard will return to its rightful place."[41]

The Shaykh's son—may God have mercy upon him—said to me, "I heard the Shaykh—may God be satisfied with him—say:

> I made a mistake and was racked with guilt inwardly and without to the extent that my spirit nearly quit my body. I went outside in a daze, fleeing like one who had committed a great sin that was now being called to account. I went up to Mt. Muqaṭṭam and sought out the places where I used to wander, crying and asking for God's help and forgiveness, but my guilt was not dispelled. So I descended to the Qarāfah cemetery and wallowed in the dust among the graves, but to no avail. Then I headed to the city of Fusṭāṭ where I entered the congregational mosque of ʿAmr Ibn al-ʿĀṣ.[42] I stood terrified in its courtyard and once again began to cry, humbling myself and asking God's forgiveness. Yet, I was still not relieved of my guilt. Then a state of anxiety came over me, the likes of which I had never experienced before, and I screamed out:
>
> Who is he who never sinned,
> who is he who does only what is right?[43]
>
> Then I heard someone between heaven and earth, whose voice I could hear though I could not see his form, say:
>
> Muḥammad the true guide, to whom
> Gabriel descended!"

The Shaykh's son—may God have mercy upon him—said to me:

> I saw the Shaykh—may God have mercy upon him—jump up and dance for a long time. He made a great show of ecstasy, and he sweated profusely until it flowed beneath his feet and fell upon the ground. He was extremely agitated, and there was no one with him there but me. Then his state subsided, and he prostrated to God most high. So I asked him the reason for his actions, and he answered, "Son, God enlightened me as never before regarding the meaning of this verse:

'Despite the skill of those
describing his beauty,
time will pass away
with what was not described!'"[44]

His son—may God have mercy upon him—told me:

The Shaykh—may God be satisfied with him—was walking in the Cairo market when he passed a group of guards who were beating time on wooden clappers and singing these verses:

Master, we stayed awake all night
seeking union with you.
But you didn't allow it, master,
so we dreamed of your phantom form.

But master, even that
didn't come,
so there is no doubt
that we're not on your mind!

When the Shaykh heard them, he screamed out, and danced for some time in the middle of the market. Many people passing by danced with him in the streets until there was a great multitude responding together. The people became ecstatic to the point where many of them fell on the ground as the guards continued to repeat the verses. The Shaykh tore off all of his outer garments and threw them to the guards, and the crowd did likewise. Then they carried the Shaykh without his clothes and turban, and clad only in his underwear, to the Azhar mosque. He remained in this intoxication for some days, lying on his back wrapped like a corpse. After he recovered, the guards came and presented his clothes to him, but he refused to take them back. People offered to buy them from the guards for a great sum of money, which some of the guards accepted, while others refused to sell their portion of the Shaykh's garments, keeping them for their blessings.

His son—may God have mercy upon him—also told me:

> The Shaykh—may God be satisfied with him—and I were walking in the main thoroughfare near the mosque of Ibn ʿUthmān.[45] A mourning woman was wailing and lamenting over a dead woman on a bier with other women responding, as the mourner cried:
>
> My lady, you've died truly died,
> Yes by God, truly truly!
>
> When the Shaykh heard her, he screamed out and fell down in a swoon. When he recovered, he began to repeat several times:
>
> My soul, you've truly died,
> Yes by God, truly, truly!

The Shaykh's son—may God have mercy upon him—also told me:

> The Shaykh was sitting at the door of the Hall of the Friday Sermon near the Friday sermon pulpit at the Azhar mosque. Sitting with him was a gathering of amirs and ascetics, including a group of Persian scholars and others who resided at the mosque. Whenever these foreigners would mention certain domestic spaces such as the "washroom" *[al-tasht khānah]*, the "bedroom" *[al-farāsh khānah]*, or similar things, they would say, "These names come from Persian terms." While they were discussing this and lauding Persian terms, the muezzins raised their voices together in the call to prayer, and the Shaykh said, "This is the Arabs' terms!" He screamed and went into ecstasy as did everyone else present until there was a great din in the mosque.

His son—may God have mercy upon him—told me:

> The sultan al-Malik al-Kāmil—may God have mercy upon him—loved scholars, and he would meet with them in a special

session for them alone. He also had an inclination for literature, and one day they were discussing the most difficult rhymes ending a verse. The sultan said, "Among the most difficult end-rhymes is the vowelless *Y*, so any of you who have memorized verse with this rhyme, let him recite it here." So they did, though no one could recite more than ten verses. But the sultan said, "I have memorized a poem of fifty verses in this rhyme." He recited them, and everyone expressed his appreciation for the sultan's recitation.

Then the judge Sharaf al-Dīn, who was the sultan's private secretary, said, "I have memorized one hundred and fifty verses using this end-rhyme in a single ode." The sultan replied, "Sharaf al-Dīn, I have in my library most of the collections of Arabic poetry from before and after the coming of Islam. I love this end-rhyme, yet I have never found an ode with the vowelless *Y* longer than the one that I recited to you. So recite to me this ode that you have mentioned." So the secretary recited the Shaykh's ode in *Y,* which begins:

Driver of the howdahs
  rolling up the desert miles,
    kindly turn aside
      at the dunes of Ṭay.[46]

Then the sultan said, "Sharaf al-Dīn, who composed this poem, for I have never heard anything like it? This is the voice of a lover!" The secretary answered, "This is the verse of the shaykh Sharaf al-Dīn ʿUmar Ibn al-Fāriḍ." The sultan said, "Where does he reside?" The secretary replied, "He used to be a resident of Mecca, but now he is in Cairo, staying at the Hall of the Friday Sermon at the Azhar mosque." So the sultan commanded, "Take one thousand of our dinars and go to him and say to him on our behalf, 'Your son Muḥammad [al-Malik al-Kāmil] greets you and requests that you accept this from him on behalf of the mendicants who come to you for aid.' If he accepts this sum, ask him to present himself to me that we may profit from his blessings." But the secretary said, "Your highness, please excuse me from this task; I cannot address him in such a fashion even though I do so on your royal behalf, for he will not accept gold, nor will he come with me to attend you. If I do this task, I will not be able to call on him ever again due to my shame!" But the sultan replied, "You must do it!"

So the secretary took the gold and left with a companion for the residence of the Shaykh. They found him standing by his door, waiting for them. Before the secretary could speak, the Shaykh said, "Sharaf al-Dīn, what's with you that you mention my name in the sultan's court? Return the gold to him and don't come back to me for a year!" So he returned and said to the sultan, "I would rather die than not see the Shaykh for an entire year!" To which the sultan replied, "There is a shaykh of this stature living here and now and I have not visited him! I must go to pay my respects and see him!"

That night the sultan along with Fakhr al-Dīn ʿUthmān al-Kāmilī descended in disguise from the citadel to Cairo, and they stayed at the residence of the Mihmandār, which stood before the Azhar mosque.[47] After the last evening prayer, the sultan and a group of his elite amirs entered the mosque and took up positions by the door to the Hall of the Friday Sermon near the pulpit. But the Shaykh had already left by another door at the rear of the mosque, so the sultan did not meet him. The Shaykh traveled to the harbor of Alexandria, where he stayed for some days in the lighthouse there. When the Shaykh returned to the Azhar mosque, the sultan was informed that the Shaykh had arrived weak and unwell. So the sultan sent Fakhr al-Dīn ʿUthmān to him to ask the Shaykh's permission to prepare a grave for him next to the sepulcher of the sultan's mother beneath the dome of the Imām al-Shāfiʿī—may God be satisfied with him.[48] The Shaykh would not permit that, so the sultan requested to build a tomb that would serve as a shrine especially for the Shaykh, but the Shaykh would not grant him that privilege either. Then the Shaykh recovered from his illness as God most high restored him to health.

I [ʿAlī] say that one day the judge Amīn al-Dīn Ibn al-Raqāqī came to pay his respects to me at my mosque.[49] He had a good opinion of the Shaykh, which he had received from his father, who had been among the Shaykh's dearest companions. Accompanying the judge was a group of dignitaries including the judge and sultan's prayer leader, Jamāl al-Dīn Ibrāhīm ibn al-Shaykh Bihā' al-Dīn ibn al-Shaykh Jamāl al-Dīn Ibrāhīm al-Amyūṭī. The judge Jamāl al-Dīn related to us the following story from his father, who had heard his own father, who had said:[50]

> I was walking with the shaykh Sharaf al-Dīn Ibn al-Fāriḍ from the Azhar mosque to Bāb Zuwaylah.[51] He told me that he was heading to the mosque of ʿAmr ibn al-ʿĀṣ in Fusṭāṭ, so I asked if I could accompany him, and he agreed. So I found a donkey driver to take us there and asked him, "How much do you charge to go to the mosque in Fusṭāṭ?" He replied, "Ride with me, and give me whatever you please as alms." To which, I replied, "No, we must agree on a price." But the Shaykh did not like this and said, "Yes, we will ride with you in exchange for alms," and so we did.
>
> Along the way we met Fakhr al-Dīn ʿUthmān al-Kāmilī, who dismounted from his horse, as did his companions from their mounts. He greeted the Shaykh—may God be satisfied with him—and tried to kiss his hand, but the Shaykh pulled his hand away and instead stroked Fakhr al-Dīn on the head and face, and blessed him saying, "Ride, and may God bless you!" Fakhr al-Dīn then mounted up and rode off. But a knight from his entourage followed after us, and he came to me for assistance saying to me, "Say to the Shaykh: 'These one hundred dinārs are to be accepted as alms from the amir Fakhr al-Dīn.'" So I told the Shaykh, who said to me, "We have ridden with the driver on the basis of alms, so these are his alms; give them to him." The knight returned to the amir and told him what had happened. The amir sent him back with one hundred more dinārs, yet when I told the Shaykh, he said, "Give them to the driver." I protested saying, "But these are an additional hundred!" But he answered, "I know; they are his alms." Then

> when we arrived at the mosque and dismounted from our donkeys, the Shaykh apologized to the driver and blessed him.

The Shaykh's son—may God have mercy upon him—told me:

> The Shaykh—may God be satisfied with him—used to undertake forty-day fasts, unbroken day or night as he neither ate, drank, nor slept. On the last day of one of these fasts, the Shaykh had a craving for a *harīsah* meat pastry.[52] So the Shaykh said, "O my soul *[nafs]*, can't you be patient for the rest of the day; then I will break the fast with *harīsah.*" But his soul refused and said, "I must have *harīsah* this minute!" The Shaykh continued, "So I bought the *harīsah*, and proceeded to the vicinity of the domed hall of al-Sharāb.[53] But as I raised the first piece to my mouth, the wall of the shrine burst open and out stepped a handsome youth with a fine form, spotless white garments, and a fragrant scent. He said, 'Shame on you!' To which I replied, 'Yes, indeed, if I eat it!' Then I threw the piece away before it touched my lips, and I left the *harīsah* behind. Leaving the sanctuary, I continued my ascetic wandering, disciplining my soul with an extra ten days of fasting so that the total was fifty consecutive days."

The Shaykh's son—may God have mercy upon him—told me:

> When the shaykh Shihāb al-Dīn al-Suhrawardī, the shaykh of the Sufis—may God sanctify his spirit—went on the pilgrimage in the year 628 [1231], many people from Iraq went on pilgrimage with him.[54] At the end of his pilgrimage, he noticed a huge crowd of people gathering around him during the circumambulation of the Kaʿbah and during the Standing at ʿArafāt, and he noticed that they imitated his words and actions. It reached al-Suhrawardī that the shaykh Ibn al-Fāriḍ—may God be satisfied with him—was there in the sacred precinct of Mecca. He longed to see him, and he wept while saying inwardly, "Do you believe that God regards me as these folk do? Do you believe that I am remembered in the

> Beloved's presence today?" Then the Shaykh—may God be satisfied with him—appeared to him and said, "Oh, al-Suhrawardī:
>
> 'Good news for you,
> so strip off what is on you,
> for you have been remembered
> despite your crookedness!'"[55]
>
> The shaykh Shihāb al-Dīn screamed and stripped off all of his outer garments, and the shaykhs and the mendicants present did likewise. He looked for the Shaykh but could not find him, so he said, "This is news from one who was in the Divine Presence!"
>
> Later, the two met there in Mecca's Noble Sanctuary; they embraced and spoke together in private for a long time. Al-Suhrawardī asked my father's permission to invest me and my brother ʿAbd al-Raḥmān with the Sufi robe according to his mystical order *[ṭarīqah]*, but my father would not permit that saying, "This is not our way *[ṭarīq]*." But al-Suhrawardī persisted until my father consented, and I was invested with the robe by al-Suhrawardī, as was my brother, together with Shihāb al-Dīn Aḥmad Ibn al-Khiyamī and his brother Shams al-Dīn, who also had my father's permission, for both of them were like sons to him. In addition, a large group of people were also invested by al-Suhrawardī there in the presence of my father and in the presence of a group of great shaykhs, including Ibn al-ʿUjayl al-Yamanī and others.[56]

The Shaykh's son Kamāl al-Dīn Muḥammad—may God have mercy upon him—told me:

> Once the Shaykh—may God be satisfied with him—was spending the entire month of Ramaḍān at Mecca's Noble Sanctuary, never going out on his ascetic wanderings, but rather fasting there and keeping awake on night vigils.

I [ʿAlī] say that the Shaykh has alluded to this when he said:

For love of you
life is a Ramaḍān
passing away
between night vigils and fasting.[57]

The Shaykh's son—may God have mercy upon him—continued:

At the beginning of Ramaḍān, my father wrapped a loincloth around his waist, as did the others staying near the Kaʿbah, for they had devoted themselves to seek the Night of Power; at times, they circumambulated the Kaʿbah, while at other times they would pray.[58] I was with them there when, one night near the end of Ramaḍān, I left the Sanctuary to go out back and relieve myself. There, I saw the Kaʿbah, the Sanctuary, the houses of Mecca, and its mountains prostrating to God most high! I saw awesome lights filling the sky, and I was scared and terrified! I hurried back to my father and told him what I had seen. Then he screamed and said to those residing there and seeking the Night of Power, "This son of mine went out to piss and saw the Night of Power!" All of the people screamed out with him, and the sounds of crying, supplications, prayers, and circumambulations rose up into a din that lasted until morning. Then my father went out to the valleys of Mecca, wandering in a daze, and he did not enter the Noble Sanctuary until the Feast several days later.[59]

His son—may God have mercy upon him—also told me:

The Shaykh—may God be satisfied with him—would frequent the mosque known as al-Mushtahā during the season when the Nile was high, for he loved to watch the river. Among the verses at the end of his *Dīwān* is this one, where he said:

My land is Egypt,
  what I want is there,
    for its Mushtahā mosque
      is the apple of my eye![60]

One day as the Shaykh was going to this mosque, he heard a fuller who was cutting a piece of cloth and beating it on the rocks as he said:

This piece of cloth
  has shredded my heart,
    but the piece remains
      neither cleaned nor cut.

The Shaykh began screaming and repeating this line hour after hour all day. He would become extremely agitated and fall to the ground; then his agitation would subside to the point that one would have thought that he was dead. But he revived and spoke to me in a mystical language the likes of which I have never heard, though I do not think it would be appropriate to pass on his words.[61] Once again he became agitated by the fuller's words as he listened closely to them and returned to his state of rapture. One of the Shaykh's close companions came in, and when he saw the Shaykh and confirmed his condition, he said:

I die when I remember you,
  then I am revived;
    how often I am revived for you,
      for how many times I've died!

The Shaykh jumped up, hugged his friend, and said to him, "Repeat what you said!" But the man was silent out of concern for him. He asked the Shaykh to go easy on himself, and he recalled to him some of what was happening to the Shaykh when he was overwhelmed by his state of rapture. Then the Shaykh said:

If God seals with His forgiveness,
then all I suffer will be easy.

The Shaykh stayed in this state caused by the fuller's words until he passed away, may God be satisfied with him!

Why the shaykh Burhān al-Dīn Ibrāhīm al-Jaʿbarī—may God give him peace—traveled from Jaʿbar to pay his respects to our Shaykh—may God be satisfied with him.[62]

The Shaykh's son [Kamāl al-Dīn Muḥammad] said:

I was in my mosque when an oppressive anxiety seized me from nightfall until the crack of dawn. I said my morning prayers at the mosque and then left, having resolved to visit the Shaykh's grave. But on the way, I passed by the mosque of the shaykh Burhān al-Dīn Ibrāhīm, and I could hear him speaking for it was his normal class time.[63] So I walked up the steps and went in the mosque where I heard him reciting this verse from the *Poem of the Sufi Way*, the ode by our Shaykh Sharaf al-Dīn Ibn al-Fāriḍ—may God have mercy upon him:

For you never loved me
so long as you were not lost in me,
and you will never be lost
without my form in you revealed.[64]

When the shaykh al-Jaʿbarī saw me he said, "There is no God but God! I have been talking about the meaning of the man's words, and so God has sent me his son!" He came over to me, and passed his blessed hand over my face and breast. Then God took the load off my chest as that oppressive anxiety left me, and I stayed at the mosque a while, feeling a sense of welcomed relief and joy. Once again, the shaykh al-Jaʿbarī spoke on the meaning of this verse, using amazing language and rare expressions. Afterward, I was told the reason for his mentioning this verse at the beginning of class. For the shaykh al-Jaʿbarī—may God be satisfied with him—had said:

> During my ascetic wanderings near Jaʿbar—or perhaps, he said, "near the Euphrates"—I was conversing with my spirit, confiding in it the pleasure I experienced when I was annihilated in love. Suddenly a man came to me like a lightning bolt and said:
>
> For you never loved me
> so long as you were not lost in me,
> and you will never be lost
> without my form in you revealed.
>
> I knew that this was the voice of love, so I rushed to the man, grabbed hold of him, and said, "Where did you get this verse?" He replied, "This is the verse of my brother, the shaykh Sharaf al-Dīn Ibn al-Fāriḍ." I said, "Where is this man?" He answered, "I used to hear his voice in the region of the Ḥijāz, but now I hear it in the region of Egypt, though he is on the verge of death. I have been ordered to go to him and attend his deliverance unto God most high, and to pray over him. I am going to him now." So when the man turned toward Egypt, I did likewise, and I smelled the man's fragrance; I followed its trace and instantly entered the Shaykh's presence as he lay on the verge of death.
>
> I said to him: "Peace, and God's mercy and blessings be upon you!" And he replied, "And upon you be peace and God's mercy and blessings, Ibrāhīm! Sit down and be glad for you are among the chosen friends of God *[awliyā']*!" I said, "O master, this is great news that you bring from God, but I would like to hear from you some proof that will put my heart at ease. For as my name is Ibrāhīm, so I share in the essence of the station of the name of the prophet Abraham as is mentioned in the Qur'ān, 'Don't you believe, [Abraham]?' He said, 'Yes, indeed, but

[a sign] would ease my heart.'"[65] The Shaykh answered, "All right, Ibrāhīm. I requested of God that a group of His chosen friends attend my death and deliverance unto Him. He has brought you as the first of them, so you are one of them."

Later, I asked the group of the chosen ones about a matter, but not one of them answered me concerning it, so I asked the Shaykh, "Master, can anyone knowingly comprehend God?" He looked at me with an awesome gaze and said, "Yes, when He encompasses them, they comprehend Him, Ibrāhīm, and you will be among them!" Then I saw the garden of paradise appear to the shaykh Ibn al-Fāriḍ, and when he saw it, he said, "Oh!" He screamed out, cried hard, changed color, and said:

If my resting place
in love near you
is what I have seen,
then I wasted my life.

A desire
seized my soul for a time,
but now it seems
just a jumbled dream.[66]

I said to him: "Master, this is a noble station!," but he said, "Ibrāhīm, Rābiʿah al-ʿAdawīyah said—and she was a woman—'By Your power! I did not worship You for fear of Your fire or in desire of Your paradise, rather in honor of Your noble countenance and for love of You!' So this station of seeing paradise is not what I sought or passed my life in trying to attain."[67] After that his agitation subsided, and he smiled, blessed me, and bade me farewell, saying, "Attend my death and prepare my corpse with the others here. Pray over my body together and sit by my grave for three days and nights. Afterward you may return to your land." Then as he devoted himself to private, intimate prayers, I heard a voice—but saw no one—say, "ʿUmar, what do you desire?" And he replied:

> I desire—though time has passed—
> one glance from you,
> but, oh, how much blood will flow
> before I reach my goal.[68]

After he spoke these words his face shone like the moon; he smiled, and expired happy and glad, and I knew that he had been given his desire. We were with him there, forming a large gathering of God's chosen ones, some of whom I knew, though not others, and among them was the man who had been the cause for my knowing the shaykh Ibn al-Fāriḍ. I attended the washing of his corpse and his funeral procession; in all my life, I have never seen a more awesome funeral procession. People crowded around to carry his bier, and I saw green and white birds hovering over it. We prayed over him at the grave site, though his grave was not completely dug until the end of the day. The people gathered there differed on what this delay might mean. One group said, "This is to chastise him for claiming such a high status in love!" But another group said, "No, indeed! This is merely the last indignity that one of God's chosen must suffer from the contingencies of this world below." Yet all of them are veiled from witnessing the Shaykh's mystical station, save those whom God wills. For by a spiritual vision granted me by God, I watched the holy and noble spirit of Muḥammad—upon whom be the greatest peace and prayers—praying as leader, and group after group of the spirits of the prophets, the angels, and God's chosen ones among humans and genies prayed over the Shaykh with the spirit of Muḥammad, the Messenger of God—His blessings and peace be upon him! I prayed with each group from the first to the last. Then the grave was ready, and he was buried in it. I stayed there three

> days and nights, witnessing what your intellects could never bear to explain regarding the Shaykh's mystical state! Then I headed for Jaʿbar, this having been my first trip to Egypt, as a voice inside me said:
>
> God rewarded your efforts well,
> though you arrived late in the day.
>
> Later, I returned to Egypt where I have lived until today.

Al-Jaʿbarī's son Shihāb al-Dīn Aḥmad[69]—may God gather the two of them together in the most praiseworthy station—once said to me [ʿAlī]:

> My father and I, together with a group of great men, paid a visit to the grave of the shaykh Sharaf al-Dīn—may God be satisfied with him. We found a lot of dirt around his grave, causing my father to scream out and say:
>
> Those poor folk of passion,
> the dirt of degradation
> covers even their tombs
> in the graveyards!
>
> My father the shaykh and the rest of us removed the dirt from [Ibn al-Fāriḍ's] stone until we had cleared away what had accumulated around the grave.

[The shaykh Ibn al-Fāriḍ]—may God be satisfied with him—passed away in Cairo at the Azhar mosque on the second of Jumādā I, 632 [1235]. He was buried in the Qarāfah cemetery at the foot of Mt. Muqaṭṭam near a stream below the blessed mosque known as al-ʿĀriḍ, which is on the highest part of mountain. I have heard that the shaykh Zakī al-Dīn ʿAbd al-ʿAẓīm, the *ḥadīth* scholar, asked the Shaykh for his date of birth, and the Shaykh replied, "It was in Cairo at the end of the day on the fourth of Dhū Qaʿdah 577 [1182]." I have heard that this was also related by the judge Shams al-Dīn Ibn Khallikān when he asked the Shaykh his birth date—may God be satisfied with all of them.[70]

So ends this preface. I have been silent regarding mention of dubious extraordinary states, fearing base criticism and disbelief. I have designated this preface as the introduction to the *Dīwān*, and I have made it a source of enlightenment for the lovers and brothers, and a memorial to the glorious deeds of the fathers and grandfathers for the sons after me. I ask God most high that He help me and them to travel His paths, and that He grant us good and blessed offspring. I give permission to the sons to relate the work from me with its chain, as I linked hearing it to the Shaykh through his son. I advise those who read it and scale its ascent that they hold fast to the *Poem of the Sufi Way* and lead a devout life by its way, which has brought great honor to the kingly ascetics. We ask God most high to open the doors to its understanding and confer on our hearts something of its knowledge so that we might move beneath its veils and reveal its hidden secrets, pulling aside its cover and drinking of its wine. For the wine jars of its rhymes are guarded by its wax seals, and the beauty of its meanings is secluded in its tents. No one can ever understand its symbols or "uncover its treasures," save "he who attains strength"[71] in his spiritual travels and enters the path *[ṭarīq]* of the poet [of this ode]. One must leave all others behind and follow [the poet] on his journey, "holding fast to his track,"[72] rendering the Moses of one's Muḥammadan heart patient for following his Khiḍr, so that one may comprehend experiential knowledge by means of his love and experience.[73]

No one is guided in these ways save one given success by God, who makes one worthy to be among those deserving to enter on these paths, and who raises one up to be a king among its kings. For these are indeed the way of him who called "to God with sure knowledge,"[74] and by following him, the paths of love were made bright. For by His leave, God most high sent him as a caller, a watchful shepherd, and vigilant protector for the worthy ones loving Him. God made him "a shining lamp"[75] for His saints, and those who followed him in love of God "received many blessings."[76] For no one saw, heard, or knew God save Muḥammad the Messenger of God—His blessings and peace be upon him!—and those who were with him. Love spread its shade over them as they drank from "its gentle and heavy showers,"[77] for they were the most worthy and deserving. Following him who holds the praised station, they drove on, and as his companions beneath the banner of this praised one, they attained the Garden. There, they drank from the river Kawthar, his drinking place, and with him they won a glance at their beloved's countenance, the utmost to be sought from the visible beloved.[78] They would never have attained this awesome station save by following their prophet, the beloved of their beloved. God bless the Prophet and give him peace, together with his family and companions, and all who submit themselves with him to God, believing in him and becoming Muslims, and upon his brothers among the prophets and the angels. As long as the wind moves and blows, as long as the lover's countenance shines and smiles with the love of God, may He bless them all with prayers lasting as long as the heavens and the earth. The tongues of Muslims of right belief and proper practice will recite these blessings for them, and these blessings will shine upon them far and wide until the day of resurrection and judgment!

Dear God, You it is "who possess the most exalted and beautiful names,"[79] and You made the word of love "like a fragrant tree firmly rooted in the earth, its branches spreading in the heavens."[80] [God] planted love's roots and branches in the lovers' hearts and caused its "peace to descend upon them,"[81] for they were the most worthy and deserving of love. [God] caused love's light "to be kindled from a blessed tree,"[82] and it is the Noble Light of Muḥammad; the angels bowed down to this light when they beheld it in Adam's countenance![83] Dear God, You have granted us the Prophet's sanctity and glory, so You have given us a place of honor before You when we follow him in worshiping and loving You. Dear God, You have made us part of his community, so we live and die holding to his faith and love of You, and we will be resurrected before You beneath the banner planted before the site where this praised Prophet stands.[84]

Dear God, You drew us as progeny from the loins before creation and made us bear witness against ourselves as You said, "Am I not your Lord?" and we replied, "Yes, indeed!"[85] And by that You made us grow, "light upon light."[86] Dear God, when You took the covenant from us with this pledge in pre-eternity, You gave us, O Lord, a "sure footing"[87] with this pledge, and what an exalted rank that is! You have graced us and made us worthy of our pledge, for You brought us forth into this Your world below, victorious in word and deed over our enemies and Yours.

You have treated us kindly and provided us with "the best and still more," and by this pledge, You exalted us over the rest of Your creation![88]

Dear God, open the doors of Your mercy to us, set us among Your necklace of gnostics, and confirm our pledge before You. For this, dear God, is Your covenant with us and ours with You. You are the judge and witness to all that is seen; "who is more faithful than God in keeping his covenant?"[89] God is a sufficient witness to the [Prophet's] praised station! Dear God, pardon and forgive us our lapses and sins, and protect us in this pledge of ours and our covenant! Have mercy on our teachers, parents, and brothers, and upon those of the other faiths who have believed in and loved You. Protect us from being frustrated, remiss, or lax, and do not give Satan power over us; keep him from our hearts, which You have made homes for Your love to dwell in. Dear God, lighten our affairs and enlighten our breasts with Your love's lights. Dear God, instruct us in the religion of loving You, and teach us the deeper interpretation of Your words. Grant us an understanding of the words of Your gnostics that we may be guided by them on the path leading us to You, following their way, which will join us to You!

Dear God, your servant [the Shaykh Ibn al-Fāriḍ] is the composer of this *Dīwān* recollecting the charms of subtle gnosis of You, and he is the interpreter of the mastery of Your noble love. Burning passion left but a fragment of his heart, though he found the shedding of his lifeblood for passion to be sweet. When the chapters of the splendid Qur'ān were recited to him, images of their beautiful meanings would appear to him. He observed the planets of gnosis, and their sun and moon were revealed to him, so he passionately loved what understanding can never grasp. He stood alone at the site of Your love, having followed Your prophet and beloved—upon whom be the greatest of prayers and peace—walking in the gathering places of passion side by side with great men; oh, what men!

Notes

INTRODUCTION

1. *Al-Mufaḍḍalīyāt*, edited by Aḥmad Muḥammad Shākir and ʿAbd al-Salām Muḥammad Hārūn, 7th printing (Cairo: Dār al-Maʿārif, 1983), 345–46. Also see Charles Lyall's translation and notes in *The Mufaḍḍalīyāt: An Anthology of Ancient Arabian Odes* (Oxford: Clarendon Press, 1918), 2:268–69, 283–85. For a finely nuanced discussion of the classical Arabic ode, see the works of Jaroslav Stetkevych, especially *The Zephyrs of Najd* (Chicago: University of Chicago Press, 1993) and "Toward an Arabic Elegiac Lexicon: The Seven Words of the *Nasīb*," in *Reorientations/Arabic and Persian Poetry*, edited by Suzanne Pinckney Stetkevych (Bloomington, Ind.: University of Indiana Press, 1994), 58–129. For translations of some of these odes, also see Michael A. Sells, *Desert Tracings: Six Classical Odes by ʿAlqama, Shanfara, Labid, Antara, Al-Aʿsha, and Dhu ar-Rumma* (Middletown, Conn.: Wesleyan University Press, 1993) and *Early Islamic Mysticism* (New York: Paulist Press, 1996), 56–74.

2. Ibn al-Fāriḍ, *Dīwān*, edited by ʿAbd al-Khāliq Maḥmūd (Cairo: Dār al-Maʿārif, 1984), 216. All translations are my own unless otherwise noted.

3. The *Maqām Ibrāhīm (Abraham's Station)* is a site a few yards from the southeast corner of the Kaʿbah holding the Black Stone; the prophet Abraham is believed to have stood on this spot to watch the construction of the Kaʿbah.

4. Ibn al-Fāriḍ, *Dīwān*, 184 (*al-Dālīyah*, vv. 30–34).

5. Concerning the noted scholar al-Qāsim Ibn ʿAsākir (527–600/1132–1203), see the *Encyclopaedia of Islam*, new edition (= EI^2), edited by H. A. R. Gibb, et al. (Leiden: E. J. Brill, 1954), 3:714.

6. Quoted by ʿAlī ibn Muḥammad al-Fayyūmī, *Nathr al-jumān fī tarājim al-aʿyān* (Cairo: Arab League Manuscript Institute, microfilm 428 [Ta'rīkh] of

ms 1746; Istanbul: Maktabat Aḥmad al-Thālith, 70b); and partially cited by Ibrāhīm al-Biqāʿī, *Maṣraʿ al-taṣawwuf* [= *Tanbīh al-ghabī*], edited by ʿAbd al-Raḥmān al-Wakīl (Cairo, 1953), 138. Jamāl al-Dīn Muḥammad ibn Yūsuf ibn Mūsā ibn Yūsuf Ibn Musdī al-Azdī was born in Granada, lived and studied for a time in Cairo, and was later killed in Mecca. Among his unpublished works is the *Muʿjam al-shuyūkh*, a biographical dictionary of his teachers and probable source for this account that, due to a scribal error, I previously attributed to Ibn al-Fāriḍ's student al-Mundhirī. See Th. Emil Homerin, *From Arab Poet to Muslim Saint: Ibn al-Fāriḍ, His Verse, and His Shrine* (Columbia, S.C.: University of South Carolina Press, 1994), 15–16, 101 n. 3. Also see ʿUmar al-Kaḥḥālah, *Muʿjam al-mu'allifīn* (Damascus: al-Maktabah al-ʿArabīyah, 1957), 12:140, and Khalīl ibn Aybak al-Ṣafadī, *al-Wāfī bi-al-Wafayāt*, edited by Sven Dedering, et al. (Wiesbadaen: In Kommission bei Franz Steiner Verlag, 1959–), 5:254–55.

7. See Homerin, *Arab Poet*, 15–24, and the translation of ʿAlī's *Proem*, below.

8. See Jawdat Rikābī, *La poésie profane sous Les Ayyūbides et ses principaux représentants* (Paris: G.-P. Masionneuve & Co., 1949), and Homerin, *Arab Poet*, 20–22.

9. See Homerin, *Arab Poet*, 20–24.

10. Ibn ʿUnayn, *Dīwān* (Beirut: Dār Ṣādir, n.d.), edited by Khalīl Mardam, 6, vv. 25–28. Also see EI^2, 3:962.

11. Regarding the divine name al-ʿAdl and its close relationship to generosity and creation within Islamic theology, see Abū al-Ḥāmid al-Ghazālī, *The Ninety-nine Beautiful Names*, translated by David B. Burrell and Nazih Daher (Cambridge: The Islamic Texts Society, 1995), 92–96. For more on this ode and the occasion for its recitation, see Aḥmad ibn Muḥammad Ibn Khallikān, *Wafayāt al-aʿyān wa-anbā' anbā' al-zamān*, edited by Iḥsān ʿAbbās (Beirut: Dār al-Thaqāfah, 1968), 5:76–79, and the translation by MacGuckin de Slane, *Ibn Khallikan's Biographical Dictionary* (Paris: Oriental Translation Fund of Great Britain and Ireland, 1842–71), 3:235–39.

12. For more on mannerism and *badīʿ* in Classical Arabic poetry, see the fine work by Stefan Sperl, *Mannerism in Arabic Poetry: A Structural Analysis of Selected Texts (3rd century AH/9th century A.D.–5th century AH/11th century A.D.)* (Cambridge: Cambridge University Press, 1989), esp. 1–7, 155–80; and also see Suzanne P. Stetkevych, *Abū Tammām and the Poetics of the ʿAbbāsid Age* (Leiden: E. J. Brill, 1991); Jaroslav Stetkevych, *Zephyrs*, and Th. Emil Homerin, "Reflections on Arabic Poetry in the Mamluk Age," *Mamlūk Studies Review* 1 (1997):63–85.

13. Ibn al-Fāriḍ, *Dīwān*, 113 (*Poem of the Sufi Way*, vv. 242–46), and see the introduction to the *Poem of the Sufi Way* below.

14. See Bashō's *The Narrow Road to the Deep North and Other Travel Sketches*, translated with an introduction by Nobuyuki Yuasa (Penguin Books, 1966), 31–33.

15. See *Laughing Lost in the Mountains: Poems of Wang Wei*, with translations by Tony Barnstone, Willis Barnstone, and Xu Haixin, and an elegant introduction by Willis Barnstone (Hanover, N.H.: University of New England Press, 1991), l–lii.

16. Ibn al-Fāriḍ, *Dīwān*, 195 (*al-Jīmīyah*, vv. 29–35). For a translation of the entire poem and its use in a Sufi meditation session, see Th. Emil Homerin, "A Saint, His Shrine, and Poetry's Power," in *Islamic Mysticism in Practice*, edited by Carl W. Ernst (Princeton, N.J.: Princeton University Press, forthcoming).

17. Quoted by Louis L. Martz, *The Paradise Within: Studies in Vaughan, Traherne, and Milton* (New Haven, Conn.: Yale University Press, 1964), 11.

18. See Louis L. Martz, *The Poetry of Meditation: A Study in English Literature of the Seventeenth Century* (New Haven, Conn.: Yale University Press, 1954); idem, *The Poem of the Mind* (New York: Oxford University Press, 1966), esp. 33–53; and idem, *Paradise*.

19. See below in this introduction, and the introduction to the *Wine Ode*.

20. Martz, *Mind*, 33.

21. See *The Poems of John of the Cross*, translated by Willis Barnstone (New York: New Directions, 1968), 46–47; and Willis Barnstone, *Laughing Lost*, liv–lvi.

22. On the relations between Arabic poetry and Islamic mysticism, see Th. Emil Homerin, "Tangled Words: Toward a Stylistics of Arabic Mystical Verse," in Stetkevych, *Reorientations*, 190–98, and "Preaching Poetry: The Forgotten Verse of Ibn al-Shāhrazurī," *Arabica* 38 (1991):87-101. Also see Sells, *Early Islamic Mysticism*, 56–57, and Barnstone, *St. John of the Cross*, 18–33.

23. See Barnstone, *St. John of the Cross*, 28–33, and *The Collected Works of St. John of the Cross*, translated by Kieran Kavanaugh and Otilio Rodriguez (Washington, D.C.: Institute of Carmelite Studies, 1979).

24. For recent translations of poems by Ibn al-Fāriḍ, see my *Arab Poet*, 4–9, "A Saint, His Shrine, and Poetry's Power," and "Ibn al-Fāriḍ: *Rubaʿiyat, Ghazal, Qasida*," in *Windows on the House of Islam: Muslim Sources on Spirituality and Religious Life*, edited by John Renard (Berkeley and Los Angeles: University of California Press, 1998), 194–200; also see Jaroslav Stetkevych, *Zephyrs*, 79–92, and Stefan Sperl, "Qasida Form and Mystic Path in Thirteenth Century Egypt: A Poem by Ibn al-Fāriḍ," in *Qasida Poetry in Islamic Asia and Africa*, edited by S. Sperl and C. Shackle, 2 vols. (Leiden: E. J. Brill, 1996), 1:65–81, and idem, "Ibn al-Fāriḍ: On Sufi Love," in *Qasida* 2:106–11.

Older translations in English include several in R. A. Nicholson's *Studies in Islamic Mysticism* (Cambridge: Cambridge University Press, 1921), 162–266, and those of A. J. Arberry, *The Mystical Poems of Ibn al-Fāriḍ*, 2 vols. (London: Emery Walker, 1952–56), whose interpretations and translations are rather idiosyncratic.

25. There are several useful introductions to Sufism, including the respected work by Annemarie Schimmel, *Mystical Dimensions of Islam* (Chapel Hill, N.C.: University of North Carolina Press, 1975).

26. Regarding these and other Qur'ānic passages see Fazlur Rahman, *Major Themes of the Qur'ān* (Chicago: Bibliotheca Islamica, 1980); Sells, *Early Islamic Mysticism*, 29–56, and below in the commentary to the *Poem of the Sufi Way*.

27. These *ḥadīth* may be found in several standard collections, including that of Yaḥyā ibn Sharaf al-Nawawī (d. 676/1277), *al-Arbaʿīn al-Nawawīyah*, edited by Ibrāhīm ibn Muḥammad (Ṭanṭa, Egypt: Maktabat al-Ṣaḥābah, 1986), 18, 47, 78, 95 (= #2, 13, 31, 40). Also see *An-Nawawī's Forty Hadith*, translated by Ezzedin Ibrahim and Denys Johnson-Davies (n.d., n.p.). For a discussion of *ḥadīth* in general, see *EI*^{2}, 3:23–29.

28. For a study of the Divine Sayings and their place in Islamic mysticism, see William A. Graham, *Divine Word and Prophetic Word in Islam* (The Hague: Mouton, 1977), esp. 53–54, 62–65, 69–72.

29. See Graham, *Divine Word*, 173–74, and al-Nawawī, *al-Arbaʿīn*, 92–93 (#38).

30. Concerning the life and work of al-Ḥasan al-Baṣrī, see *EI*^{2}, 3:247–48; for Abū Ḥanīfah, see *EI*^{2}, 1:123–24.

31. For al-Junayd and his mystical thought, see *EI*^{2}, 2:600; A. H. Abdel-Kader, *The Life, Personality and Writings of al-Junayd* (London: Luzac & Co., 1962), and M. Sell's superior translation of some of al-Junayd's writings in *Early Islamic Mysticism*, 251–65. Also see R. C. Zaehner, *Hindu and Muslim Mysticism* (New York: Schocken Books, 1969), 133–61; Roger Deladriere, *Junayd: Enseignement spirituel* (Paris: Sindbad, 1983); and M. Abdul Haq Ansari, "The Doctrine of One Actor: Junayd's View of *Tawḥīd*," *Muslim World* 73 (1983):33–56.

32. Ibn al-Fāriḍ, *Dīwān*, 142 (*Poem of the Sufi Way*, v. 496).

33. Ibn al-Fāriḍ, *Dīwān*, 112–13 (*Poem of the Sufi Way*, vv. 233–35).

34. Ibn al-Fāriḍ, *Dīwān*, 168 (*Poem of the Sufi Way*, vv. 718–21).

35. Regarding many of these scholars and samples of their work, see Sells, *Early Islamic Mysticism*. For a detailed study of al-Ḥallāj, see Louis Massignon, *La passion d'al-Ḥosayn ibn Mansour al-Ḥallāj*, translated by

Herbert Mason as *The Passion of al-Hallāj*, 4 vols. (Princeton, N.J.: Princeton University Press, 1982).

36. Concerning al-Ghazālī's life and work, see *EI*[2], 2:1038–41, and the insightful essay by Eric L. Ormsby, "The Taste of Truth: The Structure of Experience in al-Ghazālī's *al-Munqidh min al-Ḍalāl*," in *Islamic Studies Presented to Charles J. Adams*, edited by Wael B. Hallaq and Donald P. Little (Leiden: E. J. Brill, 1991), 134–52.

37. Muḥammad al-Ghazālī, *Mishkāt al-anwār*, edited by Abū al-ʿAlā ʿAfīfī (Cairo: al-Hay'ah al-ʿĀmmah lil-Kitāb, 1964). For a translation, see *Al-Ghazzali's Mishkat Al-Anwar*, translated by W. H. T. Gairdner (London: Royal Asiatic Society, 1915).

38. Regarding al-Tustarī, see Gerhard Böwering, *The Mystical Vision of Existence in Classical Islam: The Qur'ānic Hermeneutics of Sahl al-Tustarī (d. 283/896)* (Berlin: Walter De Gruyter, 1980), and his article in *EI*[2], 8:840–41.

39. For more on the Light of Muḥammad, also see Annemarie Schimmel, *And Muḥammad Is His Messenger* (Chapel Hill, N.C.: University of North Carolina Press, 1985), 123–43.

40. Ibn al-Fāriḍ, *Dīwān*, 159–60 (*Poem of the Sufi Way*, vv. 615–20).

41. See *EI*[2], 2:223–27; 8:1018–19.

42. Ibn al-Fāriḍ, *Dīwān*, 134–35 (*Poem of the Sufi Way*, vv. 430–41). Also regarding *dhikr* and the Covenant see al-Kalābādhī's comments in *The Doctrine of the Ṣūfīs*, translated by A. J. Arberry (Cambridge: Cambridge University Press, 1935), 166–67.

43. For more on the various Sufi orders, see J. Spencer Trimingham, *The Sufi Orders in Islam* (London: Oxford University Press, 1973); Schimmel, *Dimensions*, 228–58, and Th. Emil Homerin, "Saving Muslim Souls: The Khānqāh and the Sufi Duty in Mamluk Lands," *Mamlūk Studies Review* 3 (1999): 59–83.

44. Regarding Ibn al-Fāriḍ and the Muslim cult of the saints, see Homerin, *Arab Poet*. For a translation of the grandson's story, see the *Proem* below, and Homerin, *Arab Poet*, 47–49.

45. There is a growing body of fine recent research on Ibn al-ʿArabī, among which see William Chittick, *The Sufi Path of Knowledge* (Albany, N.Y.: State University of New York Press, 1989), and idem, "Rūmī and *waḥdat al-wujūd*," in *Poetry and Mysticism in Islam*, edited by Amin Banani, et al. (Cambridge: Cambridge University Press, 1994), 70–111. Also see *EI*[2], 3:707–11.

46. See Homerin, *Arab Poet*, esp. 26–32. For more on the specific commentaries and their authors, see the introductions below to the translations of the *Wine Ode* and the *Poem of the Sufi Way*.

47. In particular, see the work of Giuseppe Scattolin, including *L'esperienza mistica di Ibn al-Fāriḍ attraverso il suo poema Al-Tā'iyyat Al-*

Kubrā (Rome: PISAI, 1988); "L'expérience mistique de Ibn al-Fāriḍ a travers son poeme Al-Tā'iyyat Al-Kubrā," *MIDEO* 19 (1989): 203–23, and "Al-Farghānī's Commentary on Ibn al-Fāriḍ's Mystical Poem *Al-Tā'iyyat Al-Kubrā*," *MIDEO* 21 (1993): 331–83.

48. Concerning such readings by the major commentators, see Homerin, *Arab Poet*, 26–28; for a recent example, see the articles by Scattolin, especially "More on Ibn al-Fāriḍ's Biography," *MIDEO* 22 (1994): 197–242, esp. 228–30. Also see Nicholson's circumspect remarks on the matter in his *Studies*, 166–68.

49. For a useful general discussion of persona, see *The New Princeton Encyclopedia of Poetry and Poetics*, edited by Alexander Preminger, et al. (Princeton, N.J.: Princeton University Press, 1993), 900–902. Concerning the persona within Classical Arabic poetry, see Jaroslav Stetkevych, "The Arabic Lyrical Phenomena in Context," *Journal of Arabic Literature* 6 (1975): 55–77.

50. Ibn al-Fāriḍ, *Dīwān*, 185 (*al-Lāmīyah*, vv. 1–6).

WINE ODE

1. See Homerin, "Tangled Words," and "Preaching Poetry." Also see Arberry, *Mystical Poems*, 2:84–90, who notes poetic antecedents for several of Ibn al-Fāriḍ's images. For more on many major wine themes and images, and their poetic relationships in general see EI^2, 4:998–1009; F. Harb, "Wine Poetry," in *The Cambridge History of Arabic Literature: ʿAbbasid Belles Lettres*, edited by Julia Ashtiany, et al. (Cambridge: Cambridge University Press, 1990), 219–34; al-Sarī ibn Aḥmad al-Rifā', *al-Muḥibb wa-al-maḥbūb wa-al-mashmūm wa-al-mashrūb* (Damascus: Mājid Hasan al-Dhahabī, 1986), esp. vol. 4; and Suzanne P. Stetkevych, "Intoxication and Immortality: Wine and Associated Imagery in al-Ma'arri's Garden," *Literature East and West* 25 (1989): 29–48.

2. For a detailed analysis of the *Wine Ode*, see my forthcoming *Passion Before Me*. Also see the comments and partial translation by Martin Lings in "Mystical Poetry," in *ʿAbbasid Belles Lettres*, 235–64, esp. 255–56.

3. In particular, see the commentaries by Sibṭ al-Marṣafī, al-Ḥusrī, and al-Nābulusī cited in the bibliography. For other readings and translations of the *Wine Ode*, see ʿĀṭif Jawdah Naṣr, *al-Ramz al-shiʿrī ʿind al-Ṣūfīyah* (Beirut: Dār al-Andalus, 1983), 366–72; ʿAbd al-Khāliq Maḥmūd, *Shiʿr ʿUmar Ibn al-Fāriḍ* (Cairo: Dār al-Maʿārif, 1984), 136–43; Arberry, *Mystical Poems*, 2:84–90; R. A. Nicholson, *Studies*, 184–88; A. Safi in the *Bulletin of the School of Oriental and Asian Studies* 2:235–48; and Emile Dermenghem, *L'Éloge du vin* (Paris: Les Éditions Véga, 1931).

4. For ʿAlī's opinion of these verses, see Ibn al-Fāriḍ, *Dīwān*, 225; also see ʿAlī's account of collecting his grandfather's poetry below in the *Proem*.

5. See Homerin, *Arab Poet*, 27–31, 78–87. For al-Nābulusī, also see J. Stetkevych, *Zephyrs*, 95–98, and Shigeru Kamada, "Nābulusī's Commentary on Ibn al-Fāriḍ's *Khamrīyah*," *Orient* 18 (1982): 19–40.

6. Commentaries directly indebted to that of al-Qayṣarī include those by al-Ḥusayn al-Tabrīzī (fl. 731/1330), ʿAlī ibn Shihāb al-Hamdānī (d. 786/1384), Yaḥyā ibn Muḥammad al-Jīlānī (d. pre-897/1492), al-Jāmī (d. 897/1492), Ibn Kamāl Pashā (d. 940/1533), Sibṭ al-Marṣafī (d. 966/1559), Naṣrī ibn Aḥmad al-Ḥuṣrī (fl. 1098/1678), and ʿAbd al-Ṭawwāb al-Qūṣī (d. ?). For these and other commentaries, see the bibliography.

7. Dā'ūd al-Qayṣarī, *Sharḥ al-Qaṣīdah al-Khamrīyah*, ms 7761 (Adab) (Cairo: Dār al-Kutub al-Miṣrīyah), 320–30. For more on al-Qayṣarī's work and mystical views, see Kaḥḥālah, *Muʿjam*, 4:142; William Chittick, "The Five Presences: From al-Qūnawī to al-Qayṣarī," *Muslim World* 72 (1982): 107–28, esp. 123–24; Homerin, *Arab Poet*, 28–29; and Mehmet Bayrakdar, *La philosophie mystique chez David de Kayseri* (Ankara: Editions Ministere de la Culture, 1990).

8. The following translation is based on several manuscripts of the work at Cairo's Dār al-Kutub al-Miṣrīyah, especially ms 7761 (Adab), which I copied, with notes from mss 4502 and 4504 (Adab Ṭalʿat), and ms 366 (Shiʿr Taymūr). I have now edited and translated this commentary for publication.

POEM OF THE SUFI WAY

1. A. J. Arberry, *The Poem of the Way* (London: Emery Walker, 1952), 6; quoted by Issa Boullata in his "Verbal Arabesque and Mystical Union: A Study of Ibn al-Fāriḍ's 'AL-Ta'iyya AL-Kubra,'" *Arab Studies Quarterly* 3:2 (Spring 1981): 152–69.

2. Boullata, "Verbal Arabesque," esp. 160–66.

3. Boullata, "Verbal Arabesque," 166–69; and Arberry, *The Poem of the Way*, 6–7.

4. Ibn al-Fāriḍ, *Dīwān*, 172 (*Poem of the Sufi Way*, vv. 755, 757–58).

5. Ibn al-Fāriḍ, *Dīwān*, 143 (*Poem of the Sufi Way*, vv. 500, 502).

6. For these and other stories concerning the poem see the translation of ʿAlī's *Proem*, below.

7. See Homerin, *Arab Poet*, 26–32, 55–66, 76–78. Portions of these commentaries have been paraphrased by Nicholson in his partial translation of the ode in *Studies*, 199–266; also see Arberry's translation and commentary in *The*

Poem of the Way. For a recent examination of al-Farghānī's commentary, see G. Scattolin, "Al-Farghānī's Commentary on Ibn al-Fāriḍ's Mystical Poem *Al-Tā'iyyat Al-Kubrā,*" *MIDEO* 21 (1993): 331–83; and also see Chittick, "Five Presences," and "Rūmī and *waḥdat al-wujūd,*" esp. 79–81.

ADORNED PROEM TO THE DĪWĀN

1. Ibn al-Fāriḍ, *Dīwān*, Maḥmūd ed., 21. For remarks on ʿAlī Sibṭ Ibn al-Fāriḍ by one of his contemporaries, see ʿAlī ibn Muḥammad al-Fayyūmī (d. 770/1369) *Nathr al-jumān*, 2:70a.

2. For further discussion and analysis of the *Proem,* see Homerin, *Arab Poet*, 33–54; Issa J. Boullata, "Toward a Biography of Ibn al-Fāriḍ," *Arabica* 38 (1981): 38–56; and G. Scattolin, "More on Ibn al-Fāriḍ's Biography," *MIDEO* 22 (1995): 197–242, esp. 206–13.

3. Here ʿAlī refers to the Qur'ān 53:1–11, which, according to Islamic tradition, describes one of Muḥammad's encounters with Gabriel, the spirit of revelation. Further, Muḥammad's name is directly linked to God's "most awesome name," Allāh, in the profession of faith: "There is no deity but God (Allāh), and Muḥammad is the messenger of God!"

4. ʿAlī alludes to Qur'ān 31:20: "God has showered you liberally with His beneficence both inwardly and without."

5. This phrase is found in the Qur'ān 36:26 where it is said by a man regarding his people who obstinately remain ignorant of the truth of monotheism. ʿAlī's use of this phrase seems to imply that some in his audience might have thought his imitation to be a genuine poem by Ibn al-Fāriḍ.

6. In his introductory note to the text of this poem, ʿAlī recounts how he found the lost ode in 733/1333 during a reading of his grandfather's *Dīwān*. ʿAlī was sponsoring the reading for a group of men who wanted to become authorized reciters of the collection. One participant at the session, Jamāl al-Dīn ʿAbd Allāh ibn Majd al-Dīn Ismāʿīl al-Dimashqī, was reading ʿAlī's *Proem* and the case of the missing ode, when he realized that he had the ode in a book, though he had always thought the poem to be anonymous. Al-Dimashqī immediately went off with ʿAlī's son Ibrāhīm, and together they returned with the poem, which ʿAlī then appended to the end of his collection. Ibn al-Fāriḍ, *Dīwān*, 225–26. Jamāl al-Dīn al-Dimashqī (625–712/1227–1312) worked as a secretary in the Ayyubid chancelleries, first in Damascus, and then in Cairo, though he appears to have died prior to 733/1333; see Aḥmad Ibn Ḥajar al-ʿAsqalānī, *al-Durar al-kāminah fī aʿyān al-mi'ah al-thāminah* (Haydarabad: n.p., 1929), 2:354.

7. Several contemporaries of Kamāl al-Dīn Muḥammad were known by the patronymic Ibn Shaykh al-Shuyūkh, including four brothers whose father, Ṣadr al-Dīn Muḥammad ibn ʿUmar al-Juwaynī (d. 617/1220) had held the position of chief shaykh *(shaykh al-shuyūkh)* at the Saʿīd al-Suʿadāʾ khānqāh, Egypt's first major residence for recognized Sufis. The four brothers were Kamāl al-Dīn Aḥmad (fl. 7th/13th c.), ʿImād al-Dīn ʿUmar (d. 636/1239), Muʿīn al-Dīn al-Ḥasan (d. 643/1246), and Fakhr al-Dīn Yūsuf (d. 647/1249); all had studied Sufism and were also involved to varying degrees in the political affairs of their day. See Aḥmad ibn ʿAlī al-Maqrīzī, *Kitāb al-Muqaffā al-kabīr*, edited by Muḥammad al-Yaʿlāwī (Beirut: Dār al-Gharb al-Islāmī, 1991), 6:420–22, 715–16, and ʿAbd al-Ḥayy Ibn al-ʿImād, *Shadharāt al-dhahab fī akhbār man dhahab* (Cairo: Maktabat al-Qudsī, 1931), 5:77, 181, 218, 238–39.

8. This sentence is missing in the Maḥmūd ed. of the *Dīwān*, though it is to be found in the Tehran ms, 2b, and in other editions, as well. Ṣafī al-Dīn al-Ḥusayn ibn ʿAlī Ibn Abī al-Manṣūr (d. 682/1283) was a Sufi shaykh widely believed to have been granted mystical revelations and miracles. He was shaykh of a Sufi hostel in the Qarāfah cemetery; see al-Ṣafadī, *al-Wāfī*, 13:19, and Kaḥḥālah, *Muʿjam*, 4:37.

9. Manfalūṭ is a market town on the west bank of the Nile approximately eighteen miles (twenty-five kilometers) north of Asyūṭ. The Sufi Abū al-Qāsim al-Manfalūṭī might have been a descendent and/or disciple of the noted mystic Ismāʿīl ibn Ibrāhīm al-Manfalūṭī (d. 652/1254). See Jaʿfar al-Udfuwī, *al-Ṭāliʿ al-saʿīd*, edited by Saʿd Muḥammad Ḥasan and Ṭāhā al-Ḥājirī (Cairo: al-Dār al-Miṣrīyah lil-Taʾlīf wa-al-Tarjamah, 1966), 155–56; and Kaḥḥālah, *Muʿjam*, 2:254.

10. Qurʾān 5:54.

11. Concerning the Ayyubid ruler of Egypt al-Malik al-Kāmil (r. 615–35/1218–38), see *EI*², 4:520–21, and P. M. Holt, *The Age of the Crusades* (London: Longman, 1986), 60–65; and for the great legal scholar Muḥammad ibn al-Idrīs al-Shāfiʿī (d. 204/820), see *EI*², 9:181–85.

12. Al-ʿAzīz ʿUthmān, the son of Ṣalāḥ al-Dīn (Saladin), was the Ayyubid governor of the Cairo region from 589–95/1193–98; see Ibn ʿImād, *Shadharāt*, 4:319, and Holt, *Crusades*, 60–61.

13. Cairo's al-Azhar mosque was originally founded in 358/969 as a Shiʿī place of worship and teaching, but later the Ayyubids transformed the institution into a bastion of Sunni doctrine and practice; see *EI*², 1:813–21.

14. Founded in Cairo by Ṣalāḥ al-Dīn (Saladin), the al-Suyūfīyah was the first Ḥanafī law school in Egypt; see Aḥmad ibn ʿAlī al-Maqrīzī, *al-Mawāʿiẓ wa-al-iʿtibār bi-dhikr al-khiṭaṭ wa-al-āthār* (Baghdad: Maktabat al-Muthannā, 1970), 2:365–66.

15. Ibn al-Fāriḍ, *Dīwān*, 184 (*al-Dālīyah*, vv. 30, 32); for the Maqām

Ibrāhīm or Abraham's Station, see the Introduction above, and the *Poem of the Sufi Way*, v. 152.

16. Ibn al-Fāriḍ, *Dīwān*, 76 (*al-Tā'īyah al-ṣughrā*, vv. 57–59).

17. The scholars may have apologized for their ignorance of Ibn al-Fāriḍ's extraordinary means of traveling to and from Mecca. The al-Haram al-Sharīf or Noble Sanctuary is the immediate area surrounding the Kaʿbah and includes Abraham's Station and the Well of Zamzam; see *EI*², 4:317–18.

18. Cairo's al-Qarāfah is a large sprawling cemetery on the eastern edge of the city and surrounding the Muqaṭṭam Hills; see *EI*², 4:425–28. For al-ʿĀriḍ see al-Maqrīzī, *al-Khiṭaṭ*, 2:456.

19. Regarding saints, martyrs, and their soul-birds, see Ignaz Goldziher, "L'oiseau représentant l'âme dans les croyances populaires des Musulmans," in *Études Islamologiques d'Ignaz Goldziher*, edited and translated by G.-H. Bousquet (Leiden: E. J. Brill, 1962), 77–80. Also see Qur'ān 24:41 for birds and their praise of God.

20. For a history of Ibn al-Fāriḍ's grave and the shrine there, see Th. Emil Homerin, "The Domed Shrine of Ibn al-Fāriḍ," *Annales Islamologiques* 25 (1990):133–38. Abū al-Ḥusayn al-Jazzār (601–679/1204–81) was a prolific Egyptian poet known for his love poems, invective verse, and aphorisms; see ʿUmar Farūkh, *Ta'rīkh al-adab al-ʿArabī* (Beirut: Dār al-ʿIlm lil-Malāyīn, 1975), 3:644–46.

21. Bilāl the Abyssinian (d. 20/641), Salmān the Persian (d. 36/657), and Ṣuhayb the Greek (d. 38/659) were among the early converts to Islam and were among Muḥammad's close companions, while his uncle and protector, Abū Ṭālib (d. 619) never embraced Islam; for these men see Ibn al-ʿImād, *Shadharāt*, 1:31, 44, 47, and *EI*², 1:152, 1215; *The Shorter Encyclopaedia of Islam*, edited by H. A. R. Gibb and J. H. Kramers (Leiden: E. J. Brill, 1953), 500–501; and Maxime Rodinson, *Muḥammad* (New York: Pantheon Books, 1980), esp. 101–2, 209.

22. Concerning Abraham's dispute with his father over the latter's idolatry, see Qur'ān 9:114; 19:41–50.

23. For the story of Noah and his wayward son, see Qur'ān 11:45–47.

24. Ibn al-Fāriḍ, *Dīwān*, 55 (*al-Yā'īyah*, v. 94).

25. Shams al-Dīn Muḥammad ibn Ḥusayn ibn Muḥammad al-Armawī was an accomplished scholar of jurisprudence, who in 635/1237 was appointed military judge of the Cairo region as well as its *naqīb al-ashrāf*, the official representative of the direct descendants of the Prophet Muḥammad; he died in 650/1253. See Aḥmad ibn ʿAlī al-Maqrīzī, *Kitāb al-Sulūk li-maʿrifat duwal al-Mamlūk*, edited by Muḥammad Muṣṭafā Ziyādah (Cairo: Lajnat al-Ta'līf wa-al-Tarjamah wa-al-Nashr, 1934–58), 1:2:273, 385.

26. Ṣubayḥ ibn Bakkar ibn ʿAbd Allāh the Abyssinian was a freed slave who pursued the study of *ḥadīth* and memorized the Qur'ān. He was noted for his philanthropy, and died in 584/1188; see ʿAbd al-ʿAẓīm al-Mundhirī, *al-Takmilah li-Wafayāt al-naqalah*, edited by Bashshār ʿAwwād Maʿrūf (Cairo Maṭbaʿat ʿĪsā al-Bābī al-Ḥalabī, 1968), 1:81–83, and al-Ṣafadī, *al-Wāfī*, 16:282.

27. Shams al-Dīn Muḥammad al-Aykī (d. 697/1298) was a Persian Sufi and scholar of jurisprudence. He was appointed chief shaykh of the Saʿīd al-Suʿadā' khānqāh by the Mamluk sultan Qalā'ūn (r. 678–89/1279–90) in 684/1286. See al-Maqrīzī, *al-Sulūk*, 1:730, 851; Ibn al-ʿImād, *Shadharāt*, 5:439, and Homerin, *Arab Poet*, 40–43.

28. Al-Aykī was an infant when Ibn al-Fāriḍ died. Ṣadr al-Dīn al-Qūnawī (d. 673/1274) was a close disciple of the great Sufi theosophist Ibn al-ʿArabī (d. 638/1240). For a concise overview of the work and influence of both mystics, see Chittick, "Rūmī and *waḥdat al-wujūd*," esp. 77–79; also see *EI*[2], 8:753–55.

29. Ibn al-Fāriḍ, *Dīwān*, 170 (*Poem of the Sufi Way*, v. 743).

30. Saʿīd al-Dīn al-Farghānī was a disciple of al-Qūnawī and one of the first major commentators on Ibn al-Fāriḍ's *Poem of the Sufi Way*. In an introduction to al-Farghānī's Persian commentary, al-Qūnawī noted that he traveled to Egypt in 643/1245, during which time he read and commented on Ibn al-Fāriḍ's *Poem of the Sufi Way*, and that al-Farghānī had compiled a commentary based on these explanations of the verses. See al-Farghānī's *Mashāriq al-darārī*, edited by Saʿīd Jalāl al-Dīn Āshtiyānī (Mashhad: Dānishghāh-i Firdawsī, 1980), 5–6; Homerin, *Arab Poet*, 27–31; and Chittick, "Rūmī and *waḥdat al-wujūd*," 79–81.

31. Karīm al-Dīn ʿAbd al-Karīm ibn Ḥusayn ibn Abū Bakr al-Āmulī held the position of chief shaykh of the Saʿīd al-Suʿadā' in 701/1302, and he retained the position, with a short interruption, until his death in 710/1311. ʿUmar ibn Yaʿqūb ibn Aḥmad al-Saʿūdī was the shaykh of the Zāwiyah of Abū Saʿūd, and a Sufi of some influence among the Mamluks; he died in 707/1308. See al-Maqrīzī, *al-Sulūk*, 1:744–45, 757, 919; 2:41, 50, 83, 94–95, and his *al-Khiṭaṭ*, 2:386.

32. Jamāl al-Dīn ʿAbd Allāh (d. 743/1342) was the son of the accomplished religious scholar and judge Jalāl al-Dīn Muḥammad ibn ʿAbd al-Raḥmān (666–739/1264–1338), and on occasion served as his substitute in court. If the senior Qazwīnī composed such a commentary on the *Poem of the Sufi Way*, it has been lost for centuries; see Ibn Ḥajar al-ʿAsqalānī, *al-Durar*, 2:399–400, and Kaḥḥālah, *Muʿjam*, 10:145–46.

33. Qur'ān 18:9–27 tells the story of several young men who sought shelter in a cave and prayed to God for protection against polytheists. They fell asleep for a number of years, though when they awoke, they thought that they had slept for only a day or part of a day.

34. For an extensive analysis of this dispute and the issues and people involved, see Homerin, *Arab Poet*, 39–44. ʿAbd al-Raḥmān Ibn Bint al-Aʿazz (d. 695/1296) was a prominent legal scholar, judge, and vizier during Qalā'ūn's sultanate; see al-Kutubī, *Fawāt al-Wafayāt*, edited by Iḥsān ʿAbbās (Beirut: Dār al-Thaqāfah, 1974), 2:279–82; al-Subkī, *Ṭabaqāt al-Shāfiʿīyah al-kubrā*, edited by Maḥmūd Muḥammad al-Tanāḥī and ʿAbd al-Fattāḥ Muḥammad al-Ḥilw (Cairo: ʿĪsā al-Bābī al-Ḥalabī, 1964), 8:172–75; Ibn Taghrī Birdī, *al-Nujūm al-zāhirah* (Cairo: al-Mu'assasah al-Miṣrīyah al-ʿĀmmah, 1963), 8:82–83; and Ibn al-ʿImād, *Shadharāt*, 5:431.

35. Concerning Ibn al-Salʿūs (d. 693/1294) and his royal patron al-Ashraf (r. 690–93/1291–94), see Ibn al-Furāt, *Ta'rīkh*, 8:106–9, 122–29, and Homerin, *Arab Poet*, 40–44, 110 n. 34.

36. An *ḥadīth* of the Prophet Muḥammad.

37. Saʿd al-Din Masʿūd ibn Ahmad al-Ḥārithī (652–711/1254–1312) was a noted scholar of *ḥadīth*, and a chief Ḥanbalī judge in Cairo; see Ibn Ḥajar al-ʿAsqalānī, *al-Durar*, 5:116–17, and Ibn al-ʿImād, *Shadharāt*, 6:28–29.

38. Ibn al-Fāriḍ, *Dīwān*, 116 (*Poem of the Sufi Way*, vv. 279–85).

39. Qur'ān 24:55. The royal title al-Malik al-Saʿīd may refer to a number of individuals at this time; however, there is a strong possibility that al-Malik al-Saʿīd Khiḍr ibn Baybars is intended here. His father had been sultan prior to Qalā'ūn, and if his mother had gone on pilgrimage to Mecca, she would normally have been accompanied by a substantial retinue, including a reciter of the Qur'ān. See al-Maqrīzī, *Sulūk*, 1:828.

40. Qur'ān 8:42.

41. This statement may refer to Ibn Bint al-Aʿazz's exoneration and the restitution of his honor and positions.

42. The congregational mosque of ʿAmr ibn al-ʿĀṣ was the first mosque built in Egypt, being erected in 20–21/640–41 in the Muslim camp at Fusṭāṭ, which later became a southern suburb of Cairo; see *EI*^{2}, 2:957–59, and K. A. C. Creswell, *A Short Account of Early Muslim Architecture*, revised and supplemented by James W. Allan (Cairo: American University in Cairo Press, 1989), 8, 15, 46, 304–13.

43. In his account of Ibn al-Fāriḍ, written prior to ʿAlī's *Proem*, the biographer Ibn Khallikān (d. 680/1282) ascribes this verse to al-Ḥarīrī (d. 516/1122), to whom Ibn al-Fāriḍ refers in his *Poem of the Sufi Way*, vv. 655–59. See Ibn Khallikān, *Wafayāt*, 3:454–56, and its translation in Homerin, *Arab Poet*, 16–19.

44. Ibn al-Fāriḍ, *Dīwān*, 201 (*al-Fā'īyah*, v. 43).

45. I have not found any other reference to this mosque or its location.

46. Ibn al-Fāriḍ, *Dīwān*, 45 (*al-Yā'īyah*, v. 1). The judge and private secretary whom ʿAlī identifies only as Sharaf al-Dīn, may have been the judge

Sharaf al-Dīn Muḥammad ibn ʿAbbās (fl. 638/1240) or, perhaps, al-Qāḍī al-Ashraf Aḥmad ibn Qāḍī al-Fāḍil (573–643/1177–1245), who had extensive relations with al-Malik al-Kāmil and the Ayyubid ruling elite; see Ibn Khallikān, *Wafayāt*, 3:163, and al-Maqrīzī, *Sulūk*, 1:305.

47. Fakhr al-Dīn ʿUthmān ibn Qizil ibn Jaldak al-Turkmān al-Kāmilī (d. 629/1232) was one of al-Malik al-Kāmil's senior mamluks. See al-Maqrīzī, *Sulūk*, 1:1:283. The Mihmandār received ambassadors and important foreign dignitaries who came to Cairo to visit the sultan, some of whom were presumably lodged in this residence.

48. Fakhr al-Dīn held the office of *ustādhdār,* which placed him in charge of the sultan's estates and treasury, and so he would have been a logical choice to make financial offers to Ibn al-Fāriḍ on the sultan's behalf; al-Kutubī, *Fawāt*, 3:51.

49. Amīn al-Dīn Ibn al-Raqāqī (fl. 697/1298) was a judge during the sultanate of Qalā'ūn; al-Maqrīzī, *Sulūk*, 1:836. ʿAlī's mosque was in the al-Muʿizz li-Dīn Allāh section of Cairo; al-Fayyūmī, *Nathr*, 2:70a.

50. Ibn al-Fāriḍ's companion would have been Ibrāhīm ibn Yaḥyā al-Amyūṭī (ca. 570–656/1174–1258), a Shāfiʿī jurisprudent and judge, who also composed poetry; see al-Safadī, *al-Wāfī*, 6:167 and al-Subkī, *Ṭabaqāt*, 8:125. ʿAlī's companion would have been the latter's grandson Ibrāhīm ibn Ishāq ibn Ibrāhīm (d. ca. 757/1356), who was likewise a Shāfiʿī legal scholar; see Jalāl al-Dīn al-Suyūṭī, *Ḥusn al-muḥāḍarah* (Cairo: ʿĪsā al-Bābī al-Ḥalabī, 1967), 1:427.

51. Bāb Zuwaylah is the southern gate in the Fatimid fortifications originally surrounding Cairo; it is a logical exit for traveling south to Fusṭāṭ.

52. Traditionally, *harīsah* is believed to arouse the *nafs* ("animal soul") and to enhance one's sexual potency; see J. C. Bürgel, "Love, Lust, and Longing: Eroticism in Early Islam as Reflected in Literary Sources," in *Society and the Sexes*, edited by Afaf Lutfi al-Sayyid-Marsot (Malibu, Calif.: University of California Press, 1979), 90.

53. I have not found further reference to the Qubbat al-Sharāb.

54. For a biography and bibliography of the renowned mystic ʿUmar al-Suhrawardī (d. 632/1234) see *EI*[2], 9:778–82, and Kaḥḥālah, *Muʿjam*, 7:313.

55. Ibn al-Fāriḍ, *Dīwān*, 196 (*al-Jīmīyah*, v. 44).

56. Shihāb al-Dīn Muḥammad Ibn al-Khiyamī (602–85/1205–86) was a student of Ibn al-Fāriḍ and, subsequently, a fine poet in his own right; see al-Ṣafadī, *al-Wāfī*, 4:50–61, and Homerin, *Arab Poet*, 23–24. Aḥmad ibn Mūsā ibn ʿAlī ibn ʿUmar ibn ʿUjayl al-Yamanī (d. 690/1291) was an accomplished religious scholar, though probably he was rather young in 628/1231; see Kaḥḥālah, *Muʿjam*, 2:189. I have yet to find further references to Ibn al-Fāriḍ's son ʿAbd al-Raḥmān, or to a brother of al-Khiyamī.

57. Ibn al-Fāriḍ, *Dīwān*, 46 (*al-Yā'īyah*, v. 13).

58. Based on chapter 97 of the Qur'ān, Muslim tradition asserts that Gabriel and the angels brought the entire Qur'ān to Muḥammad on the *Laylat al-Qadr*, or "Night of Power." Qur'ān 97 declares this night to be "better than 1,000 months...peace until the crack of dawn!" This special day is believed to begin in the evening of one of the last ten days of Ramaḍān; see EI^2, 8:418.

59. The ʿĪd al-Fiṭr, or the Feast of Breaking the Fast, is celebrated at the end of Ramaḍān and features a special congregational prayer to be performed by the Muslim community; see EI^2, 3:1007–8.

60. Ibn al-Fāriḍ, *Dīwān*, 211. Al-Maqrīzī notes that a *ribāṭ* ("hostel for the poor and elderly") known as al-Mushtahā had been established on the Nile island of Rhoda; several other poets praised it as well. See al-Maqrīzī, *al-Khiṭaṭ*, 2:428–29.

61. Ibn al-Fāriḍ may have understood the piece of cloth as a symbol for the *nafs* ("concupiscence," "selfishness"), which must be broken in order to attain pure love; see Homerin, *Arab Poet*, 50–51.

62. For an analysis of al-Jaʿbarī's account of Ibn al-Fāriḍ's last hours, see Homerin, *Arab Poet*, 51–53.

63. Ibrāhīm al-Jaʿbarī (599–687/1202–88) was a Shāfiʿī scholar, Sufi, poet, and renowned preacher. He frequently delivered his sermons at his Sufi hostel *(zāwiyah)* located outside of Bāb al-Naṣr, Cairo's northeastern gate leading toward the Qarāfah and Ibn al-Fāriḍ's grave. See al-Maqrīzī, *al-Khiṭaṭ*, 2:434; al-Subkī, *Ṭabaqāt*, 8:123–24; al-Suyūṭī, *Ḥusn*, 1:523; al-Shaʿrānī, *al-Ṭabaqāt al-kubrā* (Cairo: Maktabat Muḥammad ʿAlī Ṣabīḥ, 1965), 1:177; and Ibn al-ʿImād, *Shadharāt*, 5:399–400.

64. Ibn al-Fāriḍ, *Dīwān*, 95 (*Poem of the Sufi Way*, v. 99).

65. Concerning Abraham and his faith, see Qur'ān 2:260 and *Poem of the Sufi Way*, vv. 606–7.

66. Ibn al-Fāriḍ, *Dīwān*, 239–40. For more on these verses, including an alternative reading by an opponent of Ibn al-Fāriḍ, see Homerin, *Arab Poet*, 31, 113–14 n. 55.

67. Though a vision of paradise may satisfy many believers, Ibn al-Fāriḍ desired nothing less than the beatific vision of God's countenance, as did Rābiʿah al-ʿAdawīyah (d. 185/801). Rābiʿah is regarded as one of the greatest women mystics and saints of Islam and is noted for her doctrine of total love for God; see EI^2, 8:354–56.

68. Ibn al-Fāriḍ, *Dīwān*, 75 (*al-Tā'īyah al-ṣughrā*, v. 50).

69. Shihāb al-Dīn Aḥmad ibn Ibrāhīm al-Jaʿbarī died in 702/1302; see Ibn Ḥajar al-ʿAsqalānī, *al-Durar*, 1:102.

70. Concerning Zakī al-Dīn al-Mundhirī, Ibn Khallikān, and their references to Ibn al-Fāriḍ, see Homerin, *Arab Poet*, 15–19.

71. See Qur'ān 18:82.

72. See Qur'ān 20:96.

73. For the story of Khiḍr and Moses, see Qur'ān 18:65–82, and *Poem of the Sufi Way*, commentary to v. 715.

74. I.e., Muḥammad; see Qur'ān 12:108.

75. See Qur'ān 33:45–46.

76. See Qur'ān 2:269.

77. See Qur'ān 2:265.

78. See Qur'ān 108:1–3; 75:23–24.

79. See Qur'ān 20:8; 7:180.

80. See Qur'ān 14:24.

81. See Qur'ān 48:4, 26; 9:26, 40.

82. See Qur'ān 24:35.

83. See the story of Adam's creation in Qur'ān 15:26–44.

84. According to popular Muslim belief, Muḥammad will intercede on behalf of all believing Muslims on the Judgment Day; see Jane I. Smith and Yvonne Y. Haddad, *The Islamic Understanding of Death and Resurrection* (Albany, N.Y.: State University of New York Press, 1981), 26–27, 73, 80–81. Also see the *Wine Ode*, v. 17, for Ibn al-Fāriḍ's probable reference to Muḥammad's banner.

85. See Qur'ān 7:172.

86. See Qur'ān 24:35.

87. See Qur'ān 10:2.

88. See Qur'ān 10:26; 17:70.

89. See Qur'ān 9:111.

Selected Bibliography

MANUSCRIPTS

al-ʿAjamī, Ṣāʾn al-Dīn. *Sharḥ Tāʾīyat Ibn al-Fāriḍ al-kubrā.* Ms 407 (Shiʿr Taymūr). Cairo: Dār al-Kutub al-Miṣrīyah.

Amīr Pasha, Muḥammad Amīn ibn Muḥammad. *Sharḥ Tāʾīyat Ibn al-Fāriḍ al-kubrā.* Ms 5122 (Adab). Cairo: Dār al-Kutub al-Miṣrīyah.

al-Biqāʿī, Ibrāhīm. *Tanbīh al-ghabī ʿalā takfīr Ibn ʿArabī.* Microfilm of ms 2040, 1a–38b. Leiden: Bibliotheek Der Rijksuniversiteit.

al-Farghānī, Saʿīd al-Dīn. *Muntahā al-mudārik wa-muntahā lubb kull kāmil wa-ʿārif wa-sālik.* Microfilm 519 (Taṣawwuf) of ms 1499. Istanbul: Maktabat Aḥmad al-Thālith. Cairo: Arab League Manuscript Institute.

al-Fayyūmī, ʿAlī ibn Muḥammad. *Nathr al-jumān fī tarājim al-aʿyān.* Microfilm 428 (Taʾrīkh) of ms 1746. Istanbul: Maktabat Aḥmad al-Thālith. Cairo: Arab League Manuscript Institute.

al-Ḥamawī, ʿAlwān ʿAlī ibn ʿAṭīyah. *Al-Madad al-fāʾid wa-al-kashf al-ʿāriḍ fī sharḥ Tāʾīyat Ibn al-Fāriḍ.* Ms 4558 (Adab Ṭalʿat). Cairo: Dār al-kutub al-Miṣrīyah.

al-Hamdānī, ʿAlī ibn Shihāb. *Mashārib al-adhwāq.* Ms 8 (Majāmiʿ Fārisī). Pp. 13–30. Cairo: Dār al-Kutub al-Miṣrīyah.

al-Ḥuṣrī, Naṣrī ibn Aḥmad. *Al-Nafḥah al-miskīyah ʿalā baʿḍ maʿānī al-Khamrīyah.* Microfilm of ms 4112 (1394). Princeton, N.J.: Yahuda Section, Garrett Collection, Princeton University.

Ibn al-Fāriḍ, ʿUmar. *Dīwān.* Microfilm 1559 (Shiʿr) of ms 238. Tehran: Kitābkhānah Markazī. Cairo: Arab League Manuscript Institute, and ms 3968 (Adab) and ms 1965 (Adab). Cairo: Dār al-Kutub al-Miṣrīyah.

Ibn Kamāl Pasha. *Sharḥ Tāʾīyat Ibn al-Fāriḍ al-kubrā*. Ms 62 (Shiʿr Taymūr). Cairo: Dār al-Kutub al-Miṣrīyah.

———. *Sharḥ Khamrīyat Ibn al-Fāriḍ*. Ms 660 (Shiʿr Taymūr). Cairo: Dār al-Kutub al-Miṣrīyah.

Jāmī, ʿAbd al-Raḥmān. *Lawāmiʿ-i sharḥ-i Khamrīyat-i Fāriḍīyah*. Ms 50 (Taṣawwuf Fārisī Ṭalʿat). Fols. 18b–51b. Cairo: Dār al-Kutub al-Miṣrīyah.

al-Jīlānī, Yaḥyā ibn Muḥammad. *Ḥall al-muʿḍilāt min rumūz al-mushkilāt*. Microfilm of ms 4115 (4018). Princeton, N.J.: Yahuda Section, Garrett Collection, Princeton University.

al-Kāshānī, ʿIzz al-Dīn Maḥmūd. *Kashf wujūh al-ghurr li-maʿānī Naẓm al-durr*. Microfilm of ms 4106 (3979). Princeton, N.J.: Yahuda Section, Garrett Collection, Princeton University.

al-Nābulusī, ʿAbd al-Ghānī. *Kashf al-sirr al-ghāmiḍ fī sharḥ Dīwān Ibn al-Fāriḍ*. Microfilm of ms 4104 (3223). Princeton, N.J.: Yahuda Section, Garrett Collection, Princeton University.

———. *Lumʿat al-nūr al-muḍīʾaḥ fī sharḥ al-abyāt al-sabʿah (al-zāʾidah) al-Fāriḍīyah*. Microfilm of ms 4114 (534). Fols. 44b–48b. Princeton, N.J.: Yahuda Section, Garrett Collection, Princeton University.

al-Qayṣarī, Dāʾūd. *Sharḥ al-Qaṣīdah al-Khamrīyah*. Ms 7761 (Adab). Cairo: Dār al-Kutub al-Miṣrīyah.

———. *Sharḥ Tāʾīyat al-sulūk*. Ms 4802 (Adab Ṭalʿat). Cairo: Dār al-Kutub al-Miṣrīyah.

al-Qūṣī, ʿAbd al-Ṭawwāb. *Sharḥ al-Khamrīyah*. Microfilm of ms 53. Princeton, N.J.: Garrett Collection, Princeton University.

Ṣanʿī, Ṣanʿ Allāh. *Sharḥ al-Qaṣīdah al-Khamrīyah*. Ms 56 (Adab Ḥalīm). Cairo: Dār al-Kutub al-Miṣrīyah.

Sibṭ al-Marṣafī, Muḥammad ibn Muḥammad. *Fatḥ al-Makkī al-fāʾiḍ sharḥ Yāʾīyat Ibn al-Fāriḍ*. Ms 1566 (Adab). Cairo: Dār al-Kutub al-Miṣrīyah.

———. *Al-Zajājah al-billawrīyah fī sharḥ al-Qaṣīdah al-Khamrīyah*. Ms 8764 (Adab). Cairo: Dār al-Kutub al-Miṣrīyah.

al-Suyūṭī, Jalāl al-Dīn Muḥammad ibn Ḥusayn. *Al-Barq al-wāmiḍ fī sharḥ Yāʾīyat Ibn al-Fāriḍ*. Ms 224 (Adab). Cairo: Dār al-Kutub al-Miṣrīyah.

al-Tabrīzī, al-Ḥusayn Aḥmad al-Fātī. *Risālat al-muḥabbah al-ālihīyah*. Ms 5864 (Adab). Cairo: Dār al-Kutub al-Miṣrīyah.

al-Tilimsānī, ʿAfīf al-Dīn Sulaymān. *Sharḥ Tāʾīyat Ibn al-Fāriḍ al-kubrā*. Ms 1328 (Taṣawwuf Ṭalʿat). Cairo: Dār al-Kutub al-Miṣrīyah.

SELECTED BIBLIOGRAPHY

PUBLISHED WORKS

ʿAbd al-Khāliq, Maḥmūd ʿAbd al-Khāliq. See Maḥmūd, ʿAbd al-Khāliq.

Abdel-Kader, A. H. *The Life, Personality, and Writings of al-Junayd*. London: Luzac & Co., 1962.

ʿAffīfī, Abū al-ʿAlā. *The Mystical Philosophy of Muhyiddin Ibnul-'Arabi*. Cambridge: Cambridge University Press, 1939.

Ansari, M. Abdul Haq. "The Doctrine of One Actor: Junayd's View of *Tawḥīd*," *Muslim World* 73 (1983): 33–56.

Arberry, Arthur J. See Ibn al-Fāriḍ.

Bashō. *The Narrow Road to the Deep North and Other Travel Sketches*. Translated with an introduction by Nobuyuki Yuasa. New York: Penguin Books, 1966.

Bayrakdar, Mehmet. *La philosophie mystique chez Dawud de Kayseri*. Ankara: Editions Ministere de la Culture, 1990.

al-Biqāʿī, Ibrāhīm. *Masraʿ al-taṣawwuf (=Tanbīh al-ghabī)*. Edited by ʿAbd al-Raḥmān al-Wakīl. Cairo: Matbaʿat al-Sunnah al-Muḥammadīyah, 1953.

Boullata, Issa J. "Towards a Biography of Ibn al-Fāriḍ." *Arabica* 38 (1981): 38–56.

———. "Verbal Arabesque and Mystical Union: A Study of Ibn al-Fāriḍ's 'Al-Ta'iyya Al-Kubra.'" *Arab Studies Quarterly* 3 (1981): 152–69.

Böwering, Gerhard. *The Mystical Vision of Existence in Classical Islam: The Qur'ānic Hermeneutics of Sahl al-Tustarī (d. 283/896)*. Berlin: Walter De Gruyter, 1980.

Bürgel, J. C. "Love, Lust, and Longing: Eroticism in Early Islam as Reflected in Literary Sources." In *Society and the Sexes*, edited by Afaf Lutfi al-Sayyid-Marsot, 81–117. Malibu: University of California Press, 1979.

al-Būrīnī, al-Ḥasan ibn Muḥammad. See Ibn al-Fāriḍ.

Chittick, William. "The Five Presences: From al-Qūnawī to al-Qayṣarī." *Muslim World* 72 (1982): 107–28.

———. "Rūmī and *waḥdat al-wujūd*." In *Poetry and Mysticism in Islam*, edited by Amin Banani, et al., 70–111. Cambridge: Cambridge University Press, 1994.

———. *The Sufi Path of Knowledge*. Albany, N.Y.: State University of New York Press, 1989.

Chodkiewicz, Michel. *Le Sceau des saints*. France: Éditions Gallimard, 1986.

Creswell, K. A. C. *A Short Account of Early Muslim Architecture*. Revised and supplemented by James W. Allan. Cairo: American University in Cairo Press, 1989.

Deladriere, Roger. *Junayd: Enseignement spirituel*. Paris: Sindbad, 1983.

Dermenghem, Emile. *L'Éloge du vin*. Paris: Les Éditions Véga, 1931.

Di Matteo, Ignazio. "Sulla mia interpretazione del poema mistico d'Ibn al-Fāriḍ." *Rivista degli studi orientali* 8 (1919–20): 479–500.

———. *Tā'yyatu l'kubrā*. Rome: n.p., 1917.

During, Jean. *Musique et extase*. Paris: Éditions Albin Michel, 1988.

Encyclopaedia of Islam. 1st ed. 4 vols. Leiden: E. J. Brill, 1913–1934. 2d ed. Edited by H. A. R. Gibb, et al. Leiden: E. J. Brill, 1954–.

al-Farghānī, Saʿīd al-Dīn. *Mashāriq al-darārī*. Edited by Saʿīd Jalāl al-Dīn Āshtiyānī. Mashhad: Dānishghāh-i Firdawsī, 1980.

Farūkh, ʿUmar. *Ta'rīkh al-adab al-ʿArabī*. 6 vols. Beirut: Dār al-ʿIlm lil-Malāyīn, 1975.

al-Ghazālī, Abū Ḥāmid. *Iḥyā' ʿulūm al-dīn*. 4 vols. Cairo: ʿĪsā al-Bābī al-Ḥalabī, 1957.

———. *Mishkāt al-anwār*. Edited by Abū al-ʿAlā ʿAfīfī. Cairo: al-Hay'ah al-ʿĀmmah lil-Kitāb, 1964. Translated by W. H. T. Gairdner. *Al-Ghazzali's Mishkat al-Anwar*. London: Royal Asiatic Society, 1915.

———. *The Ninety-nine Beautiful Names*. Translated by David B. Burrell and Nazih Daher. Cambridge: The Islamic Texts Society, 1995.

Ghurayyib, Mīshāl. *ʿUmar Ibn al-Fāriḍ min khilal shiʿrihi*. Beirut: Dār Maktabat al-Ḥayāh, 1965.

Goldziher, Ignaz. "L'oiseau représentant l'âme dans les croyances populaires des Musulmans." In *Études Islamologiques d'Ignaz Goldziher*, translated by G.-H. Bousquet, 77–80. Leiden: E. J. Brill, 1962.

Graham, William A. *Divine Word and Prophetic Word in Early Islam*. The Hague: Mouton Publishers, 1977.

Harb, F. "Wine Poetry." In *The Cambridge History of Arabic Literature: ʿAbbasid Belles Lettres,* edited by Julia Ashtiany, et al., 219–34. Cambridge: Cambridge University Press, 1990.

Ḥilmī, Muḥammad Muṣṭafā. *Al-Ḥayāh al-rūḥīyah fī al-Islām*. Cairo: al-Hay'ah al-Miṣrīyah al-ʿĀmmah lil-Ta'līf wa-al-Nashr, 1970.

———. *Ibn al-Fāriḍ: sulṭān al-ʿāshiqīn*. Cairo: Maṭbaʿat Miṣr, 1963.

———. *Ibn al-Fāriḍ wa-al-ḥubb al-ilāhī*. 2d ed. Cairo: Dār al-Maʿārif, 1971.

Holt, P. M. *The Age of the Crusades*. London: Longman Group Limited, 1986.

Homerin, Th. Emil. *From Arab Poet to Muslim Saint: Ibn al-Fāriḍ, His Verse, and His Shrine*. Columbia, S.C.: University of South Carolina Press, 1994.

———. "The Domed Shrine of Ibn al-Fāriḍ." *Annales Islamologique* 25–26 (1989–90): 125–30.

———. "Ibn al-Fāriḍ: *Rubaʿiyat, Ghazal, Qasida*." In *Windows on the House of Islam: Muslim Sources on Spirituality and Religious Life,* edited by John

Renard, 194–200. Berkeley and Los Angeles: University of California Press, 1998.

———. “Preaching Poetry: The Forgotten Verse of Ibn al-Shahrazūrī.” *Arabica* 38 (1991): 87–101.

———. “Reflections on Arabic Poetry in the Mamluk Age.” *Mamlūk Studies Review* 1 (1997): 63–85.

———. “A Saint, His Shrine, and Poetry’s Power.” In *Islamic Mysticism in Practice,* edited by Carl W. Ernst. Princeton, N.J.: Princeton University Press, forthcoming.

———. “Saving Muslim Souls: The Khānqāh and the Sufi Duty in Mamluk Lands.” *Mamlūk Studies Review* 3 (1999): 59–83.

———. “Tangled Words: Toward a Stylistics of Arabic Mystical Verse.” In *Reorientations: Arabic and Persian Poetry,* edited by S. P. Stetkevych, 190–98. Bloomington, Ind.: University of Indiana Press, 1994.

———. “Umar Ibn al-Fāriḍ, a Saint of Mamluk and Ottoman Egypt.” In *The Manifestations of Sainthood in Islam,* edited by Grace Smith and Carl Ernst, 85–94. Istanbul: Isis Press, 1993.

al-Ḥujwīrī, ʿAlī ibn ʿUthmān. *Kashf al-Maḥjūb*. 2d ed. Edited and translated by R. A. Nicholson. London: Luzac & Co., 1936.

Ibn al-Fāriḍ, ʿUmar. *Dīwān Ibn al-Fāriḍ*. Edited by ʿAbd al-Khāliq Maḥmūd (ʿAbd al-Khāliq). Cairo: Dār al-Maʿārif, 1984. Partially translated by A. J. Arberry. *The Mystical Poems of Ibn al-Fāriḍ*. 2 vols. London: Emery Walker, 1952–56.

———. *Sharḥ Dīwān Sulṭān al-ʿĀshiqīn Sayyidī ʿUmar Ibn al-Fāriḍ*. Commentaries by al-Ḥasan ibn Muḥammad al-Būrīnī and ʿAbd al-Ghānī al-Nābulusī. Edited by Rushayyid ibn Ghālib al-Daḥdāḥ. Cairo: al-Maṭbaʿah al-ʿĀmmah, 1888. Also see al-Nābulusī.

———. *Al-Khamrīyah*. Earlier translations of the *Wine Ode* in English include Martin Lings, in *Studies in Comparative Religion* 14:131–34; Arberry, *Mystical Poems*, 2:84–90; R. A. Nicholson, *Studies in Islamic Mysticism*, 184–88; A. Safi, in the *Bulletin of the School of Oriental and Asian Studies* 2:235–48. Translation in French: Emile Dermenghem. *L’Éloge du vin*.

———. *Naẓm al-sulūk (Al-Tā’īyah al-kubrā)*. Translated into English by A. J. Arberry. *The Poem of the Way*. London: Emery Walker, 1952. Partially translated by R. A. Nicholson. *Studies in Islamic Mysticism*, 199–266. Also translated into Italian (see Di Matteo), and into German by Joseph Von Hammer-Purgstall. *Das arabisch hohe Lied der Liebe*. Vienna: Kaiserl. konigl. Hofund staatsdrukerei, 1854.

Ibn al-ʿImād, ʿAbd al-Ḥayy. *Shadharāt al-dhahab fī akhbār man dhahab*. 8 vols. Cairo: Maktabat al-Qudsī, 1931.

Ibn Ḥajar al-ʿAsqalānī. *Al-Durar al-kāminah fī aʿyān al-mi'ah al-thāminah* (4 vols. in 2). Haydarabad: n.p., 1929.

Ibn Khallikān, Aḥmad ibn Muḥammad. *Wafayāt al-aʿyān wa-anbā' anbā' al-zamān*. 8 vols. Edited by Iḥsān ʿAbbās. Beirut: Dār al-Thaqāfah, 1968. Translated by MacGuckin de Slane. *Ibn Khallikan's Biographical Dictionary*. 4 vols. Paris: Oriental Translation Fund of Great Britain and Ireland, 1842–71.

Ibn Taghrī Birdī, Yūsuf. *Al-Nujūm al-zāhirah fī mulūk Miṣr wa-al-Qāhirah*. 16 vols. Cairo: al-Mu'assasah al-Miṣrīyah al-ʿĀmmah, 1963. Partially translated by William Popper. *History of Egypt, 1382–1469 A.D.* 8 vols. Berkeley and Los Angeles: University of California Press, 1954.

Ibn ʿUnayn. *Dīwān*. Edited by Khalīl Mardam. Beirut: Dār Ṣādir, n.d.

John of the Cross. *The Collected Works of St. John of the Cross*. Edited and translated by Kieran Kavanaugh and Otilio Rodriguez. Washington, D.C.: Institute of Carmelite Studies, 1979.

———. *The Poems of John of the Cross*. Translated by Willis Barnstone. New York: New Directions, 1968.

Kaḥḥālah, ʿUmar. *Muʿjam al-mu'allifīn*. 15 vols. Damascus: al-Maktabah al-ʿArabīyah, 1957.

al-Kalābādhī, Muḥammad. *Al-Taʿarruf li-madhhab ahl al-taṣawwuf*. Beirut: Dār al-Kutub al-ʿIlmīyah, 1980. Translated by A. J. Arberry. *The Doctrine of the Ṣūfīs*. Cambridge: Cambridge University Press, 1978; reprint of 1935 ed.

Kamada, Shigeru. "Nābulusī's Commentary on Ibn al-Fāriḍ's *Khamrīyah*," *Orient* 18 (1982): 19–40.

al-Kāshānī, ʿIzz al-Dīn Maḥmūd. *Kitāb-i Miṣbaḥ al-hidāyah*. Edited by Jalāl al-Dīn Humā'ī. Tehran: Kitābkhānah Ṣanāʿī, 1946.

Khūrī, Amīn. *Jalā' al-ghāmiḍ fī sharḥ Dīwān Ibn al-Fāriḍ*. Beirut: al-Maṭbaʿah al-Adabīyah, 1894.

al-Kutubī, Muḥammad ibn Shākir. *Fawāt al-Wafayāt*. 5 vols. Edited by Iḥsān ʿAbbās. Beirut: Dār al-Thaqāfah, 1974.

Lings, Martin. "Mystical Poetry." In *The Cambridge History of Arabic Literature: ʿAbbasid Belles Lettres*, edited by Julia Ashtiany, et al., 235–64. Cambridge: Cambridge University Press, 1990.

Maḥmūd, ʿAbd al-Khāliq. *Shiʿr Ibn al-Fāriḍ*. Cairo: Dār al-Maʿārif, 1984.

al-Maqrīzī, Aḥmad ibn ʿAlī. *Kitāb al-Muqaffā al-kabīr*. 8 vols. Edited by Muḥammad al-Yaʿlāwī. Beirut: Dār al-Gharb al-Islāmī, 1991.

———. *Kitāb al-Sulūk li-maʿrifat duwal al-mulūk*. Vols. 1–2 in 6 pts. Edited by Muḥammad Muṣṭafā Ziyādah. Cairo: Lajnat al-Ta'līf wa-al-Tarjamah wa-al-Nashr, 1934–58. Vols. 3–4 in 6 pts. Edited by Saʿīd A. F. ʿĀshūr. Cairo:

Maṭbaʿat Dār al-Kutub, 1970–73. Partially translated by R. J. C. Broadhurst. *A History of the Ayyubid Sultans*. Boston: Twayne Publishers, 1980.

———. *Al-Mawāʿiẓ wa-al-iʿtibār bi-dhikr al-khiṭaṭ wa-al-āthār*. 2 vols. Baghdad: Maktabat al-Muthannā, 1970.

Martz, Louis L. *The Paradise Within: Studies in Vaughan, Traherne, and Milton*. New Haven, Conn.: Yale University Press, 1964.

———. *The Poem of the Mind*. New York: Oxford University Press, 1966.

———. *The Poetry of Meditation: A Study of English Literature of the Seventeenth Century*. 2d ed. New Haven, Conn.: Yale University Press, 1962.

Massignon, Louis. *La passion d'al-Ḥosayn ibn Mansour al-Ḥallāj*. Translated by Herbert Mason. *The Passion of al-Ḥallāj*. 4 vols. Princeton, N.J.: Princeton University Press, 1982.

al-Mufaḍḍal al-Ḍabbī. *Al-Mufaḍḍalīyāt*. Edited by Aḥmad Muḥammad Shākir and ʿAbd al-Salām Muḥammad Hārūn. 7th printing. Cairo: Dār al-Maʿārif, 1983. Translated by Charles Lyall. *The Mufaḍḍalīyāt: an Anthology of Ancient Arabian Odes*. Oxford: Clarendon Press, 1918.

al-Mundhirī, ʿAbd al-ʿAẓīm. *Al-Takmilah li-Wafayāt al-naqalah*. Edited by Bashshār ʿAwwād Maʿrūf. 6 vols. Cairo Maṭbaʿat ʿĪsā al-Bābī al-Ḥalabī, 1968.

al-Nābulusī, ʿAbd al-Ghānī. *Kashf al-sirr al-ghāmiḍ fī sharḥ Dīwān Ibn al-Fāriḍ*. Partially edited by Muḥammad Abū al-Faḍl Ibrāhīm. Cairo: Mu'assassat al-Halabī, 1972.

———. *Al-Ṣufīyah fī shiʿr Ibn al-Fāriḍ: sharḥ al-Shaykh ʿAbd al-Ghānī al-Nābulusī*. Selected and edited by Ḥāmid al-Ḥājj ʿAbbūd. Damascus: Maṭbaʿat Zayd Ibn Thābit, 1988.

Nallino, Carlo A. "Ancora su Ibn al-Fāriḍ e sulla mistica musulmana." *Rivista degli studi orientali* 8 (1919–20): 501–52.

———. "Il poema mistico arabo d'Ibn al-Fāriḍ in una recente traduzione italiana." *Rivista degli studi orientali* 8 (1919–20): 1–106.

Naṣr, ʿĀṭif Jawdah. *Al-Ramz al-shiʿrī ʿind al-Ṣūfīyah*. Beirut: Dār al-Andalus, 1983.

———. *Shiʿr Ibn al-Fāriḍ: dirāsah fī fann al-shiʿr al-Ṣūfī*. Beirut: Dār al-Andalus, 1982.

al-Nawawī, Yaḥyā ibn Sharaf. *Al-Arbaʿīn al-Nawawīyah*. Edited by Ibrāhīm ibn Muḥammad. Tanta, Egypt: Maktabat al-Ṣaḥābah, 1986. Translated by Ezzedin Ibrahim and Denys Johnson-Davies. *An-Nawawī's Forty Hadith*. N.p., n.d.

The New Princeton Encyclopedia of Poetry and Poetics. Edited by Alexander Preminger, et al. Princeton, N.J.: Princeton University Press, 1993.

Nicholson, R. A. "The Lives of 'Umar Ibn'l-Farid and Muhyyu'DDin Ibn'l-'Arabi." *Journal of the Royal Asiatic Society* (1906): 797–824.

———. *Studies in Islamic Mysticism.* Cambridge: Cambridge University Press, 1978; reprint of 1921 ed.

Ormsby, Eric L. "The Taste of Truth: the Structure of Experience in al-Ghazālī's *al-Munqidh min al-Ḍalāl.*" In *Islamic Studies Presented to Charles J. Adams,* edited by Wael B. Hallaq and Donald P. Little, 134–52. Leiden: E. J. Brill, 1991.

al-Qushayrī, Abū al-Qāsim. *Al-Risālah al-Qushayrīyah.* 2 vols. Edited by ʿAbd al-Ḥalīm Maḥmūd and Maḥmūd Ibn al-Sharīf. Cairo: Dār al-Kutub al-Ḥadīthah, 1972–74.

Rahman, Fazlur. *Islam.* Garden City, N.Y.: Doubleday, 1968.

———. *Major Themes of the Qur'ān.* Chicago: Bibliotheca Islamica, 1980.

al-Rifā', al-Sarī ibn Aḥmad. *Al-Muḥibb wa-al-maḥbūb wa-al-mashmūm wa-al-mashrūb.* 4 vols. Damascus: Mājid Ḥasan al-Dhahabī, 1986.

Rikābī, Jawdat. *La poésie profane sous Les Ayyūbides et ses principaux représentants.* Paris: G.-P. Maisonneuve & Co., 1949.

Rodinson, Maxime. *Muḥammad.* New York: Pantheon Books, 1980.

al-Ṣafadī, Ṣalāḥ al-Dīn Khalīl. *Al-Wāfī bi-al-Wafayāt.* 18 vols. In progress. Edited by Sven Dedering, et al. Wiesbadaen: In Kommission bei Franz Steiner Verlag, 1959–.

al-Sakhāwī, Muḥammad ibn ʿAbd al-Raḥmān. *Al-Ḍaw' al-lāmiʿ li-ahl al-qarn al-tāsiʿ.* 12 vols. Cairo: Maktabat al-Qudsī, 1934.

al-Sarrāj, Abū Naṣr. *Kitāb al-Lumaʿ fī al-taṣawwuf.* Edited by ʿAbd al-Ḥalīm Maḥmūd and Ṭāhā ʿAbd al-Bāqī Surūn. Egypt: Dār al-Kutub al-Ḥadīthah, 1960.

Scattolin, Giuseppe. "Al-Farghānī's Commentary on Ibn al-Fāriḍ's Mystical Poem *Al-Tā'iyyat Al-Kubrā.*" *MIDEO* 21 (1993): 331–83.

———. *L'esperienza mistica di Ibn al-Fāriḍ attraverso il suo poema Al-Tā'iyyat Al-Kubrā.* Rome: PISAI, 1988.

———. "L'expérience mistique de Ibn al-Fāriḍ a travers son poeme Al-Tā'iyyat Al-Kubrā," *MIDEO* 19 (1989): 203–23.

———. "More on Ibn al-Fāriḍ's Biography." *MIDEO* 22 (1994): 197–242.

Schimmel, Annemarie. *And Muḥammad Is His Messenger.* Chapel Hill, N.C.: University of North Carolina Press, 1985.

———. *As Through a Veil: Mystical Poetry in Islam.* New York: Columbia University Press, 1982.

———. *Mystical Dimensions of Islam.* Chapel Hill, N.C.: University of North Carolina Press, 1975.

Sells, Michael. *Desert Tracings: Six Classical Odes by ʿAlqama, Shanfara, Labid, Antara, Al-Aʿsha, and Dhu ar-Rumma.* Middletown, Conn.: Wesleyan University Press, 1989.

———. *Early Islamic Mysticism*. New York: Paulist Press, 1996.

al-Shaʿrānī. *Al-Ṭabaqāt al-kubrā*. Cairo: Maktabat Muḥammad ʿAlī Ṣabīḥ, 1965.

The Shorter Encyclopaedia of Islam. Edited by H. A. R. Gibb and J. H. Kramers. Leiden: E. J. Brill, 1953.

Sibṭ al-Fāriḍ, ʿAlī. "*Dībājat Dīwān Ibn al-Fāriḍ*." In *Dīwān Ibn al-Fāriḍ*, edited by ʿAbd al-Khāliq Maḥmūd (ʿAbd al-Khāliq), 19–44. Cairo: Dār al-Maʿārif, 1984.

Smith, Jane I., and Yvonne Y. Haddad. *The Islamic Understanding of Death and Resurrection*. Albany, N.Y.: State University of New York Press, 1981.

Smith, Margaret. *Rābiʿa the Mystic*. Cambridge: Cambridge University Press, 1984; reprint of 1928 ed.

Sperl, Stefan. "Ibn al-Fāriḍ on Sufi Love." In *Qasida Poetry in Islamic Asia and Africa*, 2 vols., edited by S. Sperl and C. Shackle, 2:106–11. Leiden: E. J. Brill, 1996.

———. *Mannerism in Arabic Poetry: A Structural Analysis of Selected Texts (3rd century AH/9th century AD—5th century AH/11th century AD)*. Cambridge: Cambridge University Press, 1989.

———. "Qasida Form and Mystic Path in Thirteenth Century Egypt: A Poem by Ibn al-Fāriḍ," in S. Sperl, ed., *Qasida Poetry*, 1:65–81.

Stetkevych, Jaroslav. "The Arabic Lyrical Phenomena in Context." *Journal of Arabic Literature* 6 (1975): 55–77.

———. "Toward an Arabic Elegiac Lexicon: the Seven Words of the *Nasīb*." In *Reorientations/Arabic and Persian Poetry*, edited by Suzanne Pinckney Stetkevych, 58–129. Bloomington: University of Indiana Press, 1994.

———. *The Zephyrs of Najd*. Chicago: University of Chicago Press, 1993.

Stetkevych, Suzanne P. *Abū Tammām and the Poetics of the ʿAbbāsid Age*. Leiden: E. J. Brill, 1991.

———. "Intoxication and Immortality: Wine and Associated Imagery in al-Ma'arri's Garden." *Literature East and West* 25 (1989): 29–48.

al-Subkī, Tāj al-Dīn. *Ṭabaqāt al-Shāfiʿīyah al-kubrā*. 10 vols. Edited by Maḥmūd Muḥammad al-Tanāḥī and ʿAbd al-Fattāḥ Muḥammad al-Ḥilw. Cairo: ʿĪsā al-Bābī al-Ḥalabī, 1964.

al-Sulamī, Muḥammad ibn al-Ḥusayn. *Ṭabaqāt al-Ṣūfīyah*. 3d ed. Edited by Nūr al-Dīn Shuraybah. Cairo: Maktabat al-Khānjī, 1986.

al-Suyūṭī, Jalāl al-Dīn. *Ḥusn al-muḥāḍarah*. 2 vols. Cairo: ʿĪsā al-Bābī al-Ḥalabī, 1967.

———. *Qamʿ al-muʿāriḍ fī nuṣrat Ibn al-Fāriḍ*. In *Jalāl al-Dīn al-Suyūṭī wa-al-taṣawwuf al-Islāmī*, edited by ʿAbd al-Khāliq Maḥmūd ʿAbd al-Khāliq, 48–102. Cairo: n.p., 1987.

Trimingham, J. Spencer. *The Sufi Orders in Islam.* London: Oxford University Press, 1973.
al-Udfuwī, Jaʿfar. *Al-Ṭāliʿ al-saʿīd.* Edited by Saʿd Muḥammad Ḥasan and Ṭāhā al-Ḥājirī. Cairo: al-Dār al-Miṣrīyah lil-Ta'līf wa-al-Tarjamah, 1966.
Wang Wei. *Laughing Lost in the Mountains: Poems of Wang Wei.* With translations by Tony Barnstone, Willis Barnstone, and Xu Haixin. Introduction by Willis Barnstone. Hanover, N.H.: University of New England Press, 1991.
Zaehner, R. C. *Hindu and Muslim Mysticism.* New York: Schocken Books, 1969.

Index of Topics

INDEX OF TOPICS

Index of Names

INDEX OF NAMES